THE RVER'S ULTIMATE SURVIVAL GUIDE

FORWARD

Congratulations! You have just taken that very important first step that will quide you down the path towards the goal of achieving safer, more enjoyable RVing. For many RVers, there is little in our backgrounds or day-to-day lives that adequately prepares us to meet the challenges presented when we choose to travel extensively in an RV. The size and complexity of those vehicles, along with the magnitude and diversity of the travels that we undertake in our pursuit of the RVing lifestyle, often result in potentially harmful or even disastrous results when we are ill-prepared. *The RVer's Ultimate Survival Guide* has been written specifically to fill that void. It identifies the nine most obvious safety issues and discusses those topics in a clear, easy-to-understand format. It is important to recognize that this guide was prepared for RVers by an RVer; in other words, the author has been there and has successfully survived (thrived) more than 42 years of active RVing. You can do the same with the completion of this most important book. Share the information contained within this safety guide and you may become instrumental in saving the life of a fellow RVer. At the very minimum, you will have furthered the cause of the RV lifestyle, an admirable goal in itself.

DEDICATION

This book was conceived and researched over a period of years through countless conversations with fellow RVers and ultimately put into print via many more hours at the computer. This effort was only completed with the help and encouragement of many friends and family. I owe tremendous thanks to all who contributed so generously. No person was more supportive in this endeavor than Pat, my wife of 50 years and my steadfast companion for more than 400,000 wonderful RV miles. Words are simply incapable of stating how deeply I value that support. With her ongoing encouragement and God's blessings there will be many more enjoyable RV miles and perhaps additional RVing books. With my deepest gratitude,

Neil

The information in this printed book or digital version is distributed on an "as is" basis, without warranty. While every precaution has been taken in the preparation of this book, neither the author nor any other person or company involved in its preparation, publication or distribution, shall have any liability to any person or entity with respect to any liability, loss or damage caused or alleged to be caused, directly or indirectly, by the information contained in this book.

Copyright © Escapees RV Club, all rights reserved

No portion of this publication may be reproduced, stored in a retrieval system, or transmitted in any form or by any means, electronic, mechanical, photocopying, recording, or otherwise, without prior written permission of the owner.

Cover photo by Mark Nemeth.

CONTENTS

BOOK 1: WEIGHT SAFETY & LOAD MANAGEMENT 1

BOOK 2: VEHICLE TIRE SAFETY 29

BOOK 3: RV MOTOR FUEL 51

BOOK 4: PROPANE SAFETY 67

BOOK 5: ELECTRICAL SAFETY 83

BOOK 6: SAFE DRIVING 95

BOOK 7: TOWING SAFETY 125

BOOK 8: FIRE & LIFE SAFETY 149

BOOK 9: PERSONAL SAFETY 173

BOOK 1: WEIGHT SAFETY & LOAD MANAGEMENT

CONTENTS

Author's Foreword 3
What's It All About? 3

THE LANGUAGE OF WEIGHT — 04
Definitions 4
Examples Of RV "Federal Data plates" 5
It Is Possible to Exceed a Tire Rating Without Exceeding an Axle Rating 8
Total Overweight RVs 10
Overweight RVs/By RV Type 11
Which Weight Limitations or Ratings Are Exceeded 11

HOW DO "OVERLOADS" HURT YOU? — 14

UNDERSTANDING YOUR OPTIONS — 17

RVIA WEIGHT INFORMATION LABELS — 21
Summary 27

Book 1: Weight Safety & Load Management

AUTHOR'S FOREWORD

The wonderful RV lifestyle has beckoned more and more RVers (over 8+ million) to the open road. As a group, we probably spend more time behind the wheel than just about any other segment of Americans other than professional truck and cab drivers. During those long hours behind the wheel we are often witness to everything that is both good and bad about RVing in general. One of the sights that we commonly encounter is to observe an RV struggling up a hill, overheating, wallowing in dips and bumps in the road, bottoming out or dragging its rear bumper on modest hills and driveways, listing to one side or the other, smoking its brakes on downhill runs or breaking down beside the highway. We have also seen RV drivers climb from their vehicles literally "white-knuckled" after a particularly difficult run. What each of those vehicles and drivers has in common is that each of those conditions is likely the result of an overloaded or overweight RV.

> "What each of those vehicles and drivers has in common is that each of those conditions is likely the result of an overloaded or overweight RV."

WHAT'S IT ALL ABOUT?

Book 1 of *The RVer's Ultimate Survival Guide* will focus on acknowledging the magnitude of the problem, understanding the issues, and learning what positive actions we might take to correct any weight or load issues in our RV. First, we should acknowledge that RVs are the only vehicles on the road that operate at virtually 100% of their capacity 100% of the time and that RVers, by definition, are "leisure-time operators" of our rigs, not professional drivers or maintenance persons. As such, they often do not have the background, training or inclination to perform some of the tasks demanded of them. We should also acknowledge that our vehicles (no matter how expensive and nice) are derived from trucks and buses and are therefore subject to the needs and limitations of commercial vehicles.

In our discussion of RV weight issues, we will incorporate data developed by the Recreational Vehicle Safety and Education Foundation (RVSEF). They have been weighing RVs for more than 20 years to see just how RVs are used and often abused by RVers. The RVSEF database contains very accurate wheel-by-wheel weights for more than 35,000 RVs. That data, while far from all-inclusive, represents an excellent source of information on the subject of RV weight and load management. With that information we will understand where RVs and RVers commonly go awry in the weight and load management issue.

If ever there was a topic that reveals "Knowledge is King," this is it. With knowledge, the RVer has the ability to purchase the correct RV for his specific needs, has the ability to load and operate it properly and therefore has the capability to travel safely.

RVers' Ultimate Survival Guide

THE LANGUAGE OF WEIGHT
DEFINITIONS

A complete understanding of the terms used to define weight ratings is essential. That knowledge will permit you to utilize the following information to your advantage as you sort through the weight and load management issues facing you. You will also be able to discuss weight with knowledge and authority the next time you purchase an RV, and you may even play a positive role in the education of fellow RV enthusiasts.

Basic weight ratings have been around for many years; they were established during the early days of automotive development. The motivation for the establishment of weight ratings at that time was that vehicles, in particular commercial vehicles (trucks), were growing rapidly as the country sought to expand early in the 20th century. That trend was viewed then (as now) as potentially detrimental to the safety of those on the highway and for the protection of the nation's highways and bridges themselves. Governmental agencies, now the Department of Transportation (DOT), established a rating system that is still in place.

The Federal Weight Compliance Label (commonly called the federal data plate) is required for all vehicles utilized on USA and Canadian highways. This data plate is placed prominently in the proximity of the driver's area. Most generally, it is located on the driver's doorpost or pillar, but in some vehicles (particularly motorhomes) you may have to strain a little to find and read it. Note that for trailers, the data plate is generally located on the left side of the tongue or pin box or on the outside of the left front corner of the body. While manufacturers are charged with developing and installing this label, it is there by federal law. Its existence and accuracy are important to you. Generally, federal data plates are quite accurate; however, errors do occur. If an error is detected, you should seek to have the data plate corrected.

Only the manufacturer can change the federal data plate. That is a responsibility they take very seriously.

Before we begin to define weight terms, please note that most of these terms were not established for the RV industry specifically, but have been around for years as industry standards for commercial vehicles. Because of this, often they do not apply very well to our RVs. You also need to consider who determines those ratings. They are established by the manufacturer of the vehicle component (chassis, axle, tire, etc.) and probably are not directly considered, tested or approved by any government agency. It has been stated and is fairly clear that, in most cases, a single act of exceeding a rating will not result in the component failing immediately or catastrophically. Normally, ratings are based on the component achieving some defined service life or performance level. For example, in the case of a tire, it must be capable of carrying the full rated load (at the appropriate pressure) for the anticipated life of the tire, which is normally its tread life. However, when it is overloaded its casing (carcass) may no longer perform adequately and may fail well before the tread is worn away. Since tread life is how we (users) generally judge a tire's life, we could be in for a surprise in the form of a tire failure, often while the tread itself looked quite good. In a similar fashion, a mechanical component with a weight rating, such as a trailer axle, should be capable of carrying that full rated load for at least the warranted life of the product, provided it received the specified maintenance during that life. Lots more on tires later in Book 2!

EXAMPLES OF RV "FEDERAL DATA PLATES"

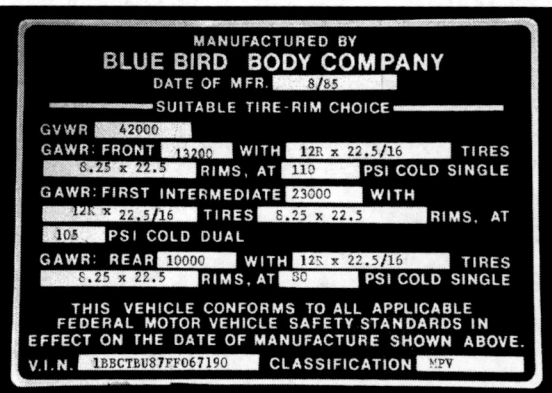

A typical example of a motorhome federal data plate, from Blue Bird Body Company, manufacturer of the Wanderlodge. Note the presence of a GAWR for the third (tag) axle, the required tire size, ply rating and pressure as specified by the vehicle manufacturer.

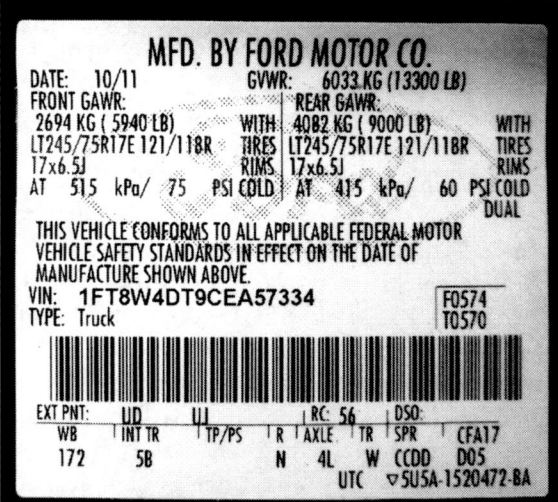

A Ford pickup (trailer tow vehicle) federal data plate. Note the sum of the GAWR for the front and rear axle exceeds the GVWR for the truck. This is a common but not universal practice giving the operator flexibility in placing his load either forward or rearward as desired, but not permitting the maximum axle load to be carried by both axles simultaneously.

This data plate, typical of data plates on many 5th wheel trailers, is mounted on the pin box (sometimes on the left front corner of the body). Note the information recorded is the same as for other vehicles; however, the two axles total far less than the GVWR of the trailer. Some manufacturers do not include pin weight in the GVWR, while others do. In this case, 2500 lbs (18%) of the trailer's total weight (GVWR) must be carried by the truck to legally operate at GVWR.

The Honda CRV is a small SUV tow car commonly used by RVers. Its data plate, like all vehicles, contains the same important safety information. As towed cars are often used as a trailer to carry extra weight (off-loading the motorhome), care must be taken to avoid overloading; without passengers in the car, an 800-1000 lbs payload should not be a problem for most "towed" cars.

Gross Vehicle Weight Rating (GVWR)

GVWR is an easily understood term. Remember that every vehicle, including cars, trucks, trailers, motorhomes and even motorcycles have a GVWR associated with them. This rating, established by the manufacturer of the vehicle, defines MAXIMUM WEIGHT AT WHICH THE FULLY LOADED MOTORHOME MAY BE OPERATED! This value is found on the federal data plate installed by the manufacturer. When you load all of your belongings, tools, fresh water, pets, etc., the unit's total weight should never exceed the GVWR when driven; you may exceed this value when parked without concern. Recall also that if you tow anything that has a tongue weight, that value must also to be included in the GVWR.

GVWR = maximum weight at which the fully loaded vehicle may be operated

Exceeding the GVWR has many potential implications. Remember that the manufacturer generally establishes the rating with consideration of service life, handling, stopping capability, acceleration and warranty coverage. When you exceed the GVWR of any vehicle, you are asking the vehicle to do more work than it was designed for. The result is that it may not last as long as it might have had the rating been respected. At the very minimum, exceeding the GVWR will hit you economically as the various components on the vehicle struggle to carry the extra load.

A common complaint that we often hear is about poor stopping performance, obviously, a very serious consideration. Note that manufacturers determine the size of the brakes they use based on how much weight the brakes must stop while providing a reasonable life and meeting all applicable performance standards. Early brake replacement is often associated with excessive operational loads. Commonly, owners who operate over GVWR will also complain about poor handling, lack of vehicle performance, ride problems, premature suspension maintenance and early driveline durability issues. Recognize, also, that operating in excess of this rating may adversely affect any manufacturer's warranty in effect and could present a legal threat should you have the misfortune of being involved in an accident.

Gross Axle Weight Rating (GAWR)

The Federal Data plate also provides a rating (GAWR) for each axle on your RV as established by the axle/chassis manufacturer. This value defines the MAXIMUM LOAD THAT SHOULD EVER BE CARRIED BY THE AXLE. Note that the GAWR is based on all of the components of the axle, including the suspension, wheels, bearings, spindles and tires. When reviewed in this manner with each of the components being considered individually, the GAWR rating is actually established based on the weakest component in the assembly. This rating seems to be straightforward and easy to understand.

GAWR = the maximum load that should ever be on the axle

However, this is a clear case where truck ratings do not apply very well to RVs. For example, consider an RV that has a front GAWR of 6,000 pounds with LT235/85R16 load Range E tires. If you check the sidewall of the tires, you will note that each tire has a maximum rating of 3,042 pounds. Since there are two tires (3,042 x 2 =6,084), the GAWR was rounded to 6,000 pounds, probably based on the tire rating.

Now consider carefully what we just did; we totaled the load rating of the two tires together to get the GAWR. With some thought we know that we can't arbitrarily load the axle so that one side has a greater load than 3,042 pounds. This now brings us to a very important conclusion: GAWR ASSUMES THAT THE AXLE IS LOADED EQUALLY ON BOTH SIDES! This is not a good assumption. In fact, this erroneous conclusion is the source of many RV tire failures. RVs are seldom loaded evenly from side to side; in our example, a side-to-side weight variation of as little as 43 pounds would result in one side of the front axle exceeding the tire's rating. In reality, 43 pounds is a very small side-to-side weight variation; it is not unusual to weigh a unit that is 2,000 pounds, or more, heavier on one side than on the other.

GAWR assumes that the axle is loaded equally on both sides!

Rightfully, you might ask, "Why then do we use GAWR for RVs?" Good question; unfortunately, the answer is because RVs are a very small segment of the automotive world, we do not have differing criteria; instead, we use standards that were designed for trucks. GAWR works quite well for trucks because they are constructed symmetrically with the load-carrying box located properly over the axles. Envision gravel flowing into a truck bed and you will note that the load distributes evenly right and left, fore and aft within the bed. In other words the load will be equally distributed on both sides of the load carrying axles. By contrast RVs may begin with a chassis that is symmetrical when delivered to the coach builder; then that company puts a very large nearly symmetrical box onto the chassis. What happens next is that the coach builder must put into that box all of the components and essentials that we value so highly. Those items are placed "around the perimeter" of the box creating a "living area" down the middle. So what we now have is a very large amount of weight placed around the edge of the RV as dictated by the floor plan. Virtually all of the remaining space in or under the box is then enclosed and fitted with a door, becoming a bin, a bay, a box, a storage area, etc. At this point, the motorhome before us is probably not balanced from side to side. Certainly, the engineers have made some attempt to spread out the load within the limitations of the chassis and components, but the construction process described has effectively dictated weight distribution. At this point, the coach builder counts on the owner to utilize their personal load to offset any weight bias that is built into the coach.

The coach builder counts on the owners to utilize their personal load to offset any bias that is built into the coach.

Now when we (RVers) purchase the RV, if we are typical, we open up one of the many provided storage areas and proceed to fill it until full. We close that door and move on to the next storage area where we repeat the process. Only when all of the bays, bins, boxes and other storage areas are full are we ready for travel. Let there be no doubt about it, we are a major contributor to the problem; we really don't want to leave home without everything we think that we might require in our travels. Where the coach builder counted on us using our personal load to offset the weight bias built into the chassis/body, we may have added to the unbalance through our unknowing loading process.

RVs must be weighed very accurately at each wheel position in order to ascertain compliance with all applicable limitations.

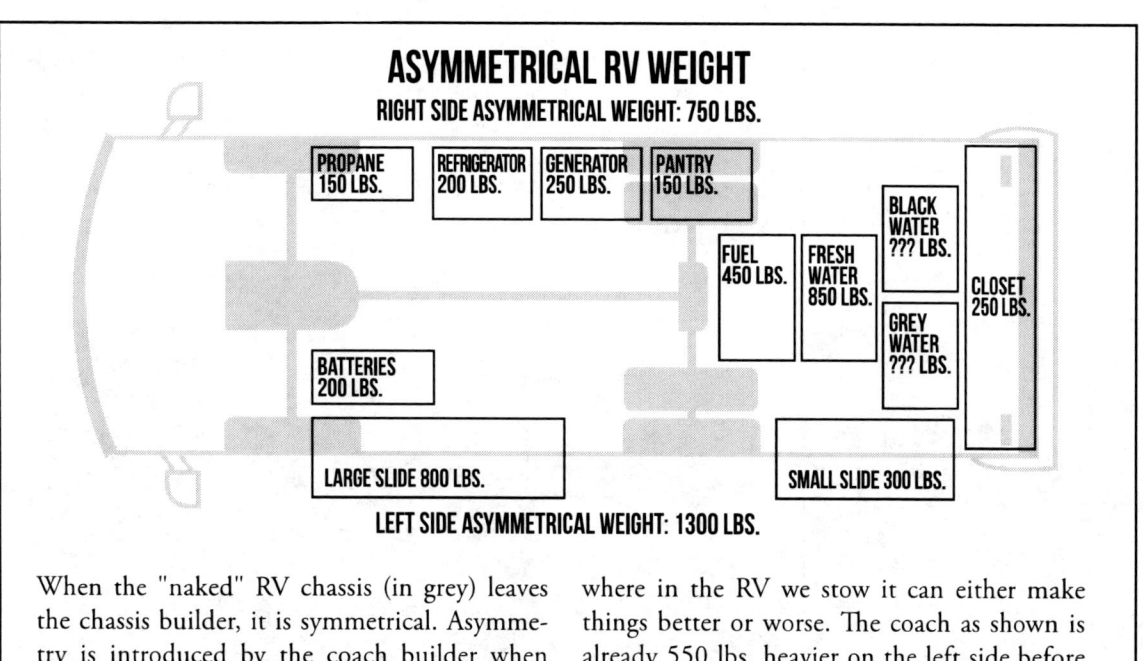

When the "naked" RV chassis (in grey) leaves the chassis builder, it is symmetrical. Asymmetry is introduced by the coach builder when the "house" is built. What we add (cargo) and where in the RV we stow it can either make things better or worse. The coach as shown is already 550 lbs. heavier on the left side before any cargo has been added.

IT IS POSSIBLE TO EXCEED A TIRE RATING WITHOUT EXCEEDING AN AXLE RATING.

Analysis of the weight and load information available for RVs reveals that 10% of the units exceeding a tire rating do so without exceeding GAWR. This is a very big potential trap for the unwary RVer. In most cases, this condition was unknown by the owner; often because they had previously taken their RV to a commercial scale, which weighs by individual axle only, and thus did NOT DETECT the tire overload. Now they depart the weight scale with a false sense of security that all is well. When they experience a tire failure down the road, they are astounded. Often they conclude that it must have been a defective tire, since they felt they were not over the GAWR. This is why RVs must be weighed at EACH INDIVIDUAL CORNER, so that not only do we determine the total weight of the unit, but its weight distribution as well.

There are literally thousands of certified weight scales around the country, some operated by state agencies while many more are private. Each provides a very valuable service to their clientele by performing accurate weighing of vehicles day in and day out. The keywords in that statement are "their clientele," generally meaning trucks because they are the ones requiring frequent accurate weighings. Since trucks are their primary market, scale operators have optimized their equipment for that specific purpose. The platform scales used work very well for trucks and axle-by-axle weighing, but they do not lend themselves well to RV or wheel-by-wheel weighing. Thanks to increased interest in RV safety, there are now several groups and organizations offering wheel-by-wheel RV weighing. RVSEF (Recreational Vehicle Safety Education Foundation) has been weighing RVs for more than 20 years. Escapees SmartWeigh has been in operation since 2010, and offers several permanent weighing sites, as well as weighing at rallies. For more information on these service providers, visit these websites:

- www.rvsafety.com
- www.escapees.com/smartweigh
- weightogollc.com

GAWR is the final vehicle rating that is contained on the Federal Data plate. However, there may be additional information on the data plate, including such things as tire size, pressure, etc. Until September 1996, this limited data was all that was readily available for the RV consumer to make judgments as to the acceptability of a particular RV for any specific usage. Recognizing that this meager information did not allow for intelligent purchase decisions or proper usage of large and complex motor vehicles, the Recreation Vehicle Industry Association® (RVIA) established a program for its members that provided additional load and weight management detail in the form of ratings, definitions, etc. This new data is in the form of an additional data plate referred to as the RVIA Data plate. Examples of RVIA weight information labels (data plates) are on page 21.

Gross Combination Weight Rating (GCWR)
Today more and more motorhomes are towing a second vehicle of one type or another. The actual percentage of those towing now exceeds 90% for motorhomes, while all truck and trailer combinations tow; therefore, most all RVers must also be concerned with GCWR. Whenever you tow anything, THE TOTAL COMBINED WEIGHT OF ALL THE UNITS MUST NOT EXCEED THE GCWR. The GCWR is related in part to the performance of the tow vehicle, so a trailer will not have a GCWR established. This is reflected in the RVIA data plate for trailers. Unfortunately, the government does not require that GCWR be posted on the Federal Data plate. However, RVs sold by members of RVIA after September 1996 will have this information provided. In addition, the GCWR can usually be found in the chassis manufacturer's manual and, in the case of some vehicles, in the manufacturer's towing guide.

<hr>

GCWR = the maximum weight of all vehicles combined

<hr>

Exceeding GCWR normally results in difficulty in stopping, poor hill climbing performance, and poor handling should an evasive maneuver be necessary. In addition to this list of potential problems, exceeding the GCWR means that the whole vehicle will be required to do more work than it was designed for. This will take a toll in terms of reduced reliability and durability, a fact that may leave you stranded by the side of the road or, at minimum, will hit you in the pocketbook as your vehicle struggles to carry and tow the extra load.

Note that GCWR by definition implies that both vehicles have active brakes. However, many manufacturers permit vehicles under a specified weight (generally 1000 or 1500 pounds) to be towed without brakes. Check your tow vehicle manufacturer's towing guide or motorhome chassis manual to determine the rules on whether or not your towed vehicle should have active brakes. For example, the Ford Motor Company® RV & Trailer Towing Guide states, "Important: The towing vehicle's brake system is rated for operation at the GVWR - NOT GCWR. Separate functional brake systems should be used for safe control of towed vehicles and for trailers weighing more than 1,500 pounds when loaded."

Further, you may want to check the laws in your state regarding the maximum allowable weight that can be towed without the towed vehicle having active brakes.

Please consider for a moment that RVs as manufactured and operated within the specified GVWR will not stop as quickly as the traffic around them. The modern automobile will stop from 60 MPH in approximately 120-130 feet; by contrast, the average motorhome will require over 200 feet to complete the same stop. This relatively poor stopping distance performance is the result of the laws of physics, the high center of gravity of the RV, the smaller tire contact area and the compounding used for truck-type tires. Any weight added to the RV, including the addition of a towed vehicle, will further increase the stopping distance, quite possibly to the point where a collision is unavoidable. The ready availability of effective and affordable tow car braking systems makes this addition to your tow car a "no brainer" to enhance your RVing safety.

(Note: More information on this subject is in Book 7.)

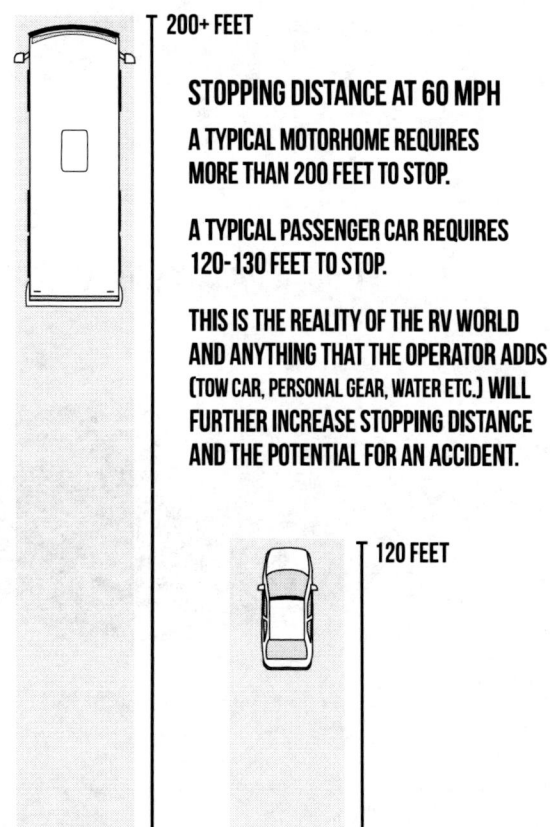

200+ FEET

STOPPING DISTANCE AT 60 MPH
A TYPICAL MOTORHOME REQUIRES MORE THAN 200 FEET TO STOP.

A TYPICAL PASSENGER CAR REQUIRES 120-130 FEET TO STOP.

THIS IS THE REALITY OF THE RV WORLD AND ANYTHING THAT THE OPERATOR ADDS (TOW CAR, PERSONAL GEAR, WATER ETC.) WILL FURTHER INCREASE STOPPING DISTANCE AND THE POTENTIAL FOR AN ACCIDENT.

120 FEET

TOTAL OVERWEIGHT RVS

Before discussing what we need to know and how to use that information, we should take a look at the magnitude of the problem itself. There is, after all, a tendency to believe that we personally are not part of the problem; it's always the other guy. For an understanding of the extent of the problem, we need look no further than the RVSEF data.

RVSEF has weighed more than 35 thousand motorhomes, 5th wheels, travel trailers, tow trucks and towed cars. The results of those weighings have been compiled into the following charts. It is important to understand that this data displays the findings from only those vehicles that have been weighed. It does not imply that this data reflects the condition of all RVs on the road. It is equally important to keep in mind that RVs are generally weighed when they are loaded with people and their possessions. Thus the information does not reveal specific details about the weight of RVs as delivered. RVers are a widely diverse group; there is no stereotypical RVer; however, you will hear more later about the retired librarian, diesel truck mechanic or rockhound as to whether or not they are typical RVers with regard to the amount of weight they carry. Probably no RVer actually carries exactly the 2000-3000 pounds that the information reveals is the average value for extended-stay and full-time RVers.

Of all of the RVs weighed to date, excepting towed cars, 58%, or almost two-thirds, were overweight. This means that they exceeded one or more of the applicable weight limitations. That clearly tells us that the problem is indeed significant. It also tells us that 42% of those vehicles weighed fully comply with all weight limitations and are being operated within all limits; those 42% are to be applauded for their efforts. They also give us hope that the other 58% can be brought into compliance by education and effort on their part. Remember, even those overweight RVers were concerned enough to pay to have their vehicles weighed rather than continue to ignore the problem. Thus, it is likely that some have already taken positive action to resolve their weight issues.

The RV industry record in this matter is shameful; we can and must do better.

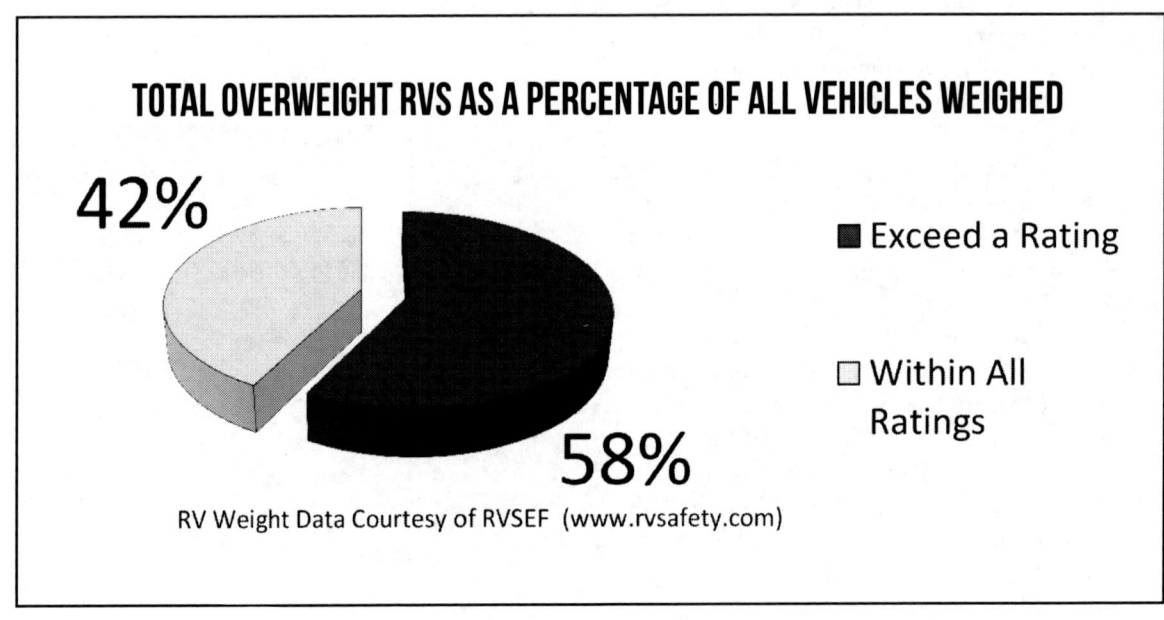

OVERWEIGHT RVS/BY RV TYPE

When the previous facts are disclosed, it is interesting to watch the audience's reaction. It is common for many to nudge their neighbor and whisper, "That's a 5th wheel or trailer problem. I drive a motorhome, so I'm OK." The trailer owner may say, "That's a motorhome problem. I'm OK since I drive a 5th wheel." You no doubt get the point; everyone thinks the problem is someone else's. The reality is shown clearly in the next chart, which breaks down the total figure into RV classes. Quickly you will observe that the problem is more or less equal among all classes of RVs. 59% of the motorhomes, 60% of the vehicles that pull trailers, 51% of travel trailers and 55% of 5th wheel trailers are identified as being overloaded. It's not so simple as blaming someone else. We all share in the overload problem.

Overloading is a general RV problem, not just related to one type of RV.

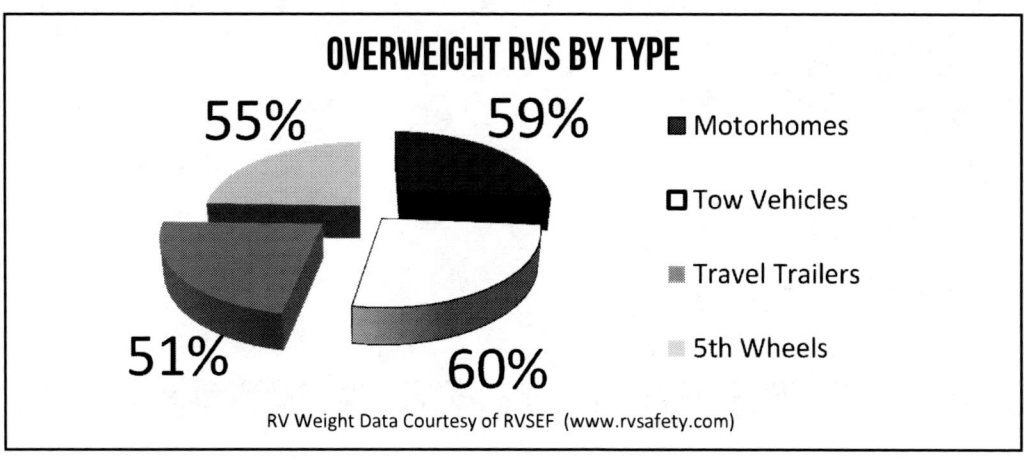

WHICH WEIGHT LIMITATIONS OR RATINGS ARE EXCEEDED

Taking a closer look at the specific weight data by RV type, our initial observation is that the problem is pretty well equal among all types of RVs, so we cannot accept the excuse that it is the other guy. It is an RV problem in general and not related to a specific type of RV. A deeper look reveals just where the problems are by identifying which ratings are most often exceeded. In some instances, mechanical overloads such as GVWR or GAWR are more prevalent, while in other cases tire overloads may be more common. Note that since many vehicles exceed the limit in more than one of the categories, summing the categories can exceed 100%.

The significance of the data breakdown by exceeded rating is very important. When we exceed a mechanical or performance-oriented limitation, such as a GVWR or GAWR, we should not anticipate that the wheels would fall off immediately. More commonly what occurs is that the vehicle will not deliver the performance or longevity that it would have had all of the weight limitations been respected. At very minimum, the result will be a greater cost of operation; at the other extreme, mechanical overloads could leave you stranded beside the road--a very unsafe place to be. The lack of "cause and effect" may lull us into a false sense of security. When informing an RVer of a serious overload, a common response is often, "We have driven this way for some time now and nothing happened, so I guess it's OK." It's not! The reality is quite different. What is actually happening is that the vehicle is being forced to do too much work, more than it was designed for. The result is a gradual degradation, a reduction in reliability and durability, if you will. Further, because of the mechanical overloads, the vehicle performance is also degraded, acceleration is poor, handling is sloppy, the ride is uncomfortable and stopping performance can be downright scary. These are real-world concerns, but are often masked by the lack of an immediate mechanical failure.

In contrast, when we exceed a tire rating, the consequences can be much more dramatic and imminent. An overloaded tire may fail immediately or it may degrade over time, failing down the road at some unpredictable and unsafe opportunity. The nature of a tire failure is also widely variable. It can be a rapid deflation (blowout), thrown tread, slow or repeated deflation, or an irregular wear pattern. In the process of failing, it may do severe damage to your coach and potentially result in personal harm. At the very minimum, it will leave you stranded by the roadside and much lighter in the pocketbook.

OVERLOADED MOTORHOMES - 59% EXCEED ONE OR MORE RATING(S)

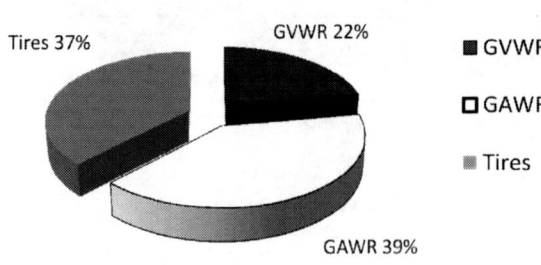

The motorhome category represents all motorhome types including Class A, B, and C. Note, the vast majority of motorhomes weighed are Class A.

OVERLOADED 5TH WHEEL TRAILERS - 55% EXCEED ONE OR MORE RATING(S)

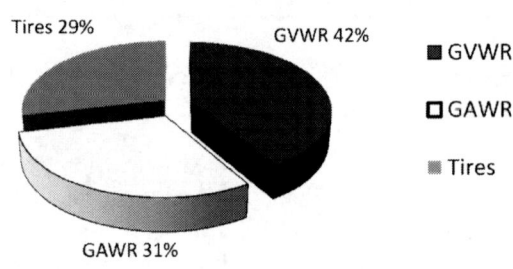

The 5th Wheel Trailer category contains all trailers of this type.

OVERLOADED TRAVEL TRAILERS - 51% EXCEED ONE OR MORE RATING(S)

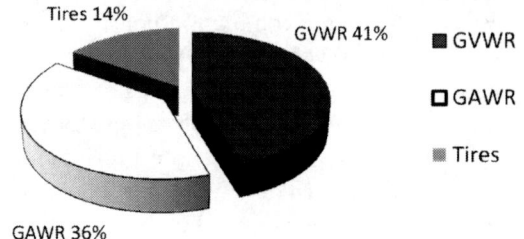

The Travel Trailer category contains all conventional tongue-type trailers.

Book 1: Weight Safety & Load Management   **13**

OVERLOADED TOW VEHICLES - 60% EXCEED ONE OR MORE RATING(S)

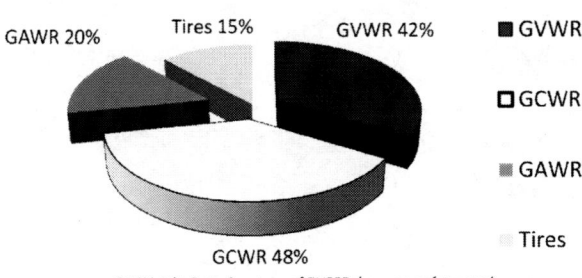

The Tow Vehicle category contains all tow vehicles including pickups, SUVs, vans, automobiles and Medium Duty Trucks (MDT) used to pull both 5th Wheels and Travel Trailers.

OVERLOADED MDT TRUCKS - 37% EXCEED ONE OR MORE RATING(S)

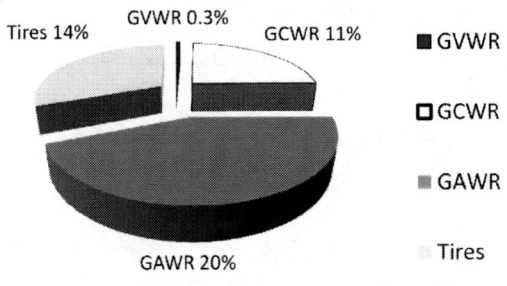

The Medium Duty Truck category (trucks over 15K GVWR) is a breakout from the tow vehicle category. The quantity is relatively small but meaningful, illustrating the benefits of this type of tow vehicle to handle the larger trailers. MDTs are overwhelmingly used to pull only the largest 5th Wheel trailers.

Now For Some Good News
This is good news for the consumer! As manufacturers address the weight issue, they produce vehicles that are more "weight friendly," resulting in fewer problems for their owners. As owners take responsibility for their role in properly loading vehicles, safety and reliability improves. All of these factors result in a healthier RV industry; everyone benefits.

To temper this euphoria somewhat, we should note that now there is a trend toward bigger, heavier and more luxurious recreational vehicles. To illustrate, where slide-outs were a novelty 30+ years ago, they are now nearly standard on today's RVs. Some manufacturers are offering four or more slide-outs per RV. This trend could slow or may even reverse the gains that have been made to date.

Choose your next RV on the basis of its weight capability first. Be prepared to trade off some desirable choices for safety, reliability and durability.

RVers' Ultimate Survival Guide

HOW DO "OVERLOADS" HURT YOU?

We have now learned that overloads in RVs are very common. With some understanding of the magnitude of the problem, it would be reasonable to question why all of those "overloaded RVs" out there are not literally destroying themselves, each other and public property at every turn. We have already approached that topic somewhat by indicating that often the damage being done is not felt immediately (lack of cause and effect), thus explaining some of the nonchalance regarding weight issues. However, there is yet another significant rational answer to the question that may add to our understanding as to just why RVers put up with the situation. Many, if not most, RVers use their RVs in pursuit of leisure activities. Most are retired and do not have to adhere to strict schedules, etc.; thus, they commonly take life at a pretty sedate pace. They often drive slowly, they avoid "rush hours," they bypass cities, they seldom drive in inclement weather, and they often limit their total mileage accumulated annually. In other words, many are somewhat successful at offsetting the damaging effects of the overload. However, not all are fully successful and they pay the price in terms of cost of operation, breakdowns, accidents and, perhaps most importantly, STRESS! Please consider fully the following charts, which summarize exactly "How Overloads Hurt You Or Your RV."

EXCESSIVE GVWRS & GAWRS

Premature driveline failures
- *Transmission*
- *Rear Ends*
- *Wheel Bearing/Wheels*
- *Lug Bolt Breakage*
- *Rapid Vehicle Brake Wear*

Premature suspension failures
- *Suspension Components*
- *Shocks*
- *Springs*
- *Ball Joints*
- *Frequent Alignments*
- *Rapid Tire Wear*

Handling difficulties
- *Sloppy Handling*
- *Wallowing*
- *Leaning*
- *Bottoming Out*
- *Rough Ride*
- *Poor Stopping Ability/Brake Fade*
- *Driver Fatigue*

Excessive cost and poor reliability
- *Poor Fuel Economy*
- *High Maintenance Cost*
- *Limited Vehicle Life*
- *Loss of Warranty Coverage*
- *Potential Legal Liabilities in Accident*

EXCESSIVE GCWR

Premature driveline failures
- *Transmission*
- *Rear End Difficulties*
- *Hitch Problems*
- *Handling Difficulties*
- *Sloppy Handling*
- *Directional Instability (Wandering)*
- *Pulling to One Side*

Operational difficulties
- *Overheating*
- *Poor Acceleration/Hill Climbing*
- *Poor Stopping*

Excessive cost and poor reliability
- *Highway Breakdowns (Road Service)*
- *Limited Life of Components*
- *Limited Vehicle Life*
- *Poor Fuel Economy*
- *Loss of Warranty Coverage*
- *Potential Legal Liabilities in Accident*

TIRE OVERLOADS

Catastrophic tire failure
Immediate Blowout
Thrown Tread
Future Failure (Days, Weeks, Months Later)

Limited tire life
Abnormal Wear Patterns
Rapid Wear

Handling problems
Pulling to One Side
Straight Line Instability (Wandering)
Poor Stopping Performance
Limited Cornering Power

Excessive tire costs
Frequent Alignment
Balance Requirement
Loss of Warranty Coverage
Rapid Wear
Potential Legal Liabilities in Accident

As a general statement, overloads of any kind present a potential threat to your personal well-being. They may leave you stranded by the side of the highway or worse, the victim of an accident. At the very minimum, they are an economic cost to you as they reduce durability and reliability of your vehicle.

Air Suspension Considerations

Motorhomes with an air suspension chassis require special attention. One of the primary tasks of the suspension is to keep the coach level at all times. To accomplish this, it varies the air pressure (volume) in the appropriate air bag(s). This process can create a severely overloaded tire position(s) that would not be identified by weighing the coach by axle, or even by weighing each side independently.

We have witnessed many examples of air suspension motorhomes with more than 2,000 pounds difference side-to-side on the front tires, while the same difference exists in the rear on the opposite side. Note that in virtually all cases the driver was totally unaware of any problem from the driver's perspective. If we dump the air pressure from the system while the coach remains on the scales, this "diagonal loading" frequently diminishes or disappears. Note that this troubleshooting procedure is not always performed because the primary concern is that the tires are carrying the loads measured initially. This apparent loading may come from actual payload, air suspension issues or possibly even from a malfunction of one of the many control mechanisms that is used with such suspension systems. A consideration in this matter is that coach manufacturers generally do not recommend any routine verification or testing to determine the proper performance of air suspension systems. Significant diagonal loading, when identified, should result in a visit to a chassis repair facility for a possible adjustment of ride height.

No matter the cause of observed load, the tires actually carry that load and must be properly sized and inflated to travel safely.

Quite often the result of this condition is a severely overloaded tire(s), which may result in tire failure and loss of control of the coach.

We strongly urge all owners of air suspension motorhomes to have their coaches weighed by individual wheel position!

Today there are more and more full-air-suspension RVs on the road. Air-suspension vehicles are equipped with multiple sensors and valves that, first, determine the vehicle height (ride height) and, second, make adjustments to those values to keep the coach level and at a constant predetermined distance from the ground. The most common method to accomplish this is to use three sensors and valves, creating the equivalent of a three-legged stool (very stable). We learned very early that an unusual distribution of the observed weight on full-air-ride RVs could be an indication of misadjustment or component malfunctions within the system. A pattern of "diagonal loading" (i.e., very heavy right front and left rear or vice versa that cannot be explained by physical observations of the RV) could be an indication of such problems. When these conditions are observed, it is suggested that you contact the coach and/or chassis manufacturer for advice.

Note that each manufacturer will have values on allowable weight asymmetry of loading applicable to their specific coach.

- If significant changes are made to your coach or should air ride adjustment be undertaken, it is our suggestion that you have the coach reweighed as soon as possible.

- If your abnormal weighing values were the result of component problems or malfunction, be cautious that those values may continue to change as you drive. Recognizing this possibility, it may be prudent to carry extra tire pressure to assure that any further degradation of the component will not result in tire overload.

Coach Leveling

When you weighed your RV, it was done utilizing a nearly level surface. Hopefully, your RV was also level when it was weighed. If your vehicle is equipped with full air-ride suspension that was properly working at the time, it would have been adequately level, as that system automatically adjusts ride height as required. If your RV rides on steel springs or rubber suspension or is equipped with air bag assists on the front or rear, it may not have been level for a couple of reasons. The actual weight distribution within your RV may have resulted in sagging at one corner or side, or the suspension (springs) may have degraded, creating a lower corner or side ride height. What is even more common is that the air bag assists may not have been properly inflated. In any case, a lower ride height at one corner or side will further shift the liquid loads in your vehicle to the lower corner or side, further adding to the loads being measured.

- If your corner loads are relatively close and you suspect that your RV still does not ride level, you should seek out a level surface (a paved parking lot) where you can safely and carefully measure the ride height of the four corners of your RV. Use a 4-foot or longer carpenter's level to verify that the lot is level within a ¼ bubble sideways and ½ bubble lengthwise before you begin. Verify that all tires are properly inflated. If you have air bag assist front or rear, be certain that they are inflated to the coach/chassis manufacturer's values and that you have your normal passenger and payload aboard (including the equivalent of your own weight). Measure the ride height of the four corners from the ground to the frame rails (body components are not always true). There should not be a significant variation side to side; greater variation between the front and rear may be okay. Check with your manufacturer for specifications. Air bag assists may be adjusted individually to correct small variations, provided the required pressure does not exceed the maximum permitted by the manufacturer.

- If additional adjustments are required, the RV should be returned to the manufacturer or to a qualified spring/suspension shop for correction. Remember that, if significant changes are made, it may be necessary to reweigh to verify the results.

- If your corner weights are not close, you should first seek to balance your load as close as possible prior to verifying ride height on the four corners of your RV as described above.

UNDERSTANDING YOUR OPTIONS

The information in this section is intended to provide guidance for RV owners when their RV is overloaded in some fashion. It is not intended to be applicable in all cases, nor is it the final word or legal authority for RVers considering their vehicle weight issues. The RV owner is fully responsible for operating a legal vehicle and for complying with all requirements placed on him or her by legal authorities and the vehicle and product manufacturers involved.

OK, So Your RV is Overweight, Now What?
If your RV has just been fully and carefully weighed and a quick look at the numbers reveals that all is not perfect, do not panic or despair. There are things that you can do to help yourselves in this situation. The following discussion provides a good starting place to, first, understand the problem and, second, to make the corrections necessary to assure continued safe travel in your RV.

Keep in mind that there are at least three (3) aspects of being overloaded that you need to understand. The first aspect is that the reliability and durability of your RV will be diminished. In effect, you are asking it, or at least some of its components, to do too much work, certainly more than they were designed for. This could adversely impact your RVing by leaving you stranded beside the road due to breakdown or component failure. What a terrible way to ruin a vacation or your annual trip south. At the very minimum, any overload condition will ultimately hit you in the pocketbook as your RV struggles to carry extra weight. Without question, overloading a vehicle can void any warranty present on your RV.

The second aspect of being overloaded is that your personal safety may be jeopardized. A failure of even the smallest component on an RV can put you at risk. The dangerous potential resulting from a blown tire is obvious, but the failure of any component on your rig could leave you stranded beside the highway with traffic whizzing by at 70 MPH or more, definitely a potentially dangerous situation.

The third aspect of being overweight that you need to consider is the legal aspect. Many of the weight limits on your RV are legally enforceable. Even if RVs do not (currently) have to go through the highway weight scales, law enforcement agencies could choose at any time to enforce the limits, as they do with the trucks that share the highways. Consider that they have recently done this in California with their enforcement of the 40-foot RV length limit, which had been widely ignored for years. Consider also that any aspect of being overweight could result in negative verdicts in the event of an accident in which you are involved. Even if you did not cause the incident or were not cited for being overweight, it still may be viewed as a contributing factor in any lawsuit resulting from the incident.

Your first step should begin immediately. Use the raw data to determine your axle weights, gross vehicle weight, tongue load, etc. for your motorhome or truck and trailer. Compare those numbers to the actual ratings contained on the data plates and components of your RV. You now know where to find this information, so this step should be easy.

If you exceed the GVWR:

- Review your total personal load to see what you do not require. Do just like wagon train families did when they moved west: they disposed of all but the necessities as the going got rougher.

- As soon as possible, dump your gray and black water tanks (properly, of course). No RVer should ever travel with gray or black water. Note that any liquid dumped in this manner will reduce your weight by 8.3 pounds per gallon.

- Dump most of the fresh water that is onboard the RV. It is recommended that you should carry no more than a quarter tank of fresh water; retain only enough for your immediate needs, to repair a broken radiator hose or for an unplanned overnight stay. Remember that water can be obtained almost anywhere, generally at no cost or for a very modest fee. There is no reason to haul water around the country if you are marginal on your load capacity.

- Consider moving what load you can from your motorhome into your tow car or from your trailer RV to the tow vehicle or vice versa. Remember, when you tow an automobile, it is not a car; it is a trailer. As a trailer, it has no passengers onboard; therefore, it can legally and properly carry as much as 800-1000 pounds of load from your motorhome. If you follow this procedure, verify that the tire pressure of your tow car is at the maximum on the tire sidewall.

If you exceed either axle rating (front or rear):
- Proceed as noted when you exceed the vehicle GVWR.

- In this case, you can move weight from one end to the other as required or, if your RV is a truck/trailer combination, you can shift weight from the trailer to the truck or vice versa as the axle loading dictates. Note that the same total weight is still present (GVWR or GCWR), but you may be able to minimize the magnitude of any individual axle overload by redistributing the load. Very few RVs are overloaded in all rated areas (front and rear).

- When you dump your tanks, consider where they are located. If your tanks are physically located where the overload exists (primarily front or rear), this may be adequate to resolve the problem. If not, it will allow weight to be moved from the heavy location into the area where the tanks are located.

If you exceed a maximum tire rating:
- The next step in the process is to determine if your RV exceeds the maximum tire load rating that is identified on the sidewall of your tires. If it does and will not be corrected by the previously listed weight reduction procedures, you should take immediate action to alleviate the situation. Tire overload is very dangerous! Proceed as follows:

- Immediately reduce all possible weight as previously discussed.

- Inflate your tires to the maximum sidewall pressure rating plus 10%. The Tire and Rim Association allows up to 10% extra pressure to provide added safety for operators. It will not increase the tire's rated load, but will allow the tire to better tolerate that overload until it can be rectified. Note that this is an interim solution only. Also, note that this may actually exceed the pressure rating of your wheel; thus, higher tire pressure must be a short-term solution only!

- Drive slowly! The slower you drive below the tires' rated speed, the higher the tires' load rating. Do not carry this to an extreme! However, driving 45-55 MPH where it can be done safely may make the difference between a successful trip and one plagued with tire failures.

- As soon as possible you should complete a long-term solution to your RV's tire overload problem. The best solution is to reduce weight to the degree that the current tire can safely carry the load. Of course, there are cases where this cannot reasonably be done. In these extreme cases you need to consider physical changes to your RV which will allow it to safely carry the extra load. For instance, it may be possible to upgrade to a higher load range tire with a greater carrying capacity. Note that there will be no gain from this unless the higher load range tire is inflated to a higher tire pressure. Higher tire pressures can exceed the maximum pressure rating of your wheels. Some wheels are stamped with the maximum load and pressure; others are not. If you can find no marking on the wheel, it will be necessary to contact the vehicle manufacturer to determine the actual rating of the wheel. If not adequate to meet the pressure requirement of the higher load range (rated) tire, they will also have to be replaced for safe operation. Another possible solution is to fit larger tires for a higher carrying capacity without higher pressure. Once again, you will have to verify that the wheel is adequate for the (larger) tire. This information (rim width requirements) can be garnered from the tire manufacturer's data book or from a tire dealer willing to help you. Note that the larger tire size will be physically larger in cross section and height; thus, you need to verify that it will still fit within the wheel well and will not interfere with the fender or suspension components even under full extremes of turning right, left and at full suspension travel. Larger tires will also have the effect of modestly decreasing the speed read on the speedometer while you drive.

- Note: Re-engineering your vehicle should be one of the last resorts in solving your overload problem. Before making extensive and/or expensive changes to your vehicle you should contact the RV manufacturer for advice. The manufacturer may already have investigated changes that will benefit your overload situation. You may come to the conclusion that there is no way your present RV will meet your personal weight requirements and desired lifestyle. Under these extremes, the purchase of a new RV may be the only practical solution.

To establish proper tire pressure:
- Use the tire load/pressure data charts developed by the tire manufacturer to establish the correct tire pressure for your specific RV. In all cases, tire pressure should be the same on both tires (four in the case of duals) on a given axle. This is the primary disadvantage of having a large side-to-side weight differential, even if it does not exceed the maximum tire rating.

- The heaviest tire establishes the tire pressure for all tires on the axle resulting in an over-inflation condition on the lighter loaded side. If you kept track of all weight changes from the time the vehicle was weighed, you will still be able to calculate and utilize actual tire loads by making adjustments to the recorded weight values to determine the required pressure. When using manufacturer's load/pressure charts, always increase pressure to the next higher column rather than using an interpolated value between two chart columns. Many tire and vehicle engineers recommend an extra 5 psi (from the manufacturer's chart) for steering tire (front) positions. Generally, this is a good recommendation. Note that, if you make a major change in the future, such as carrying extra passengers for a trip, you should reconsider your tire pressure settings.

Hitch analysis for truck/trailer combinations:
- One of the most important benefits of your precision wheel-by-wheel weighing is that the details collected present an opportunity to review (in quantifiable terms) the hitch adjustments for your truck/trailer, whether it is a 5th wheel or conventional tongue-type trailer. When your hitch was initially adjusted, it was probably done by a "rule of thumb". That means, it was adjusted until the trailer appeared approximately level to the eye. This may or may not be correct. The real purpose of the hitch adjustments is to establish proper weight distribution between all components of the two vehicles. There are two possible hitch adjustments to consider:

- Hitch height adjustments affect weight distribution between the axles (2 or 3) of the trailer. The resultant individual trailer axle loads should be very close. A difference of more than approximately 200-300 pounds calls for a hitch height adjustment of 1-2 inches or possibly more; the higher the hitch, the more the load is shifted to the rear axle. By contrast, the lower the hitch, the more the load is shifted to the front axle. This is somewhat arbitrary, but it works well and can eliminate or minimize trailer axle or tire overloads in many cases. The only caution is that for 5th wheel trailers, you must be careful not to lower the front of the trailer too far, cutting clearance to the truck bed excessively (risking contact). If further adjustment is required, it may be necessary to consider raising the trailer on its axles instead. This is not uncommon for 4x4 tow trucks.

- For 5th wheel trailers, hitch location in the bed of the truck is an adjustment. The general rule of thumb is to place the centerline of the hitch 1-2 inches forward of the axle centerline. The purpose of this is to assure that weight is not removed from the front axle of the tow truck when the trailer is attached. Weighing the tow truck twice (both with and without the trailer) to verify that a small amount of weight is added to the front axle of the truck as a result of attaching the trailer provides the information required. The actual value is small; 50-75 pounds is adequate. What is important is that weight is not removed from the front axle; that would adversely affect handling, tire wear, headlight alignment, etc.

- On very large trucks (medium-duty) this adjustment may not be essential since the truck will handle it without problem, but it is still the proper procedure. If weight is removed from the front end of the tow truck, move the hitch forward. The only limit to this occurs on short-bed trucks where contact between the cab and the trailer during sharp turns may result. In this case, there may be no practical option except for special hitches that move rearward when maneuvering sharply, such as during parking, etc.

- For conventional trailers, the transfer of weight to the front axle of the tow vehicle is controlled by adjustment of the torsion bars. If a small amount of weight (50-75 pounds) is not added to the front axle of the tow vehicle, the bars should be tightened until a positive weight gain is noted. It is not always possible to predict the total effect of this change; thus, it may be necessary to reweigh the truck/trailer to determine the effect of torsion bar adjustment. Heavier torsion bars may be required in extreme cases.

- Note that if both adjustments are required, one may affect the other; i.e., tightening torsion bars will raise the rear of the tow truck and affect trailer axle distribution. Re-weighing after adjustments are complete is recommended.

- The rule of thumb for conventional trailers is that they should carry approximately 10-15% of their total weight on the hitch. For 5th wheel trailers that value is approximately 25% of total weight on the hitch. If your trailer exceeds or falls short of this value, redistribution of trailer weight should be undertaken.

Points to consider:
- If you make significant changes in your RV's weight or weight distribution, you may wish to get re-weighed to verify the effectiveness of your changes.

- When moving weight, do it methodically; if possible, use a bathroom scale to keep track of the process.

- While not totally accurate, you can assume that weight in each quadrant of your RV will affect that quadrant primarily. In other words, 50 lbs. moved from the right front corner to the left rear corner will generally affect those corner weights by almost that exact amount.

- It is not necessary to obtain perfect side-to-side balance, but the closer you come, the better your vehicle will handle and the more satisfied you will be. Moving weight from side-to-side has double the effect in reducing the differential by twice the weight moved.

- The old RVer's adage still works: If you don't use it in six months, you really don't need it.

- Similarly, if you get rid of something old for every new item you bring aboard, you will prevent the weight gain common in RVs.

- Note that it may be possible to beef-up or bolster the suspension and tires on your RV to carry a greater load. However, that will not change the legally enforceable weight limits on your vehicle.

RVIA WEIGHT INFORMATION LABELS

Unloaded Vehicle Weight (UVW)
Although the term UVW has been around for a while, it may not be familiar to many people, particularly in its current definition as established and utilized by the RV industry. The UVW is the weight of the new RV as it leaves the factory, with full fuel, oil and coolants, as defined by the RVIA data plate.

Knowledge of the UVW of your vehicle is essential for the weight-conscious RVer. When UVW is subtracted from the GVWR, the result should be the amount of personal "stuff" that we can put aboard the RV without exceeding the GVWR of the vehicle. Since this point is so critical, we should spend a few moments fully understanding the term. The RVIA data plate samples define the term adequately (just a few pages ahead); however, when we look more closely, we realize that anything added to the motorhome after it leaves the factory is not included in the published UVW. It is not uncommon for dealers to add considerable accessories to the vehicle to assist in selling the RV. The weight of those items would not be included in the published UVW.

> **UVW = The weight of the RV as it leaves the factory, with full fuel, oil and coolants.**

Please note that RVIA is an industry organization; when putting together their program, they did not want to burden their members by requiring that they purchase and use precision weighing equipment on every vehicle. For this reason, they allow manufacturers to estimate the weight of vehicles. However, when estimates are used, they are to be identified with either an asterisk (*) or footnote indicating that the reported value was an estimate. Estimates can be accomplished in many ways, including engineering analysis, sampling production units, weighing of components, etc. Now consider that a 10% variation in a 20,000-pound vehicle would amount to 2,000 pounds, and that a 2,000-pound under or over statement of UVW will have an equal effect when we calculate the load-carrying capacity of the coach. Since many RVs have a carrying capacity of only 1,000-2,000 pounds, an error of that magnitude could totally negate its ability to carry a useful load. If the UVW is estimated, be very cautious about using that figure. Under these conditions, you would want (need) to verify the weight by taking the unit to a commercial scale prior to completing the purchase of the unit. Please note also that more and more RV manufacturers are purchasing the weighing equipment and are weighing every vehicle produced. This trend is to be applauded as it adds credibility to the RVIA Data plate.

> **If the UVW is estimated, be very cautious about using that figure.**

Net Carrying Capacity (NCC)
NCC is the TOTAL amount of weight ("stuff," INCLUDING PEOPLE) that the owner can add to the vehicle without exceeding GVWR. NCC is determined by subtracting the UVW from the GVWR. Remember that if the UVW is flawed for any reason, then the NCC (a calculated value) will be similarly flawed.

The important shortfall of NCC is that it DOES NOT tell you WHERE the "stuff" can be added without exceeding a rating. Today many coaches are being purchased on the basis of the massive storage areas offered, particularly the underfloor or bay storage. Some RVs offer one or more pass-through storage bays that cannot be fully utilized because of weight limitations in that area of the coach.

> **NCC = the amount of weight an owner can add to the vehicle without exceeding GVWR.**

The weight-conscious RVer can make some valid judgments relative to the usability of the published NCC by taking a close look at the floor plan of the coach under consideration. You can generally get a copy of the floor plan in the company's advertising brochure. Take it to a copy shop and create a larger- sized floor plan. Sketch in the location of all the heavy components (inside and out) that you can identity and add an estimated weight for each. Then make note of the location and size of all storage areas. By conscientiously following this procedure, you will be able to zero in on the weight and balance issues and how it may or may not be possible to utilize the coach. It is important that once the vehicle is loaded for travel, including passengers, that it be WEIGHED BY INDIVIDUAL WHEEL POSITION to verify that it is safely loaded! If you did your homework, there should be little to do at this point except to "fine tune" your loading.

While considering NCC, this is an excellent opportunity to discuss what your personal requirements might be. Up to this time, we have been calling your personal weight needs "stuff". While that term is descriptive, we will now shift to utilize the more definitive term, NCC. Since that value is contained on the RVIA Data plate, it allows us to make a direct correlation. The NCC, as published, does not include water, propane, passengers or personal possessions. The considerable data collected over the years leads us to conclude that the average "extended stay" RVer will carry approximately 2,000 pounds worth of personal NCC, while the average "full-timer" will require in excess of 3,000 pounds of NCC. Are you average? Probably not. The important issue here is to be very (brutally) honest with yourself. For instance, the retired librarian, diesel mechanic or rockhound probably has needs well in excess of the average mentioned. Recognize that most people have a tendency to understate their needs. What a mistake it would be to go shopping for a 2,000-pound (NCC) motorhome when your real needs are 3,000 pounds or more. One possible solution to this question, for those who own an RV, would be to unload your current coach, weighing all of your goods on a scale. Yes, this is a lot of work, but it could save you from a very expensive mistake.

Cargo Carrying Capacity (CCC)
With a revision to the RVIA data plate, that occurred in August 2000, some of the terms and definitions of this very important document changed. One of the primary motivations for the change was to allow a single data plate to comply with the varying requirements of Canada and the USA. Since most US RV manufacturers do business in Canada, and the Canadian Compliance Label, which became effective after April 1, 1999, contained differing and in some areas more stringent requirements than did the RVIA data plate, it only made good sense to merge those requirements into one document. The original RVIA data plate did not consider the weight of water, propane or passengers when it determined the NCC of the vehicle. The Canadian Compliance Label did identify those realities of RV life and subtracted them from the NCC to result in a value they now called CCC or Cargo Carrying Capacity. This is only logical since RVs do carry all of these items while traveling and the weight of those items must be taken into consideration. What remains of NCC is now identified as CCC, and it truly represents just how much of your personal goods ("stuff") can be carried on board while traveling. The term CCC, while certainly more useful than the previous value of NCC, still does not indicate where that weight may be placed, only that it can be placed somewhere "in" or "on" the RV without exceeding the GVWR. Once again, the CCC still does not include any components not installed by the factory during manufacture of the vehicle.

Sleeping Capacity Weight Rating
With the redefinition of the RVIA data plate after August 2000, manufacturers now had to consider how many people were on board their RVs when establishing the RVIA data plate values. The Canadian Compliance Label procedures and format were again followed. In its simplest definition, the quantity of people assumed to be on board for this purpose was determined by the quantity of sleeping positions in the vehicle. Further, it was assumed that all the people present would be standardized at 70 KG or 154 lbs. Thus, an RV with sleeping room for two would have a SCWR of 2 x 154 = 308 lbs. while a "bunkhouse model" with eight beds would have a SCWR of 8 x 154 = 1232 lbs. Many will argue that they do not carry extra passengers nor do they drive with full water, etc.; in this regard, everyone is unique and must apply their particulars to their personal situation. We can discuss the viability of these values and procedures forever without resolution. However, the RIVA data plate does provide the RVer looking to compare one RV to another with a standardized comparison.

RVIA Motorhome Label
(Used September 1996 through August 2000)

This is the RVIA data plate required of RVIA commercial members. It is important to look at the definition of each term, particularly the UVW and NCC. Note that UVW is defined as its weight "as it left the factory" with FULL FUEL. Therefore, the NCC truly represents how much "stuff", including fresh water, propane, and passengers, that you may choose to put into the motorhome. However, note that UVW does not include dealer-installed accessories, which means that you should add the weight of any dealer-(or previous owner)-installed accessories to the UVW and deduct it from the NCC. There is currently no provision for the dealer to change the label when he adds accessories, so "Buyer Beware!" Very encouraging, however, is the inclusion of GCWR on this label. We caution potential buyers to understand that NCC may not be what it seems and may not be the actual amount of "stuff" you can carry. Consider also the possibility that all of the available NCC may be on one axle or even on one specific corner of the RV. There is evidence of RVs that may have 2,000 pounds of NCC, but it's all located at one corner of the vehicle where there may or may not be room to store it properly.

**MOTORHOME
WEIGHT INFORMATION**

Model_____
GVWR_____
UVW_____
NCC_____
GCWR_____

GVWR (Gross Vehicle Weight Rating) means the maximum permissible weight of this motorhome. The GVWR is equal to or greater than the sum of the Unloaded Vehicle Weight plus the Net Carrying Capacity.

UVW (Unloaded Vehicle Weight) means the weight of this motorhome as built at the factory with full fuel, engine oil and coolants. The UVW does not include cargo, fresh water, LP gas, occupants or dealer installed accessories.

NCC (Net Carrying Capacity) means the maximum weight of all occupants including the driver, personal belongings, food, fresh water, LP gas, tools, tongue weight of towed vehicle, dealer installed accessories, etc, that can be carried by this motorhome.
(NCC is equal to or less than GVWR minus UVW).
GCWR (Gross Combination Weight Rating) means the value specified by the motorhome manufacturer as the maximum allowable loaded weight of this motorhome with its towed trailer or towed vehicle.

This motorhome is capable of carrying up to _____ gallons of fresh water (including water heater) for a total of _____ pounds.
Reference: Weight of fresh water is 8.33 lbs/gal; Weight of LP gas is 4.5 lbs/gal (average).

CONSULT OWNER'S MANUAL FOR SPECIFIC WEIGHING
INSTRUCTIONS AND TOWING GUIDELINES.

RVIA Trailer Label
(Used September 1996 through August 2000)

The RVIA data plate for trailers looks very much like the data plate for motorhomes except that it does not provide a listing for GCWR. This reality is because trailers most are not designed to tow anything. There is currently a trend for an increasing number of 5th wheel trailer RVers to attach a boat, motorcycles, 4x4 or automobile to the rear of their trailer. The multiple trailer combination vehicle is only permitted in some states making this legal; however, the fact remains that, excepting a few special cases, trailers are not designed to tow anything. There are structural, weight distribution and performance limits which must be fully considered before this can be undertaken safely. In addition, there are many states that limit total length to 55-60 feet or require a special driver's license to operate such a vehicle. Thus, this is a decision that should be thoroughly considered by the RVer before making such a commitment.

**TRAILER
WEIGHT INFORMATION**

Model_____
GVWR_____
UVW_____
NCC_____

GVWR (Gross Vehicle Weight Rating) means the maximum permissible weight of this trailer. The GVWR is equal to or greater than the sum of the Unloaded Vehicle Weight plus the Net Carrying Capacity.

UVW (Unloaded Vehicle Weight) means the weight of this trailer as built at the factory with full fuel, engine oil and coolants. The UVW does not include cargo, fresh water, LP gas, occupants or dealer installed accessories.

NCC (Net Carrying Capacity) means the maximum weight of all occupants including the driver, personal belongings, food, fresh water, LP gas, tools, tongue weight of towed vehicle, dealer installed accessories, etc, that can be carried by this trailer.
(NCC is equal to or less than GVWR minus UVW).

This trailer is capable of carrying up to _____ gallons of fresh water (including water heater) for a total of
_____ pounds.
Reference: Weight of fresh water is 8.33 lbs/gal; Weight of LP gas is 4.5 lbs/gal (average).

CONSULT OWNER'S MANUAL FOR SPECIFIC WEIGHING
INSTRUCTIONS AND TOWING GUIDELINES.

"New" RVIA Motorhome Label (Effective 1 September, 2000)

The new RVIA data plate is designed to conform somewhat with the "Canadian Government Compliance Label" (shown later). You will note that the term CCC (Cargo Carrying Capacity) is now used in place of NCC. This more closely equates to the realities that most owners face when they load their motorhomes. The CCC now includes full propane, full fresh water and passengers.

CCC and NCC are NOT the same!

As we have already cautioned potential buyers, they need to understand that CCC still may not be everything that it seems. CCC will tell the owner the total weight that can be legally carried without exceeding the GVWR, but it does not reveal where that weight can be located. All available CCC may be on only one axle or at one corner position. We have evidence of motorhomes, for example, that have 2,000 pounds of carrying capacity, but it's all located at the front axle where there is little or no ability to store it.

**MOTORHOME
WEIGHT INFORMATION
SAMPLE LABEL**

VIN or Serial Number _____

GVWR (Gross Vehicle Weight Rating)
    is the maximum permissible weight of this fully loaded motorhome.

UVW (Unloaded Vehicle Weight)
    is the weight of this motorhome as manufactured at the factory with full fuel, engine oil and coolants.

SCWR (Sleeping Capacity Weight Rating)
    Is the manufacturer's designated number of sleeping positions multiplied by 154 pounds (70 kilograms).

CCC (Cet Carrying Capacity)
    Is equal to GVWR minus each of the following: UVW, full fresh (potable) water weight (including water heater) and full LP-Gas weight and SCWR.

CARGO CARRYING CAPACITY (CCC) COMPUTATION

Pounds (kilograms)
GVWR 14050 (6386)
    Minus UVW 9250 (4204)
    Minus fresh water weight of 56 gallons @ 8.3 lbs/gal 880 (403)
    Minus LP-Gas weight of 14 gallons @ 4.5 lbs/gal 360 (160)
    Minus SCWR of 6 persons @ 154 lb/person 924 (420)
CCC for this motorhome* 2636 (1199)

   *Dealer installed equipment will reduce CCC

CONSULT OWNER'S MANUAL (S) FOR SPECIFIC WEIGHING INSTRUCTIONS AND TOWING GUIDELINES.

3/11/00

"New" RVIA Trailer Label
(Effective 1 September, 2000)

Once again the new RVIA data plate for trailers parallels the RVIA data plate for motorhomes. The primary difference is that this data plate does not require an adjustment to the UVW for the passenger load because there are no passengers riding in the trailer when in motion.

The term GCWR is no longer located on the RVIA data plate. As discussed earlier, this is an important issue, so you will now have to look for this information in the coach manual or contact the technical support of the coach manufacturer to locate this information.

**TRAILER
WEIGHT INFORMATION
SAMPLE LABEL**

VIN or Serial Number _____

GVWR (Gross Vehicle Weight Rating)
is the maximum permissible weight of this trailer when fully loaded. It includes all weight at the trailer axle(s) and tongue or pin.

UVW (Unloaded Vehicle Weight)
is the weight of this trailer as manufactured at the factory. It includes all weight at the trailer axle(s) and tongue or pin. If applicable, it also includes full generator fluids, including fuel, engine oil and coolants.

CCC (Cet Carrying Capacity)
Is equal to GVWR minus each of the following: UVW, full fresh (potable) water weight (including water heater) and full LP-Gas weight.

CARGO CARRYING CAPACITY (CCC) COMPUTATION

	Pounds (kilograms)
GVWR	9400 (4273)
Minus UVW	7050 (3204)
Minus fresh water weight of 56 gallons @ 8.3 lbs/gal	465 (213)
Minus LP-Gas weight of 14 gallons @ 4.5 lbs/gal	63 (28)
CCC for this trailer*	1822 (828)

*Dealer installed equipment will reduce CCC

CONSULT OWNER'S MANUAL (S) FOR SPECIFIC WEIGHING INSTRUCTIONS AND TOWING GUIDELINES.

3/11/00

Book 1: Weight Safety & Load Management

Canadian RV Compliance Labels

All RVs built or imported into Canada for sale must have a compliance label that discloses actual cargo carrying capacity (CCC). Unlike the RVIA data plate that is the standard of a trade association, this label is a Canadian government regulation. It is used to supplement the USA Federal Compliance Label (Federal Data plate).

This label determines the Cargo Carrying Capacity (CCC) based on full fuel, full fresh water including the water heater, full propane and a 70 kilogram (154 pounds) person occupying each designated seating position. It also details the weight (mass) of the waste tanks when full. The Canadian Compliance Label discloses to the operator exactly how much additional weight can be added when the vehicle is loaded for a trip with full tanks and full passenger load. Keep in mind, however, that just as with the RVIA data plate, this label does not tell you WHERE you can place your cargo. Weighing your unit by individual wheel position after you have it loaded is the only way to be certain that you are not exceeding any limitations.

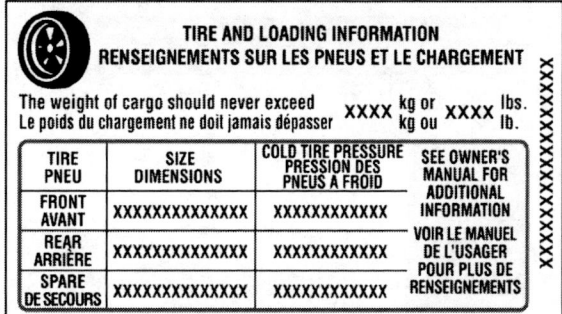

SUMMARY

Overloaded RVs are far more common than any of us would like to admit. The problem is universal across all styles and types of RVs and is generally made worse by our desire to bring our "stuff" along. Weighing your RV properly should be the first order of business for all RV owners. Your safety, and the safety of your fellow travelers, will be enhanced by ensuring that your RV is operating safely within all of its weight ratings.

RVers' Ultimate Survival Guide

RESERVED FOR YOUR NOTES.

BOOK 2: VEHICLE TIRE SAFETY

CONTENTS

Author's Foreword 31
What's it all About? 31

UNDERSTANDING & CARING FOR RADIAL TIRES — 32

Radial Tire Basics 32
The Language of Tire Markings 33
Inflation Pressure Versus Tire Life 36
Proper Tire Inflation 37
Using Tire Charts 38
Tire Pressure Monitoring Systems: Electronic 42
Tire Pressure Monitoring Systems: Mechanical 43
Speed Versus Tire Capacity 44
What is the Age of Your Tires? DOT Code 46
Tire Blocking 48
Tire Help (Assistance) 49
Summary 49

AUTHOR'S FOREWORD

Book 2 of *The RVer's Ultimate Survival Guide* thoroughly covers the topic of RV tires. Tires are the component most vulnerable to the damaging effects of an overloaded or improperly balanced RV. If you have already completed Book 1, you no doubt appreciate the job that tires must accomplish despite common overloads, under-inflation and sometimes outright abuse. Yet, despite all that a tire must do and endure, we have a tendency to take them very much for granted.

No matter how luxurious your RV, we must recognize that RVs have their roots in the truck market. Most of the mechanicals and the tires used on RVs come directly from the trucking industry. As a result, our tires are rugged, durable and able to carry a heavy load by design. However, also by design, these tires require a certain amount of maintenance. This book will help the RVer understand what is required to successfully utilize the tires on our RVs over a long period of time while deriving the maximum value from these very critical components.

WHAT'S IT ALL ABOUT?

Your tires are the only point where your RV contacts the road. As such, they have several difficult jobs to do. Tires not only support the heavy RV, but they also transfer the engine power to the road to propel the vehicle and provide the traction required to slow the RV when brakes are applied. Tires also provide 20-30% of the shock absorbing (ride quality) of your RV and the lateral traction required to steer your RV through turns. This is a bewildering collection of requirements that tires must provide day in and day out.

In order to meet these varying requirements, tires have been developed and enhanced to a high degree, making them vastly better today than ever. Much of that improvement has come about with the change to radial tire designs and the incorporation of modern materials. Today the radial design is virtually standard in the RV world; yet, for all the benefits radial tires bring to the RV world, they also require a modest amount of understanding, care and maintenance. Tire problems are not at all uncommon in RV circles. No matter whether your RV is a motorhome or a truck/trailer combination, tire failures are all too common. Sit around any campfire where RVers gather and you will hear much discussion regarding tires, tire pressure and tire failures, along with much myth and mystery regarding tires. Facts are very difficult to come by in this environment.

The primary purpose of this book is to familiarize RVers with the basics of tire design, their ratings, limitations and the maintenance required to maintain their roadworthiness. When these factors are fully understood, the result is fewer, if any, tire problems and many trouble-free RV miles to enjoy our travels safely.

"Tires are the most vulnerable component on your RV relative to overload issues."

RVers' Ultimate Survival Guide

UNDERSTANDING & CARING FOR RADIAL TIRES
RADIAL TIRE BASICS

What follows is a comprehensive discussion of everything that you as an RV owner/operator need to know about tires. We do not plan on making you a tire expert; rather, our focus is on giving you the information essential for your safety, peace of mind and to become an educated consumer.

Seminars and discussions with RV owners on the subject of tires produce more discussion than any other topic. This is reasonable because tires are the most vulnerable component in the system relative to overload issues. Tires are made of rubber and various other materials in a complicated fabrication process that takes place largely out of sight. Once sold, tires are subjected to incredible operational demands, and often they are neglected or outright abused. Therefore, it isn't any surprise when those tires fail more frequently than any other component on our RV. Recall that the RV is the only automotive vehicle type that is operated at virtually 100% of its capability 100% of the time. No other segment of the automotive world comes close to this requirement. Prevention of tire failures is not only possible, but, in most cases, simply a matter of proper selection, care and maintenance.

Before we look at tire markings and ratings, let's discuss tire damage. We all know that punctures and cuts cause tire damage, but in actual use they are only a small component of the causes of tire failure.

Overload and/or under-inflation cause most tire failures! To a tire these conditions are the same!

When a tire fails from overload and/or under-inflation, it generally occurs over a period of time. In other words, it fails from progressive damage. For each mile a tire is operated in this condition, it may be damaged internally, out of your sight and without warning. After an indeterminate period of time, it may fail, and when it does, your RV may be on the highway, traveling slowly or even sitting still at your campsite. The harder the tire is pushed, the sooner this failure is likely. Tire damage is cumulative; that is, it accumulates over a period of time until one or more components is so weakened that it can no longer do its job. Tires are not "self-healing." We should not anticipate that the simple act of removing the tire's abuse will remove the damage already inflicted upon the tire.

All this tells us that tire maintenance is extremely important beginning from the first day of usage. If you understand and operate within the capabilities and limitations of your tires and maintain them properly, it is unlikely that you will experience a tire failure. That, of course, assumes that the correct tires for the application are installed.

**PREVENTING TIRE FAILURES!
This is what the tire portion of our educational program is all about.**

THE LANGUAGE OF TIRE MARKINGS

There is a great deal of important information molded directly onto the sidewall of your tires. In fact, in the tire business jokes abound about not being able to put all of the required information on some of the smaller tire sizes. As an RVer, knowledge of much of that information is essential to assure that you purchase the correct replacement tires, to determine the correct inflation pressure and to assure appropriate maintenance procedures.

Each tire has its own distinct markings. As an example, we have chosen to utilize the LT225/75R16 LRE since it is used widely on many motorhomes, trailers and on the pickups that pull many travel trailers. Just as you have two names (first and last) that are required to fully identify you, tires also have two names. See example on previous page.

First Name = LT225/75R16
Last Name = LRE

We will discuss each term of the first name that essentially defines the size of the tire.

(LT) *stands for light truck. That is one of the tire type classifications covered by a Tire and Rim Association standard. In addition to "LT" tires, there are "P" tires that are passenger car tires and "ST" tires that are special trailer tires. One example of a tire without a prefix is 12R x 22.5 LRH. This is typical of a truck and bus tire which has no prefix.*

(225) *is a metric measurement across the section width (widest portion of the sidewall) in millimeters.*

(/) *The slash is a mathematical term indicating ratio.*

(75) *is a mathematical result of dividing the section height (depth of tire cross-section from the tread to the bead) by the section width (above). Sometimes this is referred to as the profile or series of the tire; for example, a low profile or 60 series tire. Note that ratios approaching 100% are generally associated with high carrying capacity and lower speed, while low ratios, .70 - .35, are generally optimized towards a high performance capability with high speed and handling qualities.*

(R) *This alphabetical term stands for radial tires. For practical purposes, the radial tire is the standard tire used on nearly all RVs manufactured today. In a radial tire, the cords run perpendicular to the bead of the tire directly across the crown of the tire to the opposite bead. Radial tires normally have only a single-ply of carcass material. In contrast, earlier designs were of a bias-ply design. Bias-ply tires always have more than one ply used in pairs (two at a time); for example, 2, 4, 6, 8, etc.*

(16) *The final numerical term is the diameter of the bead of the tire in inches. Bead seat diameters are manufactured in half-inch increments; thus, great care must be exercised to assure that the correct tire is selected and mounted. Your safety, and that of the mechanic doing the mounting, is at stake.*

Now for the tire's last name, which defines the load-carrying ability of the tire:

(LRE) *defines the load-carrying ability of the tire using the current terminology. The words "Load Range E" may also be used for this purpose. In years past, other terms were used for this purpose, including "xx plies" and "xx ply rating."*

It is important to understand that all tires of the same size do not necessarily have the same load-carrying capacity. Within most tire sizes, there are several "load ranges" that determine the load-carrying capacity.

To understand the background of "load range," we need to understand a little about the history of tires. Preceding current tire technology, design engineers had only one practical material to use in tire construction. That material was cotton. Cotton was an excellent, easily worked material but had only minimal strength. The various war efforts pushed the development of synthetic materials such as rayon, nylon and polyester.

Where increased load-carrying capacity was required, it was initially obtained by adding more plies, or layers of material, to the casing of the tire; thus, the familiar load-carrying term "10-ply tire." This meant that the casing actually had ten plies, or layers, of cotton material. The more layers in a tire, the greater the load-carrying capacity. With newer materials offering greater strength, engineers were then able to increase tire load-carrying ability by substituting material of greater strength. This brought with it the term "ply rating" in which fewer plies provided the equivalent strength of earlier cotton tires. With the advent of modern materials, the whole concept of tire construction changed. Today most tires that we use on RVs are radial designs and have only one ply, or layer of high strength material forming the casing.

Now, consider the problem that the tire industry faced when tire design changed. Everyone was accustomed to defining tire load capacity by the number of plies but now we use only one ply and change the strength of the casing material to vary the load-carrying capacity. To resolve this, the tire industry established the current "load range" system. The higher the letter is in the alphabet, the higher the carrying capacity. To be consistent with the older system, the load range code relates directly to the old system of plies. To "break" the code, you need only to identify the position of the letter in the alphabet and multiply it by 2. In our example, "E" is the fifth letter of the alphabet (5 x 2 = 10) or a 10-ply "RATED" tire. This means that it has the equivalent strength of a bias ply, 10-ply tire.

The next issue we must consider is the actual "load-carrying ability in pounds," which is also detailed on the tire sidewall. Let's break it down into its elements:

(MAX LOAD) *This clearly indicates just what it says: the* **MAXIMUM** *load capacity of the tire! You should not expect your tire to carry any greater load than specified in this line. Remember our discussion about progressive tire damage. Each time you operate a tire over its rated capacity, it may become damaged internally.*

(SINGLE) *This means that the stated carrying capacity only applies when the tire is installed in a single tire application. That means one tire on each end of the axle, such as the front or tag axle of your motorhome or tow truck, or the axles on your trailer.*

(2680 LBS) *This is the rated carrying capacity of this tire, in pounds, when installed in a single configuration. Do not expect it to do more!*

(AT @80 PSI) *This is the minimum air pressure required to obtain the rated carrying capacity of 2680 lbs (single). It is extremely important to understand that this tire IS ONLY RATED AT 2680 LBS. WHEN IT HAS 80 PSI OF INFLATION PRESSURE! As soon as you reduce inflation pressure, the rated carrying capacity decreases. Note also that there are times when this air pressure may be exceeded. More information on these exceptions will be given shortly.*

(COLD) *This is perhaps one of the least understood terms on the tire. This term tells us that to obtain the maximum carrying capacity of 2680 pounds the tire should be inflated to 80 psi* **WHEN IT IS COLD***! Cold, to the RV owner/operator means the temperature of the tire before we start rolling down the road or the ambient*

outside temperature (in shade). As the tire rolls under load, it flexes, which will create additional heat and pressure. If you set our example tire at 80 psi and then drive several hundred miles at 65 miles per hour, the inflation pressure will increase significantly, perhaps to as much as 90 psi or more. IT'S SUPPOSED TO DO THIS! Never reduce inflation pressure of a warm tire because it is higher than the pressure shown on the sidewall! The result may be under-inflation, which can cause internal damage to the tire.

(MAX LOAD DUAL 2470 LBS. @80 PSI COLD) *As discussed above, this tells us the maximum load-carrying capacity at 80 psi, COLD, when installed in a "DUAL" configuration, such as the drive tires on your motorhome or tow vehicle. You will note that this is the very same size tire, at the very same inflation pressure, in a dual configuration, yet it has a LOWER-RATED CARRYING CAPACITY than when used in a single configuration. This is because when two tires are installed side by side, they do not always share the load equally due to road crown (a peak for drainage), etc. The tire manufacturers compensate for this by reducing the rated load-carrying capacity when installed in a dual configuration.*

A good point to interject here, is that tires mounted in a dual configuration should be matched closely by diameter. We have learned that when duals do not share the load evenly, the tire rating must be downgraded to account for this problem. The same thing can happen when we operate tires that are mismatched in diameter from any cause. On the front or steering axle of motorhomes, diameter is equally important; here excessive differences can result in the vehicle pulling to one side or the other. Tires of differing sizes can come from several sources. A new tire (even from the same manufacturer) may be larger in diameter than is a used tire, and tires made by different manufacturers are often measurably different in diameter. The best bet is to keep your tires well matched by diameter.

As consumers wanting to make well-informed purchase decisions regarding tires, we still need to know more about tire construction. For instance, many of us tend to think of a tire as a "round and black and very expensive" thing that we put on our vehicles. In other words, the perception is that all tires are pretty much alike as long as the "first and last name" is the same. Well, nothing could be further from the truth. There are many meaningful variations in the design and fabrication of tires. In addition, the support of one brand over another is a mark of quality that should be seriously considered.

Without being a tire engineer with insider information, it is still possible to judge some quality aspects of a tire. One possibility is to determine the material used in its construction. Once again, the tire sidewall information tells us this very important quality measure along with the actual number of plies in the carcass and tread area. You will note that each tire has markings embossed on the sidewall that details this information.

In this case, you will note that the carcass (sidewall) is comprised of one steel ply (true radial) while the tread is composed of five plies of steel. This brings up another consideration. Most of our tires are now of a radial design, which is an extremely limber product (flabby, if you will). This works well in the sidewall for shock-absorbing qualities and handling; however, this would not yield acceptable tread life. For that we require a very rigid tread package. In this case, our tread surface is reinforced with five plies of steel material providing a very rigid wearing surface where the tire contacts the road. The fact that our tire example uses steel cords for both the sidewall and tread surface would indicate that this is a high quality product. All-steel designs are generally considered to be very durable, long lasting and abuse-tolerant designs.

INFLATION PRESSURE VERSUS TIRE LIFE

Tires represent one of the major ongoing expenses faced by most RVers. This reality stems from two sources: first, tires wear as a result of operating the vehicle; and second, tires have a limited life due to degradation (natural aging). Neither condition is normally covered by warranty; thus, we must purchase replacement tires periodically as long as we own our motorhome. It is understandable and in your best interest to get the maximum life out of your expensive RV tires.

All of the charts that we use in the tire portion of the seminar come from tire manufacturers' manuals or from the *Tire and Rim Association Handbook* (T&RA). The T&RA is the industry association charged with setting standards for tires, rims and valves in the United States and internationally. All of the tire charts shown apply only to radial ply tires.

You will note that our first chart plots percent of RECOMMENDED inflation pressure versus mileage (tire life) as a percentage.

Note that only when we run 100 percent of the recommended pressure (correct pressure) do we get 100 percent of the potential tire life.

You will observe that running either too much pressure or too little pressure for a given load results in loss of tire life. Obviously, more life is lost with under-inflation than over-inflation, but both conditions will cost you tire life. Keep in mind that this chart refers only to inflation pressure versus load. It has nothing to do with tire wear that is related to alignment problems, worn-out shock absorbers, etc.

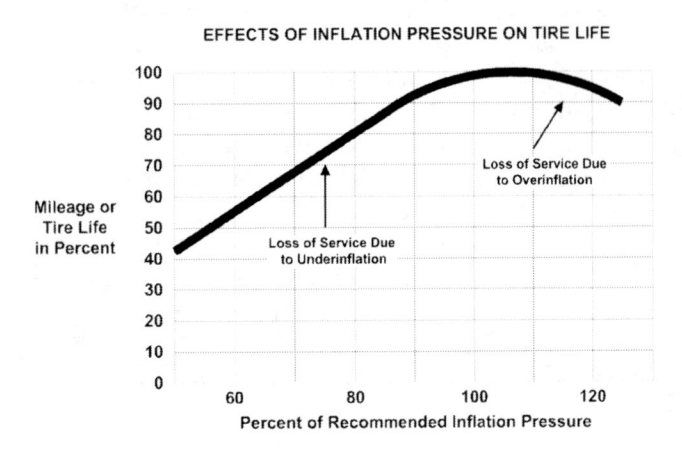

The key word is **RECOMMENDED**! The correct (recommended) pressure for tires is established by the tire manufacturer, based upon the load the tire is asked to carry and the performance standards they specify.

RECOMMENDED IS NOT:

- what your neighbor tells you based on his motorhome or experience.
- necessarily the pressure shown on the sidewall. The sidewall pressure is the pressure required when the tire is asked to carry the maximum load.
- the pressure your local tire dealer advises if he does not know your vehicle's actual weight by tire position and refers to his manufacturer's tire data sheets. Remember, the tire dealer is generally biased towards a *higher* tire pressure to minimize tire problems and warranty issues.
- necessarily what the vehicle manufacturer (or dealer) suggests that you use. The manufacturer is required to put a value for recommended tire pressure on the tire pressure placard; however, in order to do this, the manufacturer must make a guess as to how you will be operating your RV. In addition, manufacturers are generally biased towards a *lower* pressure to enhance the ride quality of the vehicle they are trying to sell.
- what your RV was delivered with. At the time it was delivered, it was empty and it may have been a while since the tire pressures were adjusted.
- what you feel is correct to result in a better ride quality. Tires are only a part of the shock absorbing system of your RV. They provide only 20-30% of the total ride quality.

RECOMMENDED IS exactly what the tire manufacturer says should be used based on the *actual* load being carried by the tire.

Now let's continue on to examine why the correct inflation pressure determines tire life and other performance considerations.

EFFECTS OF INFLATION PRESSURE ON TIRE LIFE

PROPER TIRE INFLATION

Radial tires have many performance advantages over predecessor bias-ply tires. They provide superior handling, life, ride quality and are lighter and more cost-effective. One significant advantage of a radial tire is that, when properly inflated for the load, the reinforced tread package is held rigidly flat on the road. This is true even when making severe turning maneuvers and under heavy braking or acceleration. This characteristic is optimized when the tire is properly inflated for the load being carried. Only then will we have optimum "tire patch" or contact area with the road. With this assured, we can be sure of optimum braking, acceleration, ride quality and the best tire wear.

Proper Inflation

Note on the graphic below, the example on the far right, which we have labeled "proper inflation," that the tread is flat on the road and the sidewall is bowed out slightly. This is how a radial tire should look when properly inflated.

Over-inflation

When we over-inflate the tire as shown in the center graphic, the tire stands up too straight and the edges of the tire are lifted off the road. The result is faster wear in the center of the tire because it is carrying most of the load. Over-inflation also tends to make the tire too hard, creating a harsher ride and susceptibility to damage if it strikes a foreign object or pothole while you drive. Remember that one of your tire's tasks is to function as a shock absorber. Approximately 20-30% of the shock-absorbing capability of your motorhome is derived from the tires. If it is too hard, it will not flex as designed, resulting in a harsh ride quality. Perhaps the most serious risk with over-inflated tires is the reduction of "tire contact patch." An over-inflated tire does not provide adequate contact with the road. This can reduce braking effectiveness, particularly on wet roads. The result could be a loss of control of the vehicle.

Under-inflation

If we under-inflate a tire, as depicted on the left, the tire deflects upward at the tread centerline. The result is that we get rapid wear on the outside edges and an unusual wear pattern on the center of the tread because the center of the tread is distorted.

Under-inflation's most serious consequence is heat buildup which may destroy the tire. Since the tire flexes excessively, it builds up internal heat, which causes the rubber compounds to break down, ultimately resulting in structural damage and catastrophic failure. Remember that to a tire under-inflation is exactly the same as overload.

If you are uncertain of what the correct tire pressure is for your tires, always err on the high side. Under-inflation is much more harmful than over-inflation.

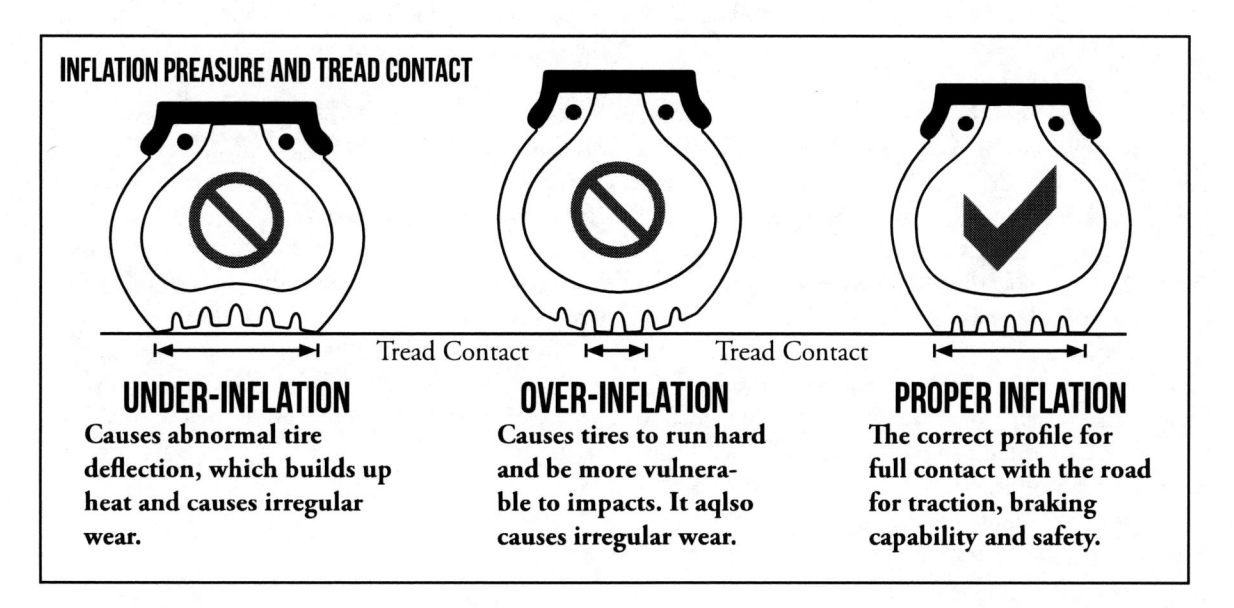

INFLATION PREASURE AND TREAD CONTACT

UNDER-INFLATION
Causes abnormal tire deflection, which builds up heat and causes irregular wear.

OVER-INFLATION
Causes tires to run hard and be more vulnerable to impacts. It aqlso causes irregular wear.

PROPER INFLATION
The correct profile for full contact with the road for traction, braking capability and safety.

USING TIRE CHARTS

With our newly found understanding regarding the importance of proper inflation, let us now examine how to determine the correct tire pressure for your RV.

Keep in mind that selection of the proper inflation is primarily a function of the load on the tire. Therefore, it follows that the only way we are going to determine the correct pressure is to weigh the RV. The most accurate way to weigh the RV for this purpose is to weigh the unit by individual wheel position. This will identify the heaviest loaded position (worst case) for each axle.

> **The heaviest (worst case) tire position determines the correct pressure for all the tires on an individual axle.**

Although there are exceptions, most tire manufacturers recommend that you run the same pressure for all tires on the same axle. Note that if you find your RV to be significantly heavier on one side or corner, you might want to contact your tire manufacturer and see what they recommend. If you are unable to weigh your motorhome wheel-by-wheel, consider taking it to a CERTIFIED truck scale where you can weigh it by axle.

To initiate our discussion, let us first examine the situation when you have obtained axle weights by having your RV weighed at a truck scale. First, locate the CORRECT TIRE CHART for the tires on your RV. Do not use a chart borrowed from others, and do not assume that because you have a chart for your size and load range tire, it is the correct one. Different manufacturers use different pressures to accomplish the same load-carrying capacity! After verification that you have the correct chart, you need to compare the maximum load and pressure shown on the sidewall of your tire with the extreme right side of the chart. If the numbers match (identical pressure and load), you probably have the correct chart.

> **Caution: Some tire charts are represented by individual tire loads, others are shown by axle loads, and some are listed by wheel position loads! All have similar numbers that vary by a factor of 2x or 4x. Be certain that you have the correct chart.**

Chart values presented by individual tire load
On these charts the value shown on the far right side of the chart will match what is molded into the sidewall of your tires for the single and dual application.

Chart values presented by axle load
Here the assumption is that the load is equal on both sides. The value shown on the far right of these charts will be twice the value shown on your tire sidewall for a single application and four times for the dual application.

Chart values presented by wheel position load
On these charts, the value shown on the far right side will be the same as shown on your tire's sidewall for single tires. However, the values shown for duals will be double that shown on the tire sidewall.

There are two ways to read a tire/load inflation chart.
If you know your tire, axle weight or wheel position weight, you can follow the chart to the right (for the single or dual application) until the published weight exceeds your actual weights. At this point, move to the top of that column and you will have identified the minimum pressure to support that tire load.

The second method is to enter the chart from the top with a specific tire pressure. Follow that column down to determine the maximum amount of weight the tire is capable of carrying at that pressure.

> **Remember, if using an axle chart, you must divide the number by two for a single tire application or four for a dual application to determine the carrying capacity of an individual tire. If you are using a wheel position chart, then the dual value must be divided by two to determine the carrying capacity of the individual tire. Knowledge of the type of chart you have is critical.**

Note: Tire load inflation charts vary widely by manufacturer, however, they all contain the same essential information!

TIRE LOAD INFLATION CHART
BY TIRE

LT225/75R16LRE

LBS PER TIRE	PSI	35	40	45	50	55	60	65	70	75	80
	SINGLE	1500	1650	1790	1940	2060	2190	2335	2440	2560	2680
	DUAL	1365	1500	1630	1765	1875	1995	2150	2220	2330	2470

TIRE LOAD INFLATION CHART
BY AXLE

LT225/75R16LRE

LBS PER AXLE	PSI	35	40	45	50	55	60	65	70	75	80
	SINGLE	3000	3300	3580	3880	4120	4380	4670	4880	5120	5360
	DUAL	5460	6000	6520	7060	7500	7980	8600	8880	9320	9880

TIRE LOAD INFLATION CHART
BY WHEEL POSITION

LT225/75R16LRE

LBS PER POS.	PSI	35	40	45	50	55	60	65	70	75	80
	SINGLE	1500	1650	1790	1940	2060	2190	2335	2440	2560	2680
	DUAL	2730	3000	3260	3530	3750	3990	4300	4440	4660	4940

To continue our discussion, let us assume that we took our RV to a truck scale and weighed the front axle. That load is determined to be 5,000 pounds. Referring to an axle chart for our LT225/75R16 LRE tires we determine that the maximum load-carrying capacity for a single application is 5,360 pounds. Since we are just within that value, we determine that we must run 75 psi in the front tires of our motorhome. If the axle load had been 4,000 pounds, then 55 psi would be the required pressure for that load. However, in both cases what we have done is assume that the load on the axle is equal on both sides!

You have learned that this is a bad assumption!

Now let us take our RV and weigh it wheel-by-wheel. The front axle still weighs 5,000 pounds, but now we determine that the left front is loaded to 3,000 pounds, and the right front load is 2,000 pounds. Still 5,000 pounds but now, when we go to the tire chart, we find that, based on its maximum rating of 2,680 at 80 psi, we are overloaded on the left tire by 320 pounds even when inflated to 80 psi.

This is the real world and the cause of many tire failures. It should be apparent that, when an RV is heavier on one side, it is imperative that we weigh it wheel-by-wheel to determine correct tire pressure and to ensure that we are not overloading a tire.

Exceptions to Tire Load/Inflation Chart Values

After having said all of the above, there are exceptions to using the specific tire pressures shown on the charts. First, when using charts note that the charts are in 5 psi increments. Most tire manufacturers recommend that you run a slightly higher pressure than that shown on the chart for STEERING AXLES. If you glance back at our graphic labeled "Inflation Preasure and Tread Contact," (pg. 37) the graphic on the right shows the tread surface sitting evenly on the ground. When turning the RV, the steering axle tires do the work for us. As we turn, the outside edge of the tire is worn away due to the high shear forces encountered. This tire wear appears much like an under-inflation wear pattern. This condition can be corrected by slightly over-inflating the tires, resulting in a more even wear pattern. The real question is, how much more? The consensus of manufacturers is to recommend 10% higher pressure than the chart value for the load. However, the selected pressure should not exceed the pressure shown on the sidewall or wheel.

In addition, the speed that you drive may also dictate the pressure you must carry in your tires. We will be discussing this issue in some depth a little later. For now, you should consider that, if you tend to drive at higher speeds (perhaps even over some speed limits), then your tires require additional air pressure.

There is yet another exception. Light truck tires (those with the size designation starting with "LT") are permitted to be inflated to a pressure up to 10 psi greater than that shown on the sidewall (20 psi for large truck and bus tires). This will result in the tire running cooler, thus better able to handle abuse, but **DOES NOT INCREASE THE LOAD-CARRYING CAPACITY OF THE TIRE!**

An additional suggested adjustment to the recommended pressure you obtain from the chart is that you should consider that the pressure shown on the charts is the MINIMUM for the load listed. Since tire pressure gauges may not always be totally accurate and many RV owners do not check their tire pressures daily as recommended, a small "margin" allowance may be prudent. This will provide a small leeway for those times that the pressure might fall before you catch it. The best way to achieve this small margin is to add about 200 pounds to the actual load per tire. Once added in this manner you can use the chart to determine recommended pressure.

Summary of exceptions to be considered when establishing tire pressure:

- *Round up to next chart value*
- *Steering tire adjustment*
- *Adjustment for abusive operation*
- *Adjustment for pressure gauge inaccuracy*

If you have any question regarding correct inflation pressure, contact the tire manufacturer!

This page is an excerpt from the current *Michelin RV Tire Guide*. Note the inflation table is now based on the owner having determined the individual wheel position weights. The emphasis is placed here because this is the only sure way to arrive at the correct inflation pressure.

The chart is entered with the heaviest single tire position on the "S" line and the heaviest dual tire position on the "D" line. The "PSI" line will provide the MINIMUM inflation pressure for the load.

Note that Michelin recommends increasing the inflation pressure 5 psi over the chart amount in order to provide a safety margin, due to the fact that the weight of an RV can vary considerably with different loading configurations. Also note that Michelin emphasizes the importance of setting ALL TIRES ON THE SAME AXLE TO THE SAME PRESSURE!

MICHELIN INFLATION CHARTS FOR RV USAGE ONLY

For RV use only, Michelin displays tire loads per axle end in the load and inflation tables, as we recommend weighing each axle end separately and using the heaviest end weight to determine the axle's cold inflation tire pressure. For control of your RV, it is critical the tire pressures be the same across an axle, while NEVER exceeding the maximum air pressure limit stamped on the wheels.

To select the proper load and inflation table, locate your tire size in the following pages, then match your tire's sidewall markings to the table with the same sidewall markings. If your tire's sidewall markings do not match any table listed, please contact your Michelin dealer for the applicable load and inflation table.

Industry load and inflation standards are in a constant state of change, and Michelin continually updates its product information to reflect these changes. Printed material may not reflect the latest load and inflation

In the load and inflation tables, SINGLE means an axle with one tire mounted on each end, while DUAL means an axle with two tires mounted on each end. The loads indicated represent the total weight of an axle end, in an RV application. When one axle end weighs more than the other, use the heaviest of the two end weights to determine the unique tire pressure for all tires on the axle. The maximum cold air pressure for each axle may vary, depending on their weights. These tables are applicable for all RV axles, whether or not they are power-driven.

WHEEL DIAMETER - 16"

LT215/85R16 LRE   XPS RIB®

PSI	35	40	45	50	55	60	65	70	75	80		MAXIMUM LOAD AND PRESSURE ON SIDEWALL			
kPa	240	280	310	340	380	410	450	480	520	550					
LBS SINGLE	1495	1640	1785	1940	2055	2180	2335	2430	2550	2680	S	2680	LBS at	80	PSI
LBS DUAL	2720	2980	3250	3530	3723	3970	4300	4420	4640	4940	D	2470	LBS at	80	PSI
kPa SINGLE	678	744	809	880	932	989	1059	1102	1156	1215	S	1215	KG at	550	kPa
kPa DUAL	1234	1351	1474	1601	1689	1801	1950	2005	2104	2240	D	1120	KG at	550	kPa

LT225/75R16 LRE   XPS RIB®

PSI	40	45	50	55	60	65	70	75	80		MAXIMUM LOAD AND PRESSURE ON SIDEWALL			
kPa	280	310	350	380	410	450	480	520	550					
LBS SINGLE	1650	1790	1940	2060	2190	2335	2440	2560	2680	S	2680	LBS at	80	PSI
LBS DUAL	3000	3260	3530	3750	3990	4300	4440	4660	4940	D	2470	LBS at	80	PSI
kPa SINGLE	748	812	880	934	993	1059	1107	1161	1215	S	1215	KG at	550	kPa
kPa DUAL	1361	1478	1601	1701	1810	1950	2014	2114	2241	D	1120	KG at	550	kPa

LT235/85R16 LRE   XPS RIB®

PSI	35	40	45	50	55	60	65	70	75	80		MAXIMUM LOAD AND PRESSURE ON SIDEWALL			
kPa	250	280	310	350	380	410	450	480	520	550					
LBS SINGLE	1740	1862	1985	2205	2315	2425	2623	2755	2910	3042	S	3042	LBS at	80	PSI
LBS DUAL	3170	3390	3610	4012	4211	4410	4762	5014	5296	5556	D	2778	LBS at	80	PSI
kPa SINGLE	790	845	900	1000	1050	1100	1190	1250	1320	1380	S	1380	KG at	550	kPa
kPa DUAL	1440	1540	1640	1820	1910	2000	2160	2270	2400	2520	D	1260	KG at	550	kPa

LT245/75R16 LRE   XPS RIB®

PSI	35	40	45	50	55	60	65	70	75	80		MAXIMUM LOAD AND PRESSURE ON SIDEWALL			
kPa	250	280	310	350	380	410	450	480	520	550					
LBS SINGLE	1700	1865	2030	2205	2335	2480	2625	2765	2900	3042	S	3042	LBS at	80	PSI
LBS DUAL	3090	3390	3690	4012	4250	4510	4762	5030	5280	5556	D	2778	LBS at	80	PSI
kPa SINGLE	790	845	920	1000	1060	1125	1190	1255	1315	1380	S	1380	KG at	550	kPa
kPa DUAL	1440	1537	1675	1820	1927	2045	2160	2280	2395	2520	D	1260	KG at	550	kPa

TIRE PRESSURE MONITORING SYSTEMS: ELECTRONIC

With our newly found understanding about the importance of tire pressure and how tires deteriorate and fail from under-inflation (or overload), it follows that we must be vigilant about checking tire pressure. In fact, the tire manufacturers are unified in the position that the tires on our motorhomes should be checked every day that we travel.

Tire pressures should be checked every day of RV travel.

Prior to weighing RVs, we ask each owner what tire pressures they utilize. The purpose of this inquiry is to enable us to determine tire ratings for their tires on their vehicle. A common answer is that the owner tells us that they "don't know," either because they don't check their tires or cannot check them due to wheel covers or some other obstruction. This is absolutely not acceptable! Not only will it cost you money should you experience a tire failure, but the personal safety implications are obvious and just not worth the risk.

The tire industry has long sought some sort of tire pressure monitoring system that would yield this information in real time, with reliability and with an accuracy that can be counted on. Tire manufacturers quite frequently are forced to pay warranty claims that are actually attributable to under-inflation. Such a system offers RV owners relief from the necessity of getting down on their hands and knees on a daily basis. Tires could then be checked for proper inflation pressure on a constant ongoing basis. This would resolve what is arguably one of the most difficult issues for most RVers.

The fairly recent development of run-flat tires for use in high performance and/or luxury automobiles has spurred the development of just such a system for RVs. Actually, there are now several such systems on the market, each with its own merits and limitations. The systems vary but most incorporate a tiny transmitter in or on the wheel that monitors inflation pressure and sometimes the temperature inside the tire. A cockpit indicator advises the driver if a tire is losing air or overheating, enabling him/her to take corrective action before the tire is severely damaged or fails. Although these systems seem expensive, in most cases the entire system is cheaper than buying one tire!

Due to the increased lengths of our RVs, it may be necessary to install a signal booster somewhere between the monitor in the cab and the actual sensors on the tires. This signal booster will boost the signal from the sensors on the tires providing a stronger signal to the monitor.

Does "peace of mind" really have a monetary value?

The usage of such a tire pressure monitoring device can prove to be particularly valuable for the vehicle that you tow. The operator of a motorhome is "disconnected" from the tow car as are truck/trailer combinations, often to the degree that a serious tire problem can occur without the driver being aware of the issue. This is proving to be one of the best benefits of a tire monitoring system, and certainly something worthy of your consideration.

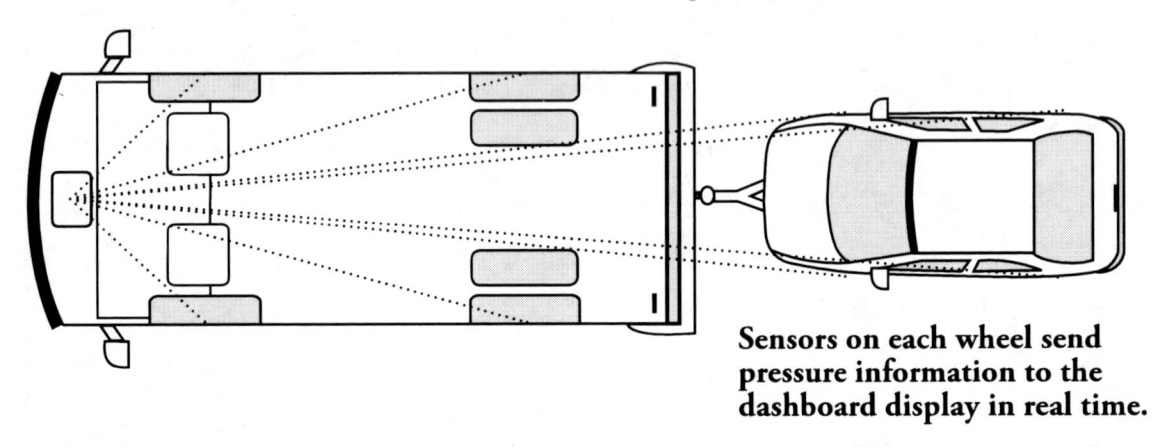

Sensors on each wheel send pressure information to the dashboard display in real time.

TIRE PRESSURE MONITORING SYSTEMS: MECHANICAL

Most RVers indicate that the most difficult task they must routinely perform is checking the tires on their dual wheels. This is particularly true for those vehicles equipped with hubcaps (wheel covers). Generally, the wheel covers and the wheels are not made by the same company; therefore, the lightening holes do not line up, making it very difficult to check tire pressure. Often the only solution for this is for the owner to modify his wheel covers, cutting away enough material to allow adequate access to the valve. The trucking industry has faced this situation for years, forcing the development of a permanent mechanical means of checking tire pressure at a glance. There are several such systems on the market for vehicles with dual wheels. They make inflation checks easier by combining the two valve stems into a common easily accessible fitting. Some even include a direct reading gauge to check the inflation pressure visually (during your walk-around) without the use of a conventional gauge. These systems are quite affordable and provide another desirable feature: they equalize the pressure between the two tires. Use caution if purchasing such a system. Verify that an air loss in one tire will not result in air loss in its mate. This is a safety feature.

Another type of tire pressure monitoring system is the monitors that replace the valve cap. These monitoring caps are pre-set from the manufacturer to a certain air pressure. If the pressure in your tire is 90 psi, then the top of the cap will show green. When the tire pressure falls by 5 psi, then the top of the cap will show yellow. When the tire pressure falls by 10 psi, then the top of the cap will show red. This type of tire pressure monitoring system is more of a passive system, and will not notify the driver of a problem while driving down the road. It is only when you stop and look at each tire that you can see a problem.

Be cautious of what you add to your wheels/tires.

Here are a few final words of caution before you add any auxiliary device to your wheels. Anything that you add to your tires and/or tire valves increases the amount of potential leaks. Valve extenders and other devices can and do fail in a variety of ways. Also, be careful about adding any system that extends beyond the side of the wheel or tire. Damage can occur to the installed system with catastrophic results, so be careful with your selection of such add-ons. Demand only the highest quality, and then monitor the tires frequently. Just because you no longer have to check the pressure in your tires daily, you must still be diligent in monitoring this very important area of your coach. The quality of your RVing lifestyle may be at stake.

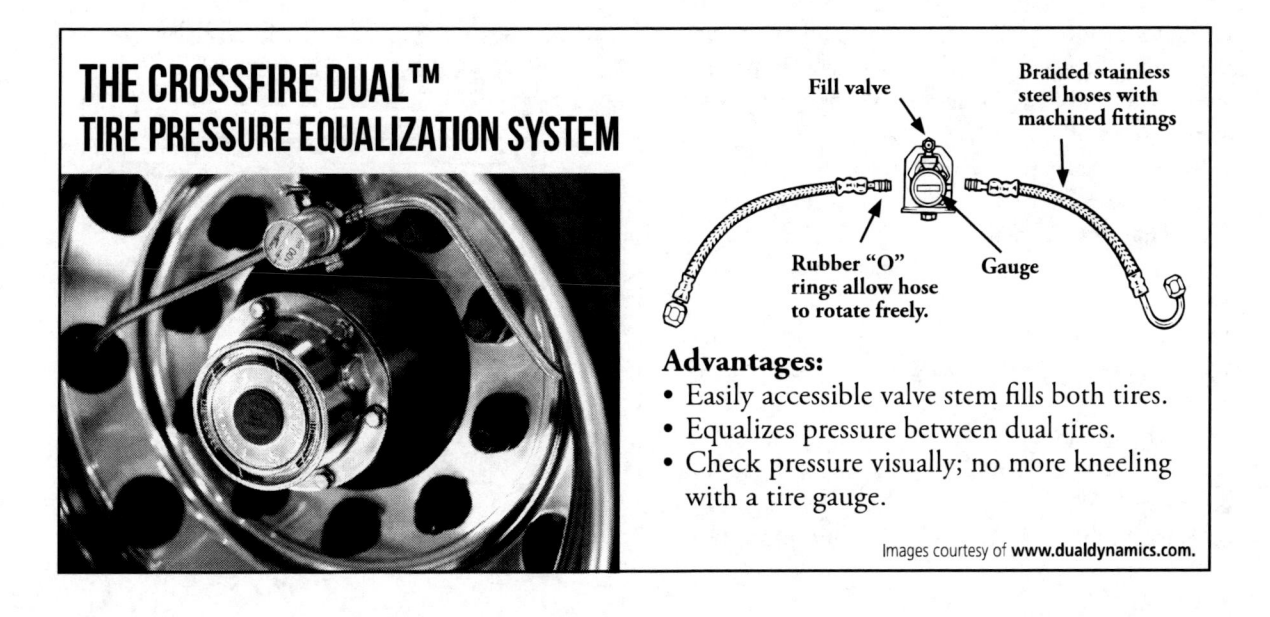

THE CROSSFIRE DUAL™ TIRE PRESSURE EQUALIZATION SYSTEM

- Fill valve
- Braided stainless steel hoses with machined fittings
- Rubber "O" rings allow hose to rotate freely.
- Gauge

Advantages:
- Easily accessible valve stem fills both tires.
- Equalizes pressure between dual tires.
- Check pressure visually; no more kneeling with a tire gauge.

Images courtesy of **www.dualdynamics.com**.

SPEED VERSUS TIRE CAPACITY

Since we have completed a thorough discussion on the subject of correct tire inflation and its ramifications, we now move on to discuss the relationship between how fast you drive and the load-carrying capacity of your tires. The faster we drive, the more tires flex, and the more they generate internal heat. This combines with the reduced time available for the tire to dissipate that heat. The inevitable result is that the tire rapidly increases its internal temperature. In a manner similar to under-inflation/overload, the internal heat in the tire continues to rise until the materials used in the tire begin to fail. To control the build-up of heat, we must either lower our speed or compensate by adjusting downward the load-carrying requirement on the tire (carry less weight).

Most RV highway tires are designed to do their job between 56 and 75 mph. Know the speed rating of your tires!

When we deviate from this speed range, we use the following load/speed charts to determine how the load-carrying capacity changes. These charts plot the relationship between tire speed and load.

At high speeds, the tire is no longer capable of the performance depicted in the load/pressure charts and on the sidewall of the tire.

The first load/speed chart (to the right) is for light truck (LT) tires. Notice that speed, in miles per hour, is plotted against the required load rating change in percentage. In other words, it defines the change to the rated load capacity of the tire chart as a result of speed. You will observe that at speeds between 56 and 75 mph, the chart indicates "NONE," reflecting no change. This simply means that the tires will accomplish their job in accordance with the applicable tire chart.

However, when we operate at sustained speeds above 76 mph, the chart reflects a minus 10% load change. Now we must reduce the load-carrying capacity of the tire by 10%. When we apply that to our LT225/75R16 LRE example, that tire will no longer carry 2,680 pounds at 80 psi without the risk of damage. It now has a load-carrying capacity of only 2,412 pounds (10% less than 2,680). This is a significant reduction that must be considered if you drive at sustained speeds in excess of 75 mph. Equally important, please observe that the chart also requires that tire pressure must be raised 10 psi over chart values at any speeds in excess of 65 mph. This is required to remain within the limits that are also reduced for speeds in excess of 75 mph.

There is a real cost to pay if you elect to fly with the eagles in the fast lane.

Fortunately, most RV owners do not drive much over 65 mph, so let us look at the other side of the chart depicting speeds below 55 mph. It is apparent that as we slow down the allowable load adjustment increases, yielding tires with increased carrying capacity. To illustrate this phenomenon, at 55 mph you would get a 9% INCREASE in carrying capacity for your light truck tire. The slower we go, the greater the increase in tire-carrying capacity. The important message here is:

If you are concerned about tire overload or you just want to extend the life of your tires, slow down!

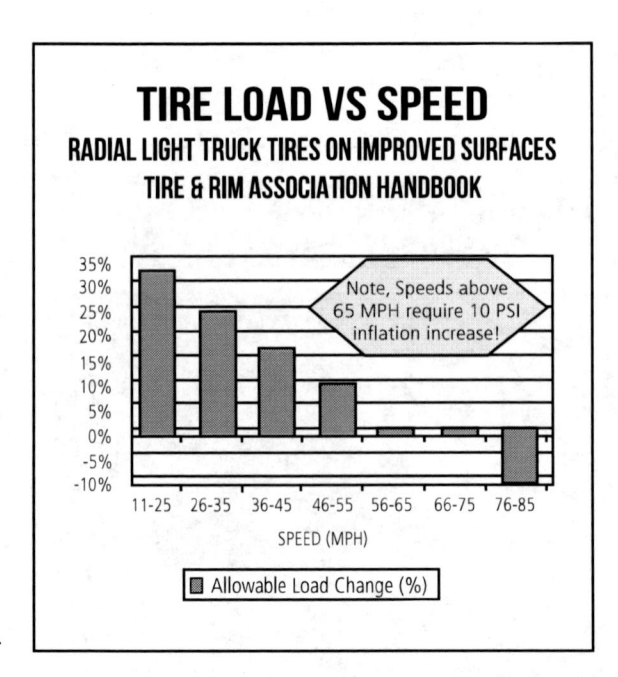

TIRE LOAD VS SPEED
RADIAL LIGHT TRUCK TIRES ON IMPROVED SURFACES
TIRE & RIM ASSOCIATION HANDBOOK

Note, Speeds above 65 MPH require 10 PSI inflation increase!

Speed (MPH)	Allowable Load Change (%)
11-25	~33%
26-35	~25%
36-45	~18%
46-55	~10%
56-65	0%
66-75	0%
76-85	-10%

At the extreme left of the chart, note that you would get a 32% increase in carrying capacity at 25 mph. Keep this option in mind in the event of failure of a dual tire. Changing the tire or waiting for a tow truck at the side of the highway may be a very unsafe thing to do. Remembering the tire load/pressure and load/speed charts, you now know that you can generally slowly drive your vehicle to a safer location! Driving slowly (36-45 mph) you gain considerable load-carrying capacity on the remaining tire.

The next load/speed chart (below) is similar to the previous one but covers the truck and bus tires that are often used on larger motorhomes. The important difference is that, in this case, we begin to lose carrying capacity when we drive faster than 65 mph. The effect is significant with the loss of 4% between 65-70 mph and fully 12% for speeds between 70-75 mph. In addition, at these speeds the tires now require a 5 psi increase in inflation pressure. Again, the left side of the chart is similar, but note that we require a 15 psi increase in inflation pressure at speeds below 21 mph if we want to attain the 32% increase in carrying capacity. On the larger rigs, this may not be as difficult as it sounds because most of the larger motorhomes have an onboard source of air allowing this to remain a practical option in the event of a dual tire failure.

Do not carry this to an extreme by driving so slowly that you present a traffic hazard to others on the road or yourself.

The final load/speed chart (below) is for tires rated at 75 mph or above. Note that these tires do not lose capacity above 65 mph. But alas, speed in this range may cause you other problems such as with local law enforcement officers and your co-pilot.

All of this is interesting, but the key point is:

THE FASTER YOU DRIVE, THE HARDER YOU ARE WORKING YOUR TIRES!

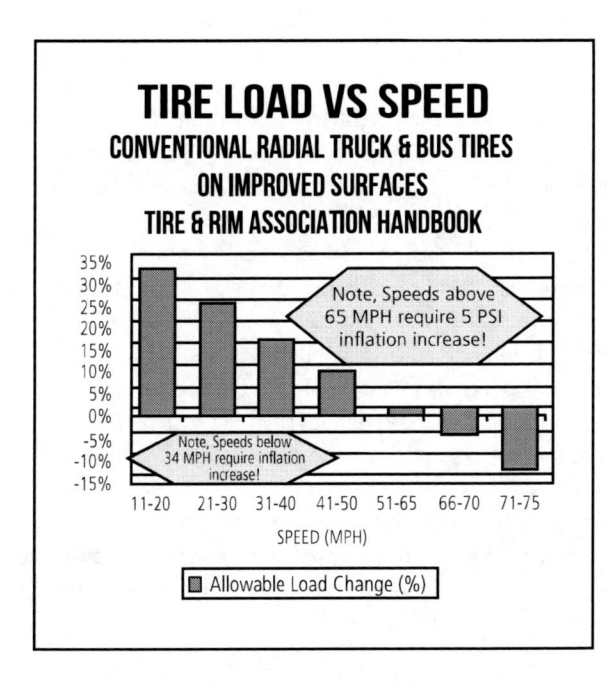

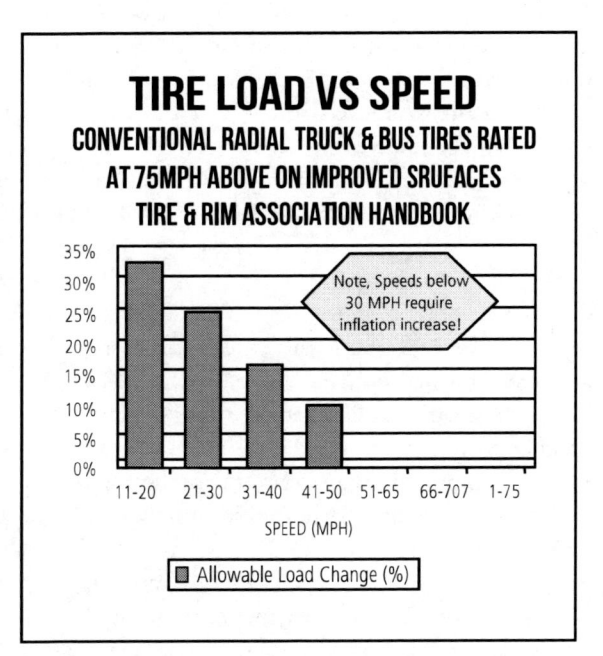

TIRE LOAD VS SPEED
CONVENTIONAL RADIAL TRUCK & BUS TIRES ON IMPROVED SURFACES
TIRE & RIM ASSOCIATION HANDBOOK

Note, Speeds above 65 MPH require 5 PSI inflation increase!

Note, Speeds below 34 MPH require inflation increase!

TIRE LOAD VS SPEED
CONVENTIONAL RADIAL TRUCK & BUS TIRES RATED AT 75MPH ABOVE ON IMPROVED SRUFACES
TIRE & RIM ASSOCIATION HANDBOOK

Note, Speeds below 30 MPH require inflation increase!

WHAT IS THE AGE OF YOUR TIRES? DOT CODE

Tires are made primarily of rubber, and we intuitively know rubber ages and deteriorates over time. It follows that TIRES DO NOT LAST FOREVER! The life expectancy of a tire in RV service is not easily predicted. In this case, we are speaking of the casing life as opposed to the tread life. The difficulty of this is that the life of a tire carcass depends to a great degree on how the tire is utilized and maintained. For instance, a tire exposed to the rays of the sun for extended periods of time, or stored in the presence of high levels of ozone, may have a relatively short life. Similarly, a tire operated near, at, or over its rating may also have a relatively short life. Recalling that under-inflation is the same as overloading, poor maintenance practices will also adversely affect the tire life.

Tread life is easy to measure. When the tire is worn excessively, it is time to replace the tire. Simple! However, the tire's useful carcass life is much more difficult to determine.

Rubber products are cured during the manufacturing process using a process called "vulcanization." During this process, the rubber changes its state from a tacky soft material to the pliable yet strong material we are used to seeing in our tires. The process of vulcanization is initiated in the mold by a combination of heat and chemicals. At a specific point in the process, the tire is removed from the mold. This eliminates the heat; however, the chemical action continues. Therefore, the curing continues throughout the life of the tire. This accounts for much of the ongoing deterioration we observe in our RV tires.

The good condition and/or appearance of the tire's tread does not indicate that the tire is still useful. In fact, tires operated on a regular basis will generally enjoy a longer carcass life than tires that sit statically for a high percentage of the time. This is because tires contain compounds that keep the rubber supple. Tire flexing and internal heat activates these compounds. If the tire is not used regularly (flexed), it dries out quickly! Visit an automobile museum to see this principle in action. Many of the automobiles there were restored using new tires. After several years in a fully protected environment, the tires are deteriorated and cracked. The infrequent usage of RVs somewhat parallels this action.

Other factors affecting RV tire life include the improper usage of chemicals. RVers commonly use chemicals to polish the sidewall of tires to enhance their appearance. Often this causes or accelerates damage because of harmful components contained in the "tire dressing." The tire manufacturers suggest using nothing but mild soap and water to maintain the tire's appearance. While they do not endorse any individual products, they do specifically state that any product that contains petroleum distillates, silicon or alcohol should not be used. If you elect to use any product on your tires, carefully check the container for these materials. If they are listed or there is no ingredient listing, do not use the product. Consider also, if you are using a tire dressing to enhance the tire's appearance, it is fine but do so cautiously. If you are looking to prolong the life of your tires, you may be wasting your time and money; you just cannot coat all areas of the tires inside and out that are acted on by ozone and ultraviolet. Meanwhile, the vulcanization process continues.

When considering negative effects on tires, we should also think about the practice of storing our RVs for long periods. This practice hurts tires two ways: first, the tire is not flexed regularly, activating the chemicals in the rubber placed there to retard deterioration; and second, we often park our RVs on surfaces paved with either asphalt or concrete. These materials will leach those same chemicals from the tires with the effect of shortening its life. When storing your vehicle, there should be a "barrier" of some sort between the tire and the asphalt or concrete surface. This can be as simple as a piece of wood or plastic. Check this effect for yourself. The next time you park on concrete for a week or more, note the black marks on the concrete when you move. The black contact patches where your tires were are the chemicals that have been leached from your tires. The same would be true with asphalt except it cannot be seen because of the black color of the asphalt.

Summary of Aging Effects on RV Tires
Vulcanization process

Exposure to ultraviolet rays

Limited usage

Effects of chemicals

Storage on asphalt or concrete surfaces

High operational demands

Tires have a limited life. How can I tell how old they are?

Once again, the tire's sidewall markings provide this essential piece of information. Keep in mind that your tires, even those that were delivered on the RV when you bought it, may well be several years older than your RV. It's important to keep track of the age of your tires just as you would with any other product that deteriorates with time.

On all tires manufactured or imported (legally) into the United States or Canada, a code is required by the Department of Transportation (DOT) to be molded into the tire. This code tells us when the tire was made or, more specifically, when it was in the mold.

Look for a series of letters and numbers beginning with "DOT." Look to the end of the string. There you will find four numbers. The first TWO of these numbers are the CALENDAR WEEK the tire was in the mold, beginning with week 01 in January, and so on through the year. The LAST number(s) (one or two digits) tells us what year the tire was made.

In our example, the tire was in the mold in the 17th week of 2015. Rarely, you may encounter a tire with a 3-digit date code. This means the tire was manufactured prior to the year 2000. Such a tire is years past its mandatory replacement age and should be removed from service immediately.

> **The date code is found on only one side of the tire, so the ideal time to locate it is when you or your mechanic are working on or under your RV. When you find the date code, make a note of it for future reference.**

So, how long will a tire last?

We will never get a manufacturer to tell us precisely the life of a tire because they cannot control its environment. However, most tire manufacturers agree that five to seven years of age is the norm for RV service. Now, does that mean that you should panic and immediately throw away your tires when they reach the five-to-seven-year age? No. What a knowledgeable RVer should do at this point is to become more diligent and watchful of the tires on his/her RV. That means you should be especially observant of the sidewall (both sides), looking for deterioration or cracks that might expose the carcass material (cords) to the atmosphere. Do not forget the bottom of the tread grooves, and look for blisters or bulging on the sidewalls. Watch air pressure closely, because an unexplained or recurring air pressure loss could be deterioration of the inner liner of the tire. Obviously, should any tire fail, all should be reviewed closely if they are in this age bracket. When any of these signs of deterioration begin to show, that is the time to go shopping for tires. At minimum, plan on replacing all tires of a similar age. Hopefully, this proactive approach will afford you the opportunity to shop for tires in a more convenient manner and avoid the very costly and dangerous potential of failing tires one at a time while on the road.

> **Most tire manufacturers agree that five to seven years of age is the norm for RV tire service! If you have any doubt about the condition of your tires, take your RV to a tire dealer and have them inspected!**

TIRE BLOCKING

The modern radial tire is constructed of a combination of rubber, steel and sometimes other materials designed to make them superior in strength and to dissipate heat quickly. Steel is always used for tire beads (the steel bands that anchor the tire to the rim) and may also be used for the carcass construction and for the tread reinforcing belts. Other materials may also be used for the carcass and tread reinforcing belts. When steel is used for the casing and tread reinforcing belts, the resultant product is commonly called an "all-steel radial." All-steel radial tire construction is generally considered to be a superior product, offering long life and excellent reliability and durability; in other words, a premium product. As is the case with many specialized products, the all-steel radials that we are discussing here do require a bit of understanding and extra care.

All-steel radial tire construction is generally considered to be a superior product, offering long life and excellent reliability and durability; in other words, a premium product.

As was often demonstrated in high school physics classes, you can take a metal paper clip in your hands and bend it back and forth. After many such cycles, it will break, especially if you bend it to an extreme angle. What has happened is that the steel material has "fatigued" due to being bent beyond its elastic limit. Had we not bent the clip beyond its elastic limit, it may have lasted for many thousands of cycles. This very same phenomenon will occur in all-steel radials if we severely bend or kink the tiny wires in the sidewall of the tire beyond what they were designed to endure.

This may be caused by an unknowing RV owner while attempting to level his rig by using blocks of wood or some other material placed under the tires. It is vital to ensure that you do not distort the tire excessively, either in the tread or in the sidewall, as is depicted in our illustrations. To do so will invite damage to the steel wires, which in turn may result in a tire problem. Just like the paper clip, kinked wires may not result in failure right away, but more commonly will fail later on down the road after you have traveled for some period of time. Often this failure will occur long after you have forgotten about how you blocked the tires on this particular day, denying you the understanding of a cause-and-effect relationship.

It is good procedure for all tires, especially for all-steel radials, to avoid the incorrect blocking shown in our illustrations. Be very certain that your blocks cover the entire footprint of the tire and have a proper lead-in (angle). For duals, the blocking should span both tires evenly, covering the entire footprint.

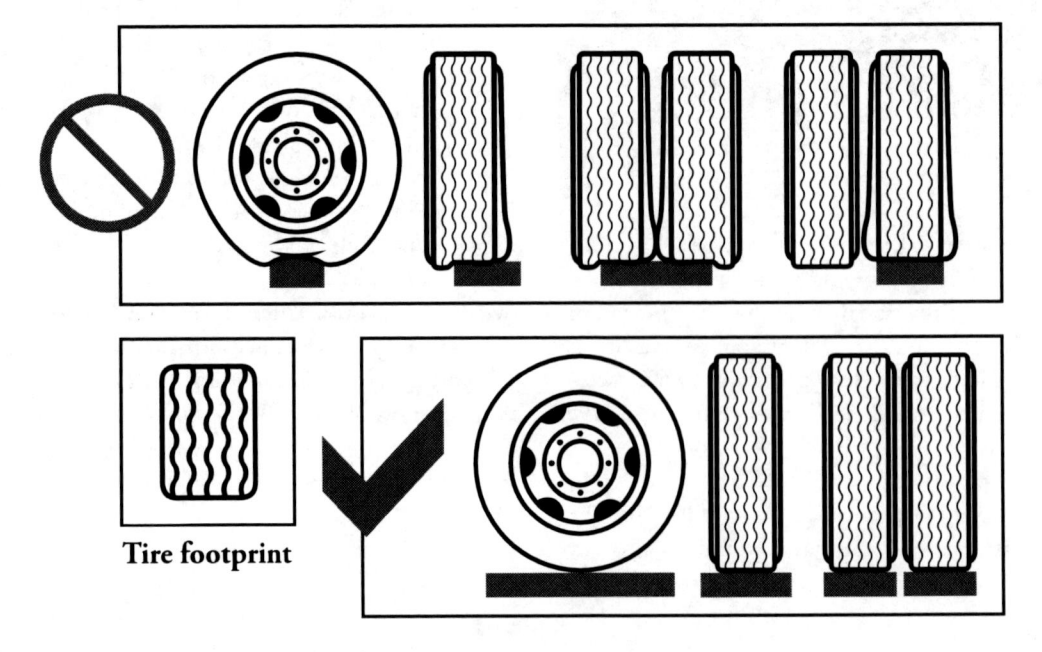

Tire footprint

Note: if you are unsure whether or not you have all-steel radial tires, look to the tire sidewall. The sidewall markings will inform you of the quantity of plies and the material utilized for the carcass and tread-reinforcing package in clear language. Our example illustrates an all-steel radial design with one steel ply in the carcass and five steel plies in the tread. We also discussed one "informed consumer" usage of this important information during our discussion under the "Language of Tires Markings." (pg. 35)

TIRE HELP – (ASSISTANCE)

Tires are technically complex products produced in a series of complicated procedures largely out of sight. The result is a product that can and does provide a service life remarkably free of problems. Our automobiles tires are a largely forgotten item. They may or may not be checked and serviced when the automobile itself is serviced approximately every six months. In contrast, our RV tires are routinely placed under extremes of service and have greater maintenance requirements, yet are almost as trouble-free day in and day out; yet RV tire problems do arise. It is nice to know that, when needed, there is help available at the other end of a phone line. If you have any questions about your tires, the tire manufacturers have a staff of tire experts trained specifically about RV tires. To reach them, simply call their 800 numbers. Be prepared to provide your tire size, load range, pressure, weights, etc. as they will question many of these areas seeking a solution to your problem.

Michelin Tires Consumer Hotline
866-866-6605

Goodyear Tires Consumer Relations
1-800-321-2136

Toyo Tires Customer Assistance
800-442-8696

Bridgestone Tires Service Center
844-659-5820

Firestone Tires Service Center
844-658-0724

SUMMARY!

Our tires are one of the most critical factors affecting our safety, yet they are commonly given only cursory care and attention. Under-inflation and/or overloading is the cause of the majority of tire failures. An understanding of the language of tires, and proper maintenance and care, will go a long way towards making your RV travels trouble-free.

Tire load inflation charts are available on the SmartWeigh page at www.escapees.com.

RESERVED FOR YOUR NOTES.

BOOK 3: RV MOTOR FUEL

by Mello Mike.

CONTENTS

Author's Foreword 53
What's It All About? 53

UNDERSTANDING MOTOR FUELS — 54
All About Motor Fuels and Your Safety! 54
Gasoline and Diesel Fuel Advantages 54
Gasoline Is Highly Flammable and Diesel Fuel Is Combustible. 56
An Empty Gasoline Fuel Tank is More Dangerous than a Full Tank! 56
Fuel Spills and Vapor 58
Any Change to the Fuel System Should Be Clearly Thought Out 59
Handling Motor Fuels Always Demands the Greatest of Respect 60
The Fueling Process 61
Summary 62

FREQUENTLY ASKED QUESTIONS (FAQ) — 63
Should I use a premium gasoline in my RV? I plan to keep my RV for a long time and want to take particularly good care of it. 63
What are all of the various gasoline ingredient acronyms
I see at gas pumps around the country? 63
I store my gasoline-powered RV for extended periods of time. Do I need to take special precautions? 63
How do I know what grade of diesel fuel to use? 64
Why do diesel engines smoke? 64
How can I avoid having filter-plugging problems with my diesel? 64
How does water get into diesel fuel and what problems can it cause? 65
What should I do to my diesel fuel to adjust for cold winter temperatures? 65
How long can I store diesel fuel? 65

AUTHOR'S FOREWORD

It requires a great deal of energy to move a heavily-laden RV from place to place. If there is any doubt about that fact, check your fuel receipts or just try to push your RV for even a brief distance. The energy to accomplish that task comes in a highly concentrated liquid in the form of gasoline or diesel fuel. In addition to being highly flammable, fuels are explosive under the right conditions, highly toxic to humans and animals, as well as being potentially destructive to the environment in which we all must live. With knowledge of fuel comes the ability to utilize it safely for the purposes for which it is intended.

WHAT'S IT ALL ABOUT?

Gasoline and diesel fuel are absolutely essential to enable our RV travels. Most of us have been around these fuels our entire lives and with familiarity comes complacency. There are significant hazards associated with these fuels, and safe handling of fuels is critical to your safety. RVing can offer additional safety challenges when we deal with fuels, due to the onboard RV systems, and also due to the way that RVers utilize their vehicles. Here we will discuss how fuels behave, cover the relative flammability of common fuels and discuss safe handling procedures. We will also cover common fuel issues that RVers may face, such as service station safety procedures, how to store fuels for long periods of time and how to safely transport additional fuels for your toys. We will also discuss what to do in case of a fuel spill and the environmental issues that may be of concern if a spill happens. Motor fuels are safe when handled properly. If you take the information in this book to heart, and follow the safe handling procedures contained within, you will prevent any fuel-related mishaps from impacting your RV life.

"All motor fuels must be treated with respect and care for our own safety, that of the people and things around us and for the environment as a whole."

UNDERSTANDING MOTOR FUELS
ALL ABOUT MOTOR FUELS AND YOUR SAFETY!

Without much debate, most recreational vehicle enthusiasts would acknowledge that the availability and affordability of motor fuel for our RVs is probably the single biggest factor in our continuing enjoyment of the RV lifestyle. That is a true statement regardless of whether our motorhome or truck and trailer rig uses gasoline or diesel fuel for its motive power. An automotive or RV engine burns fuel as its source of energy. Various types of fuels will burn in an engine: gasoline, diesel fuel, gasohol, alcohol, liquefied petroleum gas, liquified natural gas and other alternative fuels. However, once engineered for a specific fuel, automotive (RV) engines can only utilize that fuel for continuing operation.

As a source of motive power, we do not have many viable choices for our RVs. While there may be a few specific instances of a heavy RV operating on compressed natural gas (CNG), liquified petroleum (LPG), electric power, or some other alternative fuel, for the vast majority of RVs the fuel of choice is gasoline or diesel fuel. These fuels possess the combination of qualities that make them hard, if not impossible, to replace.

GASOLINE AND DIESEL FUEL ADVANTAGES

Very High Energy Content (BTUs)
Diesel fuel produces approximately 130,000 BTUs of power per gallon. Gasoline produces a little less. Propane produces approximately 90-95,000 BTUs. This is one of the reasons for the fuel mileage advantage of large diesel-fueled vehicles. Most alternative fuels have a much lower energy content (30-50% compared to gasoline or diesel fuel) meaning that the range of a vehicle using that fuel will be greatly reduced or more fuel will have to be carried aboard the RV to assure similar range. The lower the energy content of the chosen fuel, the greater the requirement for adequate room to store the fuel and the tanks to contain it properly. In addition, an expanded fuel distribution system across the country will be required. Some fuels (i.e., LPG and LNG) are in a liquid state only under pressure. This creates a requirement to have a fuel system (storage tank and lines) with adequate structural integrity to safely contain that pressure. Liquid/gas conversion equipment and pressure regulators are also required to convert the liquid to a gas and to provide the pressure required by the engine.

Easily Vaporized
All currently utilized internal combustion engines operate with a fuel in the vaporous state. Thus, one of the primary qualities of a motor fuel is that the liquid (or solid) be readily convertible to the vaporous state and that the energy required to complete this transformation not be prohibitively high. Both gasoline and diesel fuel are liquid at normal temperatures, while LPG and LNG are not.

Readily Available
Motor fuels must be in widespread distribution to be a practical fuel choice. Today only gasoline and diesel fuel have a distribution system in place to meet this requirement for the automotive market. LPG and LNG have just begun to establish a nationwide distribution network; however, it will be years before it comes even close to meeting the needs of the mobile RVer.

Affordable
Affordable motor fuel is a prerequisite of RVing. Without affordable motor fuel, RVing as a lifestyle would be much diminished, as it was during earlier fuel crises in the USA. Even though we all complain about the high cost of motor fuel, there is little doubt that gasoline and diesel fuel are a tremendous value. This is particularly true recognizing where the raw materials come from, what processing is involved in the final product and the amazing distribution system that assures that the product is available on almost any street corner in the USA.

Safe to Use
Many of the potential alternative fuels being considered for future generation motor fuels require the use of liquid fuel maintained at high pressure and/or very low temperatures. This requires large heavy containers and fuel system support equipment that could impose some risk to operators during fueling, operation or in the event of a crash.

Despite all of these advantages, gasoline and diesel fuels also have notable drawbacks that we must consider when we operate our vehicles with these fuels on a daily basis.

Gasoline and diesel motor fuels are also:
- Flammable/combustible
- Toxic
- Poisonous
- Environmentally destructive
- Often expensive
- Increasingly rare
- Dirty and just plain smell bad

Actually, the bad smell of these products is purposeful and is a blessing in that the offensive smell alerts us to its presence in an unconfined state and prevents us from using it more haphazardly. Yet, it is a fair question to ask why we put up with all of the problems and inconvenience of gasoline and diesel fuel. The equally obvious answer remains that there is no practical alternative. Further, since there is no viable substitute in the foreseeable future, it behooves RVers to understand motor fuels in order to utilize them safely in support of our RVing lifestyle.

Both gasoline and diesel fuels are manufactured from petroleum (crude oil) which reside deep underground. Oil deposits occur in many, but not all, regions of the earth. Many of those natural deposits of crude oil are found in remote areas of the world, requiring first that the product be located, then tapped, pumped and finally transported to more populated areas for processing into useful fuels for our vehicles. Virtually all of these steps are politically and sociologically controversial, further limiting the available quantity of the crude oil product.

Typical fractionating tower allows crude oil vapors to condense into separate collection systems.

Fractionating Column

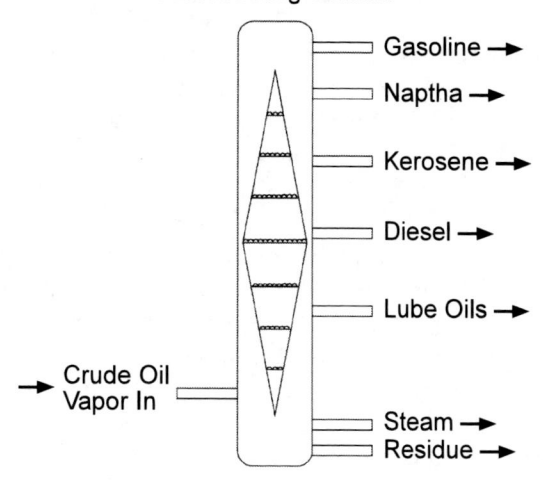

- Gasoline →
- Naptha →
- Kerosene →
- Diesel →
- Lube Oils →

Crude Oil Vapor In →

- Steam →
- Residue →

Once transported to areas where the refineries are located (normally by pipeline or huge ocean-going tankers), the petroleum is processed through a distillation procedure. This process separates the petroleum into various fractions or parts. LPG, gasoline, kerosene, motor fuel oil, heating oil, lubricating oils and many more products result from this process. After distillation, additional processes purify these products, add various additives for specific applications and stabilize the products for distribution and usage.

As an RVer, we do not have a choice of what product to use. We already made that choice when we purchased our motorhome or truck-trailer RV. From that point forward, our primary concern is to operate the vehicle correctly and in accordance with the engine manufacturer's recommendations. The engine manufacturer makes very specific engine fuel requirements for safe, economical and long-term operation of their products. In most cases, the manufacturer's warranty (if any) is dependent upon the exclusive usage of the stipulated fuel. The RVer needs to be very familiar with all of those requirements as well as the proper handling of the fuels used.

GASOLINE IS HIGHLY FLAMMABLE AND DIESEL FUEL IS COMBUSTIBLE.

Recall that back during your high school physics classes you learned that motor fuels are flammable only in the gaseous (vapor) state. In essence, it is the vapor (gas) that burns (or explodes), not the liquid fuel. However, since gasoline vaporizes at a much lower temperature than diesel fuel and that temperature corresponds to the normal atmospheric conditions in our RVing life, the burning or explosion hazard is much more likely and common than with diesel fuel. Another way to state this is that gasoline fumes can be ignited outside a closed fuel tank at any temperature where a person commonly would be working with gasoline or the vehicle itself. That is not necessarily true for diesel fuel because it requires temperatures of 150°F to vaporize. To the RVer, this means that we must exercise great caution when we fuel our RVs, especially those fuelled by gasoline. We must avoid the possibility of a gasoline or diesel fuel spill. Always use the automatic fuel shutoff on the pump, and do not top off your tank as this often results in the tank overflowing. Should a fuel spill occur from malfunctioning pump equipment, broken hose, failure of shutoffs or from dropping the fuel nozzle, proceed as follows as quickly and efficiently as possible:

- Take all fuel spills very seriously and treat any fuel spilled as hazardous material.

- Above all, do not start your vehicle.

- Remove all passengers from your RV, including any pets on board.

- Notify the station operator immediately (they will call the fire department if the condition dictates).

- Locate a suitable fire extinguisher (class B, for flammable liquids) and familiarize yourself with how to use it properly.

- Contain the spill by spreading an absorbent material as soon as possible.

- Shut off the refrigerator and water heater along with any other device that might be a source of ignition.

- Move your vehicle only when the spill is adequately contained, permitting your vehicle to be moved safely.

AN EMPTY GASOLINE FUEL TANK IS MORE DANGEROUS THAN A FULL TANK!

Any container that has held gasoline, but is now empty will still contain residual fumes and enough oxygen to be a potentially lethal bomb if ignited. All it takes is an ignition source, which might be a spark, a cigarette, static electricity or, as commonly occurs, a spark or flame from a welding torch being used to seal a leak during vehicle maintenance. Note that a tank with a measurable amount of gasoline in it cannot explode from an internal spark because the vapor pressure is so high that it keeps out air, depriving the gas of an adequate supply of oxygen. Without oxygen in the proper ratio, you cannot ignite the gasoline fumes! This condition is why an electric fuel pump is permissible in a gasoline fuel tank but not in a diesel fuel tank. The gases from evaporating diesel fuel are much less than that of gasoline, so that with a partially full tank of diesel fuel there may still be enough oxygen present from outside air to provide a volatile condition, and an explosion can then result from any available ignition source. It is only common sense and good practice to consider any empty fuel container to be much more dangerous than one that is full or partially full.

In general, it is recommended that RVers not carry extra motor fuel for the above reasons. However, many RVers do carry with them motorcycles, boats, automobiles, airplanes, scooters and many more self-powered toys for transportation and enjoyment. Recognize that each of these "toys" has a fuel tank that should be treated exactly the same as a spare gas can because it presents the same potential hazards. It is best to keep all such "toys" full of fuel and in good repair to prevent fuel leakage.

RVers who must carry additional fuel to support other vehicles, hobbies or trips into remote areas should be very cautious where this fuel is carried. First, be absolutely certain that you utilize only properly certified safety fuel containers. No fuel containers should be carried within the living compartment of the RV under any circumstances. However, placing them on the rear bumper could prove to be equally bad since this area could be severely damaged in any rear-end-type collision. The idea is to place spare fuel containers where they are not readily damageable in a collision and will not collect liquid or gaseous vapors if the tanks leak from any cause. Probably the best place to carry the extra tanks would be in anything that is towed by the RV whether it is a trailer, boat, car, etc. because that vehicle is not inhabited when traveling along the highway. Barring this, perhaps storage in an outside compartment that does not contain a floor (or has had the floor removed) would be the next best choice. One possibility is the propane compartment as this area is also subject to similar precautions, thus it is constructed as described. Of course, suitable attachment points will have to be constructed to secure the tank in this area. Another possibility would be to carry them under the RV in an open rack fabricated for this purpose. In this case, the area must be protected from damage from road debris, rocks, curbs, etc. Think this issue through thoroughly before proceeding. Your RV, your life and the lives of your loved ones may be at stake.

RVers commonly add additional fuel tanks to tow trucks (occasionally motorhomes) used to pull their RVs. This is a logical thing to consider for increasing the range of the RV providing added flexibility to our RVing lifestyle. Additional fuel capacity can be added to many trucks in several ways, provided there is adequate load-carrying capacity.

Purchase optional fuel tanks when purchasing the vehicle new.
Probably the best way to add fuel capacity to a tow truck is to purchase the factory optional (OEM) equipment tanks for those vehicles that offer them. For an existing vehicle, the purchase of OEM parts to duplicate the optional (OEM) configuration should be considered.

Add commercially available aftermarket fuel tanks.
Such tanks might be located either under the body (OEM location) or in the bed of the truck. This option places the engineering burden and requirement to follow industrial and governmental standards regarding auxiliary fuel systems onto the supplier of the tanks. Professional installation provides the same assurances for the RV owner and, in most cases, assures proper workmanship, etc. In all cases, the RVer should satisfy himself that good workmanship procedures were followed, that quality materials were utilized and that all industry requirements have been met.

Use loose (separate) fuel containers placed in the truck bed.
This option is probably the least desirable approach for adding fuel capacity. If this approach is pursued, it is absolutely essential that the containers be safety certified fuel containers. In addition, they must be properly stored upright and adequately restrained in the bed of the truck; they must not be overfilled (for expansion), and care should be exercised when transferring fuel from the extra tanks into the tow truck or auxiliary vehicle to prevent spills. RVers should not pump or pour fuel from containers while they are in the bed of the truck. Place them solidly on the ground before dispensing fuel.

If you must have a motor fuel around your RV: a few simple reminders regarding your safety:
- Always store it in approved safety containers. These can be expensive, but they are cheap "fire insurance."

- Always have a fire extinguisher marked for "B"-type fires (gasoline and other flammable liquids) readily accessible. Be sure you know how to use it!

- Always carry only the minimum amount of fuel required to meet your immediate requirements.

- Always store the motor fuel containers in a cool and well-ventilated area.

- Keep all fuel containers away from any source of heat or sparks such as water heater, electric motors or car engines.

- Always store the containers externally in a vented compartment rather than inside the RV.

- Never carry motor fuel in the trunk of your tow car.

- Always keep motor fuels away from children.

- Never siphon motor fuel by sucking the hose; motor fuels can be fatal if swallowed. There are small commercially available siphons available to transfer motor fuels when needed.

- Never use gasoline as a cleaner, charcoal starter or as a solvent.

- If motor fuel is spilled on clothing, remove the clothing and dispose of carefully.

- Should you or your child swallow a motor fuel, move away from the motor fuel source; safely secure the fuel; call your doctor or Poison Center immediately; alternatively call 911 for assistance.

- Do not induce vomiting if a motor fuel is ingested. This is also true for kerosene, lighter fluid or diesel oils (fuels) as well.

- If motor fuel is spilled on the skin, use lots of warm soapy water to reduce the risk of chemical burns.

- If you experience a gasoline fire and don't have a "B"-type fire extinguisher, get everyone a safe distance away from the fire. Call the fire department by dialing 911.

- Never use water to put out a motor fuel fire; it will only spread the fire.

- Stay calm!

FUEL SPILLS AND VAPOR

Gasoline fumes are heavier than air.
If gasoline is spilled or leaked, the fumes will tend to congregate in the bottom of any contained area. A commonly recognized hazard is fuel leaking on a boat because the vapors tend to collect in the bilge of the vessel. Here, the fuel vapor can mix with air, similar to the empty fuel can that was discussed earlier. This effectively becomes a bomb waiting to explode! The United States Coast Guard (USCG) has actively campaigned on this subject for many years as explosion and fire on a boat is an acknowledged and common hazard. Many individuals die each year from this source. As responsible RVers, we must recognize that while gasoline itself evaporates quickly and, therefore, may not be present in the liquid state, the resulting vapor can remain in the immediate area (particularly in the low points of the vehicle or compartment). Fuel vapors will remain there until moved away or diluted to a noncombustible fuel/air ration by air currents. During this period, a spark from striking metals or any other ignition source while gasoline fumes remain trapped in the low point may cause an explosion. Often this type of explosion is unanticipated by the people involved because they do not relate the hazard to something that occurred earlier, i.e., the original liquid fuel spill.

Diesel spills evaporate but will not explode unless the temperature of the vapor in the area is over 150 degrees F.
Diesel motor fuels also present a special hazard and potential danger. Where gasoline will vaporize at temperatures that are normal and comfortable for human beings, diesel fuel requires fairly high temperatures to vaporize before becoming a potential fire or explosion source. Note that, in the case of diesel fuel, ambient temperatures are normally not adequate to vaporize the fuel. However, subsequent operation of the RV may provide adequate temperatures in the engine compartment sufficient to vaporize spilled or

leaked diesel fuel, presenting a potential hazard as we drive. In an otherwise "tight" fuel system, a leak from the fuel filter (or any other fuel system component), such as might result from the opening of a drain valve and not closing it tightly, can present a future hazard. Because diesel fuel filters require periodic draining to assure adequately clean fuel and that no water enters the engine, they are a common source of leakage in the engine compartment. Similarly, reassembling a fuel filter after changing a filter element, etc., but with an error in properly placing one of the seals, can also result in leakage. Certainly one of the most common, yet unrecognized, potential maintenance failures is to leave a fuel filter in place from the previous season or to ignore the need to change the filter regularly. Since some water is almost always present (the removal of water is one of the main purposes for the fuel filter), the potential of a leak resulting from corrosion over a period of time is very real. Just because the engine was not used much for any reason, all fuel filter elements should still be changed at least once a year. This is a must. Note: Most engine maintenance schedules call for such maintenance as a minimum!

Many RVers do not personally perform maintenance on their RVs; thus, they are not commonly subject to such maintenance-oriented issues. However, some RVers can and do routinely maintain their RVs, requiring that they remain diligent as to the requirement for proper maintenance techniques. At a very minimum, all RVers must understand what is dictated by good maintenance practices and select only companies willing to do quality work and to oversee the work that is actually performed on their RVs.

All liquids, especially motor fuels, require room to expand without spilling.
It should not be necessary to point out that all fuel containers need tight fitting covers and should not be fully filled. The extra room at the top of the container provides room for expansion to prevent pressurizing the container with the expanding liquid which might result in leakage. 10-20% of the tank should be left empty for this reason. Certified fuel containers are designed to prevent overfilling, generally by locating the filler opening down from the top of the container.

ANY CHANGE TO THE FUEL SYSTEM SHOULD BE CLEARLY THOUGHT OUT

If changes are contemplated to the factory fuel system of your RV, whether powered with gasoline or diesel fuel, great care must be exercised to assure that the result will be free of any leaks. Both types of engines shake (vibrate) measurably at various operating speeds. Engines are commonly installed with rubber isolation bushings (motor mounts) to prevent those engine vibrations from being transmitted to the RV and its passengers. As a result, any fuel line that is run between the RV itself and the engine assembly must contain a flexible section to prevent the hard metal lines from vibrating, work hardening and ultimately failing from that cause. While flexible lines are a necessity in a fuel system, they are also a hazard in themselves. Because they are designed to flex in order to do their job, they are also subject to developing a leak from repeated usage and vibration. By industrial and governmental standards, there are limits to the length of flexible fuel lines to be used, for safety reasons. If flexible fuel line is used, it must be protected from external damage. This is normally accomplished with a solid shield of some type.

A common addition or modification to fuel systems completed or contemplated by many RVers is the replacement or addition of a different fuel filter assembly. If this is done, whenever possible the fuel filter should be mounted in the original factory location such that the original supply and fuel delivery lines will remain intact. In addition, the fuel filter must never be installed in such a way that it will be pressurized when the RV is not operating either from a pump or by installing it at a location lower than the fuel tank (gravity). The purpose for this is to prevent continuing fuel spills into the engine compartment or onto the ground, should a leak develop in the filter or fuel lines or in the event of a crash. In most cases, this type of addition is best left to professionals, yet it remains the responsibility of the RV owner to assure that the work is done properly.

Over time, engine vibrations can do strange things to mechanical components.
It seems that time and usage takes a toll on mechanical components and humans alike. In the case of mechanical components that contain a hazardous material such as fuel, that truism seems to work overtime. Constant movement from engine vibration and road conditions will ultimately loosen everything on your RV.

Ultimately, it may appear that you will spend a great deal of time tightening screws, nuts and bolts, and replacing items that have fallen off your RV or failed from this cause. Nowhere is that more obvious than in fuel system components. The very act of tightening filter water-separating bowls, drain valves and fittings for routine maintenance seems to make leakage all the more common. Fuel filters should be installed in the most vibration-free area (on solid RV structure; not the engine or body sheet metal) and checked daily for wetness, drips or any other noticeable discrepancy. Resist putting a wrench on the fuel system fittings to check their tightness as this will actually increase the likelihood of leakage as the fitting becomes distorted after being repeatedly over-tightened. Your eyes are a better way to verify the integrity of the fuel system, especially after maintenance is performed.

HANDLING MOTOR FUELS ALWAYS DEMANDS THE GREATEST OF RESPECT

Gasoline and diesel fuel should only be used for the purpose that they were designed for. They should never be used as a fire-starting aid, no matter what the situation! There are countless products designed to safely assist in starting fires that will do a much better job of starting your campfire or barbecue while not placing you and your RV in danger. Gasoline or diesel fuel should also never be used as a solvent to clean anything.

Any motor fuel spill should be cleaned up promptly and properly.
Motor fuels are strong solvents that can destroy paint, some plastics, asphalt paving material, plants, and many other materials they come in contact with. Gasoline or diesel fuel that is spilled onto something should be wiped up as soon as possible with an absorbent material, after which the area should be washed with detergent/water and thoroughly dried in a well-ventilated area. If an indoor spill occurs, be certain to open all windows, doors, etc. to provide adequate ventilation. Use rubber gloves to avoid touching motor fuel with bare skin because of its toxicity. Additionally, many people have allergic reactions to motor fuels, making them even more sensitive. If the spill is onto the ground, first use an absorbent material to collect as much of the material as possible, then wash the area down with water and/or with a water/detergent solution as soon as possible. A motor fuel that has spilled into a body of water will generally float on the surface where an absorbent material can collect it. The addition of a detergent will assist in dissipating the motor fuel. Note that all of the above pertains only for very minor spills of motor fuel such as might occur at home when attempting to fill a lawn mower or other tool with fuel. If rags or other absorbent material are used to collect spilled motor fuel, they also become hazardous material. Keep any such material outdoors in a well-ventilated area until the odor is gone; then dispose of it properly.

If any significant quantity of fuel is spilled, the legal, safest, and proper action is to call the fire department. They will then take charge of the situation, assuring the safety of those in the area and the proper cleanup.

Ecological concerns mandate that care should be taken that fuel of any kind is never spilled!
Motor fuels present a well-documented hazard to the environment. Even what we might consider insignificant amounts of gasoline and diesel fuel escaping into the air, earth or water can create environmental chaos and must be avoided at all costs. There are many pertinent laws on the subject of contamination by motor fuels that are far too complex and comprehensive to discuss here. It is sufficient to say that as responsible RVers and citizens we must do our part in preventing motor fuel contamination. Our primary means of accomplishing this is to take great care during the fueling process for our RVs, automobiles and motor fuel-powered toys.

THE FUELING PROCESS

It is often stated by RVers that the worst thing about diesel as a motor fuel is the fueling itself. The process is perceived to be dirty, smelly and, in general, more disagreeable than the same process with gasoline. What is true is that diesel fuel is generally bought from fuel retailers who normally deal with trucks and buses as their primary clientele. Thus, RVers, who commonly have other backgrounds, find that the "truck stop" is different and often somewhat distasteful. The reality is that, while the process is essentially the same, the difference is in the details.

Note that many experts in the field recommend that RVers use truck stops for fueling to assure that the fuel purchased is fresh and clean. A small neighborhood automotive service station that pumps only a small amount of diesel fuel from a pump "out back" may not sell enough of the product to provide such assurances.

Many RVers' concerns have to do with the dirty environment of the truck stop and its equipment combined with the smell of the fuel itself. Utilizing the RV fuel islands now available at many truck stops can largely offset these concerns. The use of "throwaway" plastic gloves will also keep much of the offensive smell off your hands and out of your RV. A small entry mat can be stored in a bay alongside the fuel tank inlet, providing a clean place to stand while completing the fueling process and helps prevents the tracking of fuel into your RV when the process is complete. Diesel fuel nozzles at the RV-specific fuel islands are generally smaller than they are at the truck pumps and will pump at a slower rate of flow. Using these pumps will require a little longer to complete refueling but will minimize the likelihood of a fuel spill due to "fuel blowback." This is largely an RV problem because the location of tanks within the RV requires the usage of hoses, pipes, etc. to reach its often remote location. In contrast, trucks generally have large "saddle mounted" tanks with very large openings on the top to permit the rapid refueling possible with the truck diesel fuel pumps. The design of fuel inlets for RVs sometimes makes holding the pump nozzle in the tank difficult. When this is the case, a simple bungee cord can be rigged inside the inlet that will hold the nozzle, freeing the RVer to watch the process safely away from any fuel blowback. Procedures such as these will be tolerated at the RV island but might be frowned on at the actual truck fuel islands.

Remember fueling etiquette at the truck pumps. After fueling, pull ahead prior to going in to pay. This frees the pump for the next truck that is frequently on a tight timetable.

Gasoline (unleaded fuel) pump nozzles used for our RVs are the same as those used for automobiles. They have the same small diameter spout designed to fit only unleaded fuel tanks. In most states fuel pumps are equipped with devices (latches) to hold the pump on while providing an automatic shutoff when full. These devices will make the job easier and prevent "fuel blowback."

Many RVs are equipped with locking fuel compartments for security. In all cases, the fuel requirement should clearly state "diesel" or "unleaded gasoline." Due to the remote location of the fuel tanks in many RVs, the fuel inlet is through pipes or flexible tubing into the centrally-located tank. This often results in "fuel blowback" out of the inlet when a high flow rate is used. This is particularly true for diesel fuel, which foams when dispensed from the pump at high speed.

Note the use of a bungee to hold the fuel nozzle in the tank opening. This relieves the necessity to hold the nozzle and keeps the RVer away from any fuel that might be blown back out of the tank. A bungee of this type can be mounted inside the fuel inlet compartment of many RVs.

The diesel fuel tanks for large trucks are designed to provide ease of filling. The large-diameter inlet is located at or near the top of the tank, making it very easy for the driver to fill the tank with the high flow rate pumps provided at truck stops. The large inlet hole permits the driver a visual indication of the amount of fuel in the tank. The penetration of the tip of the nozzle into the tank establishes the automatic shut-off point to prevent overfilling. Note the use of a bungee here to hold the nozzle while the driver sets up the pump on the other side of the rig or completes other tasks such as washing the windshield, etc.

SUMMARY

The handling, storing and utilization of gasoline is far more dangerous than the same activities when using diesel fuel. Yet, since most of us have grown up with vehicles using gasoline as a fuel, we are familiar with it and comfortable with the special care that it commands. While many RVers do not have the same comfort level with diesel fuel, it is actually more forgiving in many regards than gasoline making the transition an easy one. The bottom line is that all motor fuels must be treated with respect and care for our own safety, for the people and things around us and for the environment as a whole.

FREQUENTLY ASKED QUESTIONS (FAQ)

Should I use a premium gasoline in my RV? I plan to keep my RV for a long time and want to take particularly good care of it.
Premium fuels, in essence, offer a higher octane rating to control knocking or pinging in high-performance or other engines requiring it. Some premium fuel products also contain a different additive package (more detergent, etc.) enhancing its performance when compared to the normal fuel product. To determine what octane your engine needs, you should check your owner's manual. Most RVs only require the use of a quality fuel with an octane rating of 87 (regular) and will operate on that fuel satisfactorily if it is in good operating condition. Normally, your RV will not benefit from using higher octane than is recommended in the owner's manual. Knocking may occur under certain conditions. If your engine knocks or pings at the recommended octane level, you may require a higher-octane gasoline to prevent the knock. A small percentage of RVs may knock more than others due to the manufacturing tolerances of engines (even within the same model). Knocking is also possible because of an unusual buildup of engine deposits during the first 15,000 miles of driving. Other factors, such as extremely hot weather, changes in altitude or hard driving conditions (such as towing a heavy load), may also cause knocking either intermittently or permanently. Note that many modern RVs are equipped with an electronic device that detects and eliminates light knocking even before you hear it. These devices suppress the knock by retarding the spark. RVs with such systems may experience some deterioration of acceleration performance, without knocking, when operating under high engine demand conditions due to the retardation of the ignition spark.

If your RV experiences knocking or pinging when operating with the proper fuel grade, first verify that it is in a good "state of tune" and that all systems are correctly operating. If the knocking or pinging continues, then you might try a different brand of fuel. This is often very helpful. If all reasonable efforts fail, then the only possible solution would be to utilize a higher-octane gasoline as excessive knocking or pinging can be quite harmful to your engine.

What are all of the various gasoline ingredient acronyms I see at gas pumps around the country?
There are several ingredients used in gasoline in various parts of the country, that are essential to meet local, state or federal requirements. Many gasoline pumps carry such ingredient information in order to fully inform the operator of the product that he/she is purchasing. Several terms are commonly found in the USA:

- RFG (reformulated gasoline) is a special-blend fuel that is designed to reduce harmful automotive emissions. RFG must be marketed in those areas of the USA where air quality does not meet the ozone requirements of the Clean Air Act Amendments. It has a lower benzene content and must contain oxygenates like ethanol or MTBE.

- CBG (California cleaner burning) gasoline is a type of reformulated gasoline also designed to reduce emissions. It reduces the emissions of NOX and volatile organic compounds, has lower benzene and sulfur levels and limits the amounts of aromatic and olefinic compounds in the blends. It is required throughout the State of California.

- MTBE and ethanol, as well as several other alcohols, are classified as oxygenates. These are required in many parts of the country and are used in larger quantities in most RFG formulations. Most states require labeling of dispensers when ethanol-blended gasoline is provided.

I store my gasoline-powered RV for extended periods of time. Do I need to take special precautions?
There is no one answer to the question of how long gasoline can be kept in storage, because the answer depends upon the conditions under which it is stored. Gasoline can deteriorate in two ways: it may vaporize and/or oxidize. In addition, gasoline blended with ethanol can absorb water and separate into two layers as a result.

The vaporization of gasoline is largely a function of the initial compounding of the fuel. Gasoline prepared for sale during the summer months has a higher vaporization temperature, while that to be used during the winter has a decreased vaporization temperature to meet the needs of engines operating under those specific conditions. While vaporization does occur under almost all conditions, it is minimized in a filled container and at lower storage temperatures.

The oxidation of gasoline is a chemical reaction impacted by a number of factors. The storage temperature, the amount of airspace in the container and the presence of a stabilizing additive are the primary factors contributing to this process. Oxidation causes deposits to form in the gasoline that might drop out as fine sediment, plug fuel filters or form a lacquer-like coating on the fuel-wetted surfaces of the fuel system. Quality gasoline will last longest during winter months and in full, tightly sealed containers.

Gasoline blended with ethanol can absorb water from the air, eventually accumulating enough to cause the mixture to separate into two phases: an ethanol/water phase and another gasoline-only phase. The key to avoiding this "two phasing" is to keep the fuel container tightly sealed, thereby keeping any humid air from contact with the fuel.

Summarizing, gasoline should generally be used within a few months of purchase. For RVers specifically desiring storage for the winter (2-6 months), the best procedure would be to fully fuel the vehicle (be certain to allow adequate space for fuel expansion when it heats up in the spring) with a quality fuel, and then leave it alone. For extensive storage (beyond six months), the best procedure is to drain the fuel and then run the engine until it stops due to fuel starvation. There are fuel stabilizing compounds that can be added to fuel to enhance its storage properties. Such products should be used cautiously due to possible effects on the engine and its fuel and exhaust system components.

How do I know what grade of diesel fuel to use?
Most diesel engines are designed to operate on ASTM No. 2-D grade diesel fuel. Thus, most diesel engine RVs require the use of No. 2 diesel fuel. Note that there may be other grades of diesel fuel available routinely or seasonally at some truck stops. Generally, the pumps are clearly marked. However, the definitive answer to this question is simple: follow the recommendations of the engine manufacturer. The diesel engine operator's manual that came with your RV will provide the information that you require. If such a manual was not provided at the time of your RV purchase, take the time to obtain one as soon as possible. Most engine manufacturers have a sales and service facility in most middle- to large-sized cities making this task easy. If not, search the Internet for a website that will point you to the location of the closest facility where you can obtain one. Most engine manufacturers attend the large RV shows and rallies, making this another source of information.

Why do diesel engines smoke?
Diesel engine smoke is caused by incomplete combustion. White smoke is caused by tiny droplets of unburned fuel resulting from engine misfiring at low temperatures, sometimes encountered when starting on a cold morning. This smoke should drastically decrease almost immediately and disappear completely as the engine warms up. Black smoke could be caused by a faulty injector, insufficient air (check the condition of the air filter or filter indicator) and overloading or overfilling the engine. Blue-gray smoke is the result of burning lubricating oil and may be an indication that the engine is in poor mechanical condition.

How can I avoid having filter- plugging problems with my diesel?
Diesel engine fuel filters can plug up from a variety of causes. In the winter (cold temperatures), small amounts of water in the fuel can plug filters, or the use of a fuel with inadequate low temperature fluidity may also cause filter plugging. At other times (normal temperatures), common dirt and fuel

distribution debris can cause filter-plugging. Additionally, if a fuel storage facility is not properly maintained, bacteria and algae can grow in the fuel and cause filter problems as well. With the exception of the fuel with inadequate low temperature fluidity, most of these problems can be effectively avoided by keeping the fuel storage system clean and dry. Purchase your quality diesel fuel from a large-volume dealer who is constantly moving products from his tanks to customers. Take a look (or ask) to see if he changes fuel filters routinely. Note that if you find a specific diesel fuel pump to be particularly slow, it could be a sign that excessive contaminants are being pumped through that pump from some source. BE CAUTIOUS!

Be sure to drain water accumulation in your fuel system frequently--once a week is probably about right. However, if water is found, then you may want to increase that frequency until all signs of the problem disappear. That will also avoid icing problems along with minimizing bacterial growth in your tanks. There are fungicides and antibacterial additives available for use in your diesel fuel, but, it is far better to avoid the conditions that cause and perpetuate this than it is to treat the problem after it occurs.

How does water get into diesel fuel, and what problems can it cause?
Water gets into diesel fuel storage and vehicle tanks in several ways--by condensation of humid air, during transportation from refineries to service stations, by leakage through faulty fill pipes or vents, and by careless handling. Water can cause injector nozzle and pump corrosion, bacteria and fungi growth and fuel filter-plugging with the materials resulting from corrosion and microbial growth. Water can also cause an icing problem for RVs operating in cold country during winter months. Both vehicle and storage tanks should be checked frequently for water and drained or pumped out as necessary. In extreme cases, biocides may be required to control bacterial growth. In cold northern winters, ice formation in fuels containing water creates severe fuel line and filter-plugging problems. Regularly removing the water is the most effective means of preventing this problem; however, small quantities of alcohol may be used on an emergency basis to prevent fuel line and filter freeze-ups.

What should I do to my diesel fuel to adjust for cold winter temperatures?
Certainly, most RVers minimize this situation by avoiding cold weather entirely, but, if that is not possible, the best solution is to purchase diesel fuel that has been winterized for your area. In areas that routinely experience very cold temperatures, this "winterized fuel" should be readily available. Non-winterized diesel fuel will not generally cause problems as long as temperatures are at or above 10°F.

How long can I store diesel fuel?
If kept clean, cool and dry, diesel fuel can be stored 6 months to 1 year without significant quality degradation. Storage for longer periods can be accomplished through the use of periodic filtration and the addition of fuel stabilizers and bactericides.

RESERVED FOR YOUR NOTES.

BOOK 4: PROPANE SAFETY

CONTENTS

Author's Foreword 69
What's It All About? 69

UNDERSTANDING RV PROPANE SYSTEMS — 70
Propane: The "Lifeblood" of the RV 70
The RV Household Propane Fuel System 72
Propane Safety 77
The OPD Valve and the RVer 78
Important Safety Reminders 79
Summary 79

FREQUENTLY ASKED QUESTIONS (FAQ) — 80
In very cold weather, my furnace does not seem to produce
the amount of heat it normally does or does not light at all. 80
I have noticed that the flames at my cook stove are yellow. Is this OK? 80
The pilot light on my water heater will not stay lit more than a few seconds. What is wrong? 80
Why do the windows in my RV collect condensation when we cook or bake in cold weather?. ... 80
The flame pattern on the burners of my stove appears not to be connected to the burner itself. 80
The electrical ignition device for my range has stopped working. Can I ignore this
condition and just use a match to light the burners until I can obtain a replacement unit? 81
I know that the LPG system probably should be checked annually for preventive maintenance,
but how do I know that I am not getting ripped off with needless service? 81
Would an RV Propane leak detector be a good investment? 81

AUTHOR'S FOREWORD

There is no doubt that, without the LPG system in our RVs, the lifestyle that we have chosen would not be nearly so appealing. The LPG system goes a long way to making our life on the road "just like home" without being so burdensome that it detracts from the quality of life. The basic Propane gas has inherent potential to be dangerous; yet, through years of engineering effort and development of the systems in place today, it has evolved into a very safe and convenient household power source for RVs. The maintenance requirements for modern LPG systems are minimal. A little preventive maintenance and a constant alertness for anything wrong is all that is required. Sleep well tonight!

> "A little preventative maintenance and a constant alertness for anything wrong is all that is required."

WHAT'S IT ALL ABOUT?

RVs are complex machines containing both automotive and household systems to meet our varying needs and requirements. Not only must they carry us down the road from destination-to-destination, but they must also provide all of the comforts of home when we ultimately arrive at those destinations. For the most part, they are "not connected" to support systems to meet those ongoing needs. We stop for fuel and oil occasionally to provide the automotive needs for our RVs. Similarly, when we stop to spend the night at various locations around the country, we are generally able to "plug in" to 110 VAC (household electricity) providing the basic electrical needs of our RVs, yet we must carry with us our household fuel requirements in the form of "liquefied petroleum gas," LPG, or "Propane," as it is commonly referred to. There are other "bottled gas" products that are quite similar to Propane that are also referred to as "liquefied petroleum gas" and, thus, are often confused. The most common of these is Butane, which is also a gas liquefied by pressure and utilized by various portable or mobile applications. Some of the differences will be discussed later where they relate to the RVer.

The Propane that we carry generally provides the energy to cook our food, cool our refrigerators, heat our RVs, heat our water, power our barbecue, run the generators in many RVs and, in some cases, provide some or all of our lighting requirements. Of course, we can only carry a limited quantity of Propane to provide our needs for a reasonable period of time before we must refuel that system as well. This book deals with Propane SAFETY and provides the information you need to be safe while traveling down the highway and refueling.

UNDERSTANDING RV PROPANE SYSTEMS
PROPANE: THE "LIFEBLOOD" OF THE RV

Propane is a very useful and convenient fuel for RV purposes. It has a unique blend of qualities that makes it almost ideal for our mobile application. When used carefully, including proper system maintenance, Propane is very safe, yet it does pose some risk and demands understanding and special handling from RVers who utilize this fuel. Most RVs today contain from 10-40 gallons of Propane, which, when combined with the automotive fuel (gasoline or diesel fuel), represents a major potential fire or explosion threat. Thus, much of our concern and care should be to minimize that danger.

Propane itself is a derivative of the distillation process of motor fuels and natural gas that we utilize in our vehicles and homes. It is one of the lightest factions of the fractionating procedure coming out of that process as a gas. In order for it to be utilized as a convenient fuel, it must be liquified. This is accomplished by compressing the gas. To liquify the gas, it is compressed approximately 270 times by volume. As long as the "liquified petroleum gas" is maintained under pressure, it remains in the liquid state. For these reasons, the storage and usage of Propane requires the use of heavy steel or aluminum tanks capable of withstanding the high pressure required to maintain the gas in a liquid state.

Propane has a high energy content.
Propane will produce approximately 91,500 BTUs of energy for each gallon of fuel burned. This high-energy content produces more than adequate heat for use in the various RV systems without requiring excessively large quantities of the gas to be stored and transported by the RVer. In contrast, Butane contains more energy (approximately 102,500 BTU per gallon) which would appear to make Butane a better choice for our RVs. However, Butane has the negative quality of not vaporizing (boiling) at temperatures below 30ºF, making it impractical for RVs that occasionally must endure lower ambient temperatures (Propane will vaporize down to -44ºF). If the gas will not boil (vaporize), it will remain in the tank, where it does no good.

In actual practice, some commercial suppliers of Propane provide a mixture of the two gases creating a product that we can utilize successfully with good heat content and an acceptable operating temperature range. This is one reason that the energy content of the Propane we purchase seems to vary. This same reality (varying mixtures) means that in very cold temperatures the combination of the two gases will have an unpredictable degree of vaporization. To the RVer, that could mean that his Propane systems might freeze up today when it did not do so the last time he or she encountered the same very low temperature.

Propane has a widespread distribution network in place.
No household fuel would be ideal for RVers if it were not widely available in every city, large and small, throughout the country. Propane has the distinction of having a very widespread distribution network throughout the country. That distribution system is in place not because of the RVer and his mobile lifestyle, but, because Propane is in great demand for both mobile and fixed facilities throughout the country. Where natural gas is not available for household usage, Propane is normally the next best choice. In addition, many commercial and industrial operations utilize Propane because it burns clean, allowing them to meet the ever-tightening EPA requirements. Many companies view Propane as being just about the ideal fuel. LPG has also gained some acceptance as a motor fuel. It is commonly used in plant (indoor) environments and "on the road" where its clean burning qualitiy is appreciated.

Propane fuel is easily vaporized.
In order to be utilized in our RV appliance systems, fuel must first be vaporized. It is the vapor of the fuel that is flammable and is burned to operate those appliances. In this critical aspect, Propane excels because it is easily vaporized at any temperature above

-44ºF. The conversion to the gaseous state requires no energy from the system and does not decrease the available fuel. Vaporization does result in a chilling of the Propane system. However, at the limited rate of usage in most RVs, that chilling does no harm and will easily dissipate into the atmosphere. In very cold conditions, the slowed rate of vaporization, combined with the low ambient temperature, might result in the Propane system freezing up, and not providing adequate quantities of gas to meet our needs. Note that the empty space reserved at the top of the Propane tank is there to provide room for the liquid gas to vaporize and to accommodate the expansion of the liquid Propane when the outside temperature rises. These are the reasons that Propane tanks are limited to 80% of their volume when filled to the maximum level permitted by law.

Propane fuel is affordable.
Historically, Propane has always been a reasonable value in terms of its cost per BTU of heat content. To a large degree, this was the result of the fact that Propane is a by-product of the production of automotive fuels that are in far greater demand. When combined with the limited usage of Propane, the result was an oversupply and a relatively low price. With the advent of tightening of EPA regulations, increased industrial demand and the change in demographics around the country where more and more households are opting for a rural lifestyle, the demand for Propane is burgeoning. With that increase in demand, the cost has risen to the point where the fuel is actually more expensive than its primary competition--natural gas. To the RVer, the cost of the Propane is less a concern than is its distribution network and convenience of use.

Propane is safe and convenient to use.
With virtually every RV (6 million plus) using Propane day in and day out as its household fuel of choice, RVers know that Propane is both safe and convenient. Yet every year RVs are damaged or destroyed by fire and explosion directly related to the Propane system. Further, many more RVs are damaged to a greater extent because of the Propane carried onboard the RV when a crash or incident triggers involvement by the Propane. One common illustration of this secondary involvement is that Propane lines are often run through or adjacent to the wheel well in our RVs where a blown tire or thrown tread could break the line, possibly resulting in fire. Knowledge of Propane and its proper usage and handling, along with a full understanding of RV weight and tire issues (see Books 1 and 2 regarding RV Weight Safety and Tire Safety) are generally adequate to virtually eliminate any risk.

RV and mobile home Propane systems are designed for long, safe and trouble-free operation. A tremendous amount of engineering effort has gone into the prevention of Propane accidents. The safety record of the industry proves the adequacy of those efforts. Propane gas has an odor added providing users with its most important safety feature. The offensive garlic smell is unique and should alert you to the presence of Propane. If the odor is present, take immediate appropriate action to counter the danger of fire or explosion. We will have much more on Propane safety later.

Many RVers use camp stoves, barbecues and outdoor lights which are also powered by Propane. In this case, the Propane generally does not come from the RV system; but from small one-pound cylinders.

The usage of these small containers could not be simpler. They are merely screwed in place and disposed of when depleted. The containers themselves are readily available wherever sporting goods are sold and can be stored for some period of time before being used. The one-pound Propane cylinders are very trouble-free in operation, but still contain a significant amount of potential energy; thus, they should be treated with care.

- Treat one-pound Propane cylinders with the same respect you treat your RV Propane system.

- Remove the fuel containers when not using the appliance.

- Do not attempt to refill the Propane cylinders.

- Store extra Propane cylinders outside the living area of the RV.

- Keep cylinders away from heat sources.

- Dispose of used cylinders properly.

THE RV HOUSEHOLD PROPANE FUEL SYSTEM

With full recognition of the unique qualities of Propane, engineers have gone to great lengths to assure that the product can be used safely in the hands of RVers. The primary considerations in this engineering effort are based on recognition that:

- Propane is pressurized in the tank.

- Propane will easily vaporize if released.

- Propane is heavier than air; thus, it will settle in low points of the RV if released.

- Propane liquid will expand measurably when heated.

When used in the RV, the Propane supply connection is normally standardized. It is most commonly located on the tongue of a conventional trailer, in a compartment under a 5th wheel trailer hitch, or in a Propane tank compartment generally on the left side of the rig for an ASME tank in a motorhome. This standardization of location provides ready access in the case of an emergency involving the RV and fire or the Propane system. Lines connecting the regulator and the various appliances must meet industry standards for low-pressure gas applications. The regulator, the cylinder supply valve (3 types are commonly used, including the POL valve, standing for Prest-O-Lite, being the most common valve type),

and connections in between must meet industry standards for high-pressure gas connections. The Propane tank must meet the standards established by either DOT (Department of Transportation) or ASME (American Society of Mechanical Engineers). The regulator must be a two-stage device to reduce the high tank pressure to 11 inches of water column (approximately 1/2 PSI). In addition, there may be additional components to accommodate the specific application. In some cases, additional regulators are located at each appliance for safety in case the primary regulator fails. They are used along with shut-off valves placed strategically to shut off various appliances for safety (in case the primary regulator fails). This very simplistic explanation of your RV's Propane system and its components greatly understates reality, since today's RVs are actually quite complicated with literally hundreds of components and potential leak sources.

The DOT or ASME cylinders (also called bottles) and tanks which contain the liquid Propane come in a variety of sizes: 20, 30 and 40 gallons are common sizes for motorhomes, while 5, 6 and 10-gallon sizes are common on trailers (often in multiples) to meet the RVers' requirements. In all cases, the rated capacity is the full or theoretical volume of the tank. All Propane tanks are limited to 80% of that amount to provide an empty or unwetted space for the Propane to vaporize and to allow for the liquid Propane to

ASME Container

- Fill Valve
- Level Gauge
- 80% Valve
- Capacity Label
- Vapor Service Valve (POL) and Pressure Relief

DOT Container

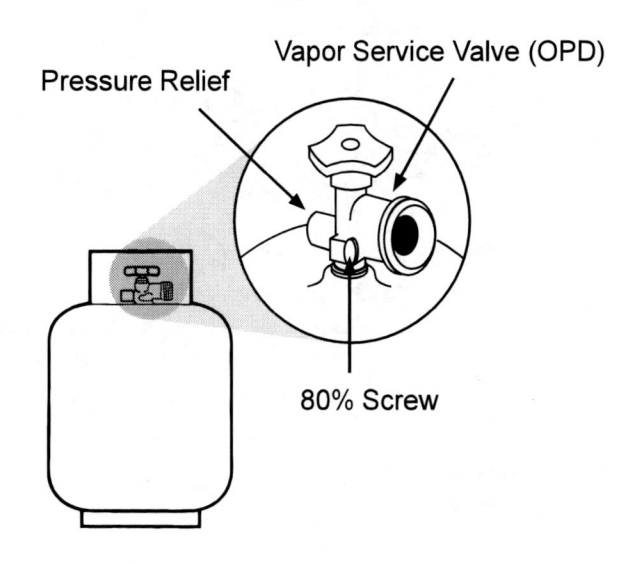

- Pressure Relief
- Vapor Service Valve (OPD)
- 80% Screw

expand without leaking should the ambient temperature rise.

Regulations limit the total amount of Propane that can be carried aboard RVs. For motorhomes it is approximately 45 gallons, while trailers are limited to approximately 20 gallons. If you require more than this amount, the most common solution is to purchase or rent large tanks that can be hooked up to the RV. The location of the tanks within the RV is closely controlled. In no case should the Propane tank be installed inside the RV where leaking gas could collect and potentially explode. When installed in an external Propane compartment, the compartment itself should be vapor-tight to the RV interior and must be vented both above and below to release and safely dissipate any leaking gas liquid or vapor. This is particularly important because of the two safety valves that are designed to reduce internal pressure, assuring the tank integrity by releasing gas. When mounted on the tongue of a trailer, Propane tanks require secure straps that can be released to permit tank filling. The vapor service valve of all Propane tanks must be protected from damage; hence, the familiar shield surrounding the valves, etc.

All Propane tanks must be fitted with a vapor withdrawal valve. On ASME tanks, it is a separate valve, while DOT tanks use the supply or OPD valve for this purpose. The OPD valve is also used for filling the DOT tanks and shutting it off when no gas is to be delivered. Note that the OPD valve itself contains a pressure relief valve for safety. An eighty percent (80%) valve is also provided to indicate when the tank is completely filled. The safety valve opens if pressure inside the tank builds to dangerous levels. All of these components are safety items and must be maintained in good condition. Propane tanks are designed to operate either vertically or horizontally. Tanks may not be used in a position different from that for which they were designed. Propane tanks may also be equipped with various types of gauges to indicate the level of fuel in the tank for the convenience of the RVer.

Regulators are devices that reduce the internal tank gas pressure to that required by the RV's appliances. By regulation, they are two-stage components designed to prevent high pressure from ever reaching the RV appliances that operate at a much lower pressure. Propane regulators designed for use on trailers equipped with two tanks often have an integral change-over valve incorporated. Additional regulators may be used within the RV to assure that excessively high pressure or liquid never reaches the RV appliances where damage could be done.

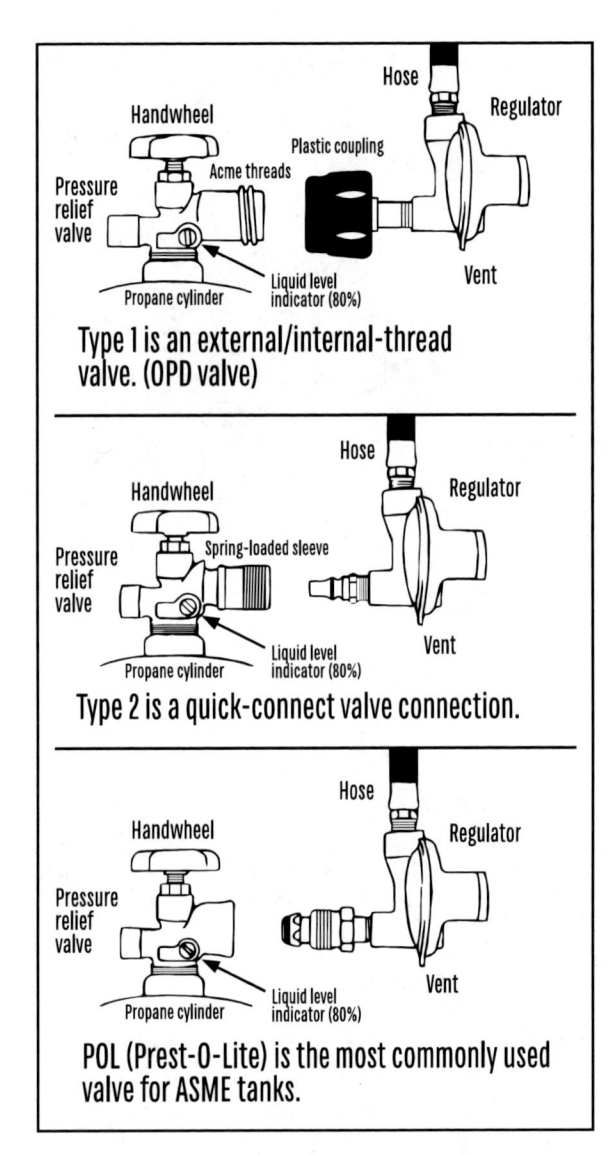

Type 1 is an external/internal-thread valve. (OPD valve)

Type 2 is a quick-connect valve connection.

POL (Prest-O-Lite) is the most commonly used valve for ASME tanks.

The piping used to distribute Propane throughout the RV may be of differing material and designs: LPG standards pertain to whatever material is chosen. Threaded pipe and fittings fabricated from steel, wrought iron or brass may be used with proper workmanship rules applying. Copper tubing with flare-type fittings is commonly used for Propane systems. Steel tubing externally treated to minimize corrosion is another possible choice when used with flare-type fittings. By far, the most common material utilized by RV manufacturers is copper tubing because of its flexibility. Its flexibility makes it a good choice for operation in an RV that travels the highways with all of the road shock and vibration that are involved.

Our discussion of the various components and safety devices required for each is intended to be only a brief explanation for the RVer's familiarization. This discussion is not intended to be exhaustive or complete since Propane systems are among the most controlled on your RV. For this reason, RVers should approach any changes or repairs cautiously. The RVer should be knowledgeable about what is required by regulation, select only quality companies to work on their systems and closely inspect all work completed.

Filling the RV Propane System

By law, filling Propane systems is not a do-it-yourself operation. The trained attendant will do it for you. Your job is to observe and to assure that it is done correctly to protect your rig and the lives of those on board.

Filling Propane tanks is a simple operation for the RVer. In the case of a motorhome, the vehicle is positioned next to the Propane tank of the service facility. Those with trailers will have to remove and carry their tanks to the service facility. This is accomplished by closing the OPD valve (hand tighten only) and disconnecting the union that connects the pressure regulator to the OPD valve. Disconnect the tie-down strap and transport the tank to the service facility. Never carry the tank (empty or full) in the trunk of an automobile. If transported in the bed of a truck, secure the tank to prevent it from falling out or doing damage to the tank itself if unexpected turbulence is encountered en route. At this point, the attendant will take over. He will attach a hose to the OPD valve and open the 80% valve. The tank should be filled until liquid spurts out the 80% valve indicating that it is full. Never allow the attendant to fill past this point, since there will not be adequate room for the liquid fuel to vaporize properly or to expand without over-pressurizing the tank. At this point, the Propane supply is shut off and both the OPD and 80% valve closed. With removal of the fill hose the process is complete allowing the RVer to return the full tank to their RV.

The RVer's responsibility during this process is to be sure that his or her RV is properly set up for Propane refueling. For motorhomes, this entails properly positioning the RV within reach of the refueling hose, but not too close, shutting off the engine and generator (if operating), and shutting off all appliances that operate on Propane or could provide a source of ignition for Propane fumes that might collect in the area. Further, all passengers and pets should be removed from the RV and kept a safe distance away. The RVer's responsibility also extends to reviewing the refueling station to be certain that the equipment is in good repair, that a proper fire extinguisher is readily available and that the attendant appears to know what he/she is doing. With all of that assured, the RVer should also keep his/her distance from the fueling site in case something goes wrong.

For trailers the process is simpler because only the empty tank is delivered to the fueling site. At that point it must be removed from the bed of the truck and placed on the ground within reach of the Propane pump. The truck itself should be positioned a safe distance from the refueling site and be shut down during the refueling process. The trailer RVer's responsibility then extends to reviewing the whole refueling site to be certain that it is in good repair, that a proper fire extinguisher is readily available, and the attendant is qualified to dispense Propane. With this assured, the RVer should remain a safe distance from the refueling operation in case something goes wrong. When the refueling process is complete, the now-filled Propane tank can be placed back into the bed of the truck and secured for the trip back to the trailer. When transported, a Propane tank should be carried in the same orientation (horizontal or vertical) for which it was designed to operate on the trailer.

Operating with a Propane System
Living with Propane systems in our RVs is just about the easiest possible thing that we can do. The RVer simply has to turn on the system by opening the vapor supply valve located at the tank or cylinder. The rest is virtually automatic. The system is ready for use. Yes, there may be shut off valves located at the individual appliances, but these are to be used only to isolate that specific appliance should it malfunction or require repair. The rest of the time, those shut off valves are left ON.

The individual appliances may also require that a switch be turned ON or that the pilot light be lit before the unit becomes fully functional. Many modern appliances, including cook stoves, refrigerators and water heaters, are equipped with pilotless systems to conserve Propane and to eliminate the heat load produced by the pilot in the RV. If the appliance requires lighting the pilot, be certain that you practice that operation when the conditions are good. There is nothing quite like trying to light a balky heater in the dark while you are shivering from the cold. A good place to start is with the directions that came with the appliance. Note also, that if the RV has not been used for some time with the Propane shut off, it might take a while for good gas to reach the pilot burner. If the appliance does not light after a reasonable amount of time once you smell the distinctive odor of Propane at the appliance, you should take the RV in for service.

The RVer should also make certain that all of the safety detectors provided with the RV are in good working condition. This includes the LP leak detector, the carbon monoxide detector and the smoke alarm(s). If battery-operated, carry spare batteries to assure that these vital safety devices are functioning correctly at all times when the RV is occupied.

The refrigerator in most RVs uses 110 VAC electricity or Propane to maintain the cold temperature. These are referred to as two-way units. Some refrigerators can also use a 12 VDC source of electricity, making them a three-way unit. In general, these units are designed (prioritized) to use 110 VAC power whenever it is available, since it is the cleanest, most effective and economic power source, and it operates without noise or distraction. When 110 VAC is not available, such as when parked without hookups (dry camping) or driving down the highway, a two-way refrigerator generally switches automatically (sometimes manually) to use Propane as the power source. This would be the next "best" choice of power available. Under the conditions of dry camping, the three-way refrigerator would also switch to Propane, however, while driving it would switch over to use 12 VDC power. The logic here is that the power requirements of a refrigerator are so high that a 12 VDC source (batteries) would be quickly depleted running the refrigerator while dry camped.

Using Propane for refrigeration while driving bothers many RVers and experts in the field. In order to do this, the Propane system must be on, thus, it provides gas throughout the RV and potentially creates a dangerous situation if there is an accident, or a leak developes. For this reason many experts recommend that the Propane system be shut down while traveling by shutting off the vapor supply valve. This will leave the refrigerator without a power source, but, by keeping it tightly closed and limiting the time spent in this condition, it is generally possible to keep it cool enough to prevent food spoilage.

There are no laws restricting the use of the Propane system while in transit, so it is an individual RVer's decision to do so or not. Note that there are some tunnels in the USA that prohibit Propane systems from being used while traveling through them, or restrict Propane-carrying vehicles from using the tunnel or bridge. This is logical based on the knowledge that Propane is heavier than air and will, therefore, settle into low points, possibly collecting until the concentration reaches the proper ratio for combustion or explosion.

When it comes time to refuel your RV, the Propane system should once again be shut down for safety. This is best accomplished at the vapor supply valve. The obvious purpose of this precaution is to eliminate a potential source of ignition should a gasoline or diesel fuel spill occur. This is only required if you travel with the Propane system open and functioning.

Traveling Safely with Extra Propane
RVers, particularly those who "boondock" or settle in at a given location for an extended period of time, often wish to carry extra propane for their RVs. Their motivation for this is to extend their stay at a location, limit trips for refueling, or to save expense by fueling where it is more economical. While there is nothing inherently wrong with these goals, it does present some serious safety considerations. Motorhome RVs come equipped with a well-designed fully integrated propane system utilizing a tank mounted permanently in a secure, protected location on the RV. Similarly, trailer-type RVs are equipped with up to two propane tanks securely mounted to the tongue or stowed internally in a forward compartment of the trailer. A major factor in the engineers selecting these locations was that tanks placed there are secure and well protected from external damage.

In contrast RVers carrying extra propane often place the tanks in locations where they are very vulnerable to damage in the event of a crash or loss when traveling down the road. This picture illustrates clearly how not to carry extra propane; the tank is located on the rear bumper where it is subject to damage in even the most minor rear-end collision. Recognize that the rear-end collision is the most common type of automotive accident. In addition, the propane tank itself is poorly attached to the RV. It is sitting in a plastic crate and held in place by "bungee cords," presenting an opportunity to bounce out with only a minor bump. A tank positioned in this manner is also subject to any act of vandalism, and it is in full sunlight that may cause the liquid to expand, resulting in the venting of explosive propane gas. RVers should seriously consider all of the ramifications of carrying extra Propane and weigh it against the relatively small benefits obtained before making a decision.

PROPANE SAFETY

Safety is vitally important for anyone working with or using Propane and its systems. Propane is flammable, explosive under pressure and can freeze human skin if the liquid comes into direct contact with it. For the RVer, using Propane safely depends on correct refueling procedures, preventive maintenance and constant alertness. We have already discussed the refueling process in some detail, so we will now focus on preventive maintenance issues and operator awareness.

Preventative Maintenance
The RV Propane system can be rather complex, with many appliances, safety devices, storage tank(s) and the essential distribution system. For the most part, RV manufacturers do not have a recommended maintenance schedule for the Propane system, yet many experts suggest that the entire Propane system should be checked at least once a year, whenever a condition is suspected and prior to every trip after the RV has been in storage.

The annual check of the entire RV Propane system can be accomplished by a professional RV service technician by using a leak detector device attached adjacent to the regulator. When all of the Propane appliances are shut off, any leakage, indicated by small bubbles or pressure loss, should be investigated and corrected prior to RV usage. A testing of the Propane system's operating pressure and lockup pressure should be undertaken with adjustments or repairs completed as indicated. When followed with a cleaning and functional testing of each appliance individually, the RVer should feel very secure that the Propane system is OK.

The test of the Propane system following a significant storage period is quite similar in that the system is leak tested as a complete system, and each appliance is functionally tested as well. What is different is that the physical system is carefully reviewed to assure that no critter or insect(s) has found its way into the various orifices and vents where they might adversely affect the operations of the appliance.

The final factor in our preventive maintenance program is to seek a system check by professionals whenever we suspect that something is wrong. Any malfunction of a Propane appliance, such as a pilot light that will not stay lit or a refrigerator that does not cool properly, might be an alert that your Propane system requires professional service. If your gas leak detector (if equipped) sounds an alert, even if it is only momentary, have the system checked. The most common cause of such suspicions is when we detect the pungent (garlic) odor associated with Propane. The odor is purposely put into Propane to provide us with an olfactory indication that there is something wrong. Note, however, that there are conditions when the smell of Propane or our ability to detect it is missing. Please consider that:

- Some people (especially the elderly) are unable to detect the smell of Propane gas.

- Colds, allergies, sinus congestion and the use of tobacco, alcohol or drugs may diminish your sense of smell.

- Cooking odors or other strong odors can mask the smell of gas.

- Propane gas can lose its odor if a leak occurs underground.

- On rare occasions, Propane gas may lose its distinctive odor. This is called "odor fade." Air, water and rust in a Propane tank or cylinder may weaken the gas odor, especially if valves were left open after the container was emptied.

- Odorant in a leaking gas can be absorbed by various materials (unpainted or untreated masonry, rough wall surfaces, furniture, fabrics and drapes) and by the walls of gas piping and seldom used Propane storage containers and distribution systems.

Also consider that some people wrongly believe that the smell of Propane is a signal that their tank is nearly empty and should be refilled. When a tank is low, you may get a momentary whiff of gassy smell when stovetop burners are ignited. However, if the smell of gas lasts more than an instant, then the continuing gas odor means that you may have a serious Propane gas leak. Any persistent gassy smell is your signal to TAKE IMMEDIATE EMERGENCY ACTION.

The potential consequences of a Propane leak are so severe that we must be ever vigilant and never overlook the subtlest clue that something is amiss.

THE OPD VALVE AND THE RVER

Most trailers use Propane cylinders certified under DOT rules that are temporarily mounted on the trailer. Most motorhomes use Propane tanks constructed under ASME standards that are permanently mounted under the vehicle or in a dedicated compartment. Effective October 1, 1998, all DOT portable tanks must be equipped with an "Overfilling Prevention Device" (OPD). The permanently mounted motorhome ASME tanks already meet this requirement as they have been equipped with OPD valves for many years.

Most RVers today will never encounter a non-OPD-equipped propane tank, as most of the old-style tanks have aged out or been converted to the new valve. The OPD valve is easily recognized by its tri-lobular valve handle.

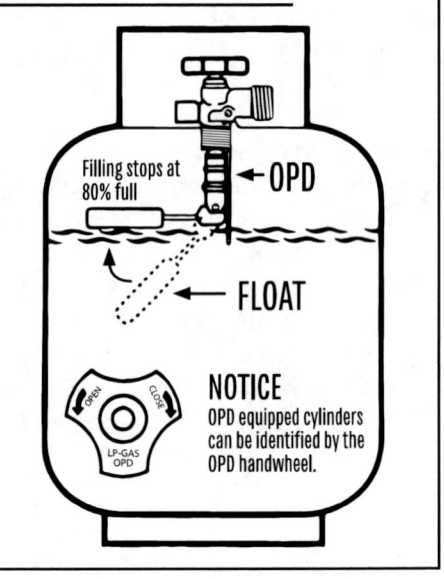

Filling stops at 80% full ← OPD

← FLOAT

NOTICE
OPD equipped cylinders can be identified by the OPD handwheel.

IMPORTANT SAFETY REMINDERS!

- Do not smoke when filling a Propane tank or when near the Propane dispenser.

- Extinguish appliance pilot lights during Propane refueling. The pilot lights might act as a source of ignition and result in an explosion.

- Use only certified appliances.

- Leak-test your system annually, after storage or whenever you suspect a problem might be present.

- Keep Propane turned off when you are on the road. When possible, use your RV electrical system to keep the appliances you require running.

When transporting and handling Propane:
- When transporting Propane tanks or cylinders, keep the POL valve tightly closed and secured by a plastic POL plug.

- Keep tanks and cylinders upright in their normal operating position and well ventilated at all times.

- Handle tanks and cylinders gently and with care.

- Use only properly approved tanks and cylinders.

- Extinguish or remove all ignition sources before handling, transporting or installing Propane cylinders.

Propane storage:
- Note that it is not legal to store cylinders with a capacity of more than five pounds indoors. Store all cylinders outside, away from sources of heat and ignition with the outlet valve closed and safety plugs installed.

If you smell Propane:
- Remove all sources of ignition, including cigarettes.

- Do not enter an area where you suspect a gas leak. If you are in such an area, leave immediately. Open windows or doors to provide a flow of fresh air.

- Shut off all appliances and the Propane tank or cylinder valves.

- Do not turn the lights ON or OFF. Any spark or flame in the area where Propane is present may ignite the gas. The spark in a light switch, telephone, appliance motor or static electricity from walking around the room can present a fire or explosion hazard.

- Immediately get everyone out of the RV and safely away from the area.

- If the smell of Propane continues after the valves have been shut off, call for qualified assistance. Do not call from your own RV or home.

SUMMARY

There is no doubt that, without the LPG system in our RVs, the lifestyle that we have chosen would not be nearly so appealing. The LPG system goes a long way to making our life on the road "just like home" without being so burdensome that it detracts from the quality of life. The basic Propane gas has inherent potential to be dangerous, yet by years of engineering effort and development of the systems in place today, it has evolved into a very safe and convenient household power source for RVs. The maintenance requirements for modern LPG systems are minimal. A little preventive maintenance and a constant alertness for anything wrong is all that is required. Sleep well tonight!

FREQUENTLY ASKED QUESTIONS (FAQ)

In very cold weather, my furnace does not seem to produce the amount of heat it normally does or will not light at all.
Propane fuels vary considerably in their chemical makeup. Often suppliers might add varying amounts of Butane to the mixture. Both products are excellent fuels; however, Butane does not boil or vaporize well in very cold weather. The resultant mixture will vaporize somewhere between the -44ºF of Propane and the 15-30ºF of Butane. Often RVers do not use much Propane while traveling great distances across the country. The LPG prepared for one part of the country may not perform well in another as a result.

I have noticed that the flames at my cook stove are yellow. Is this OK?

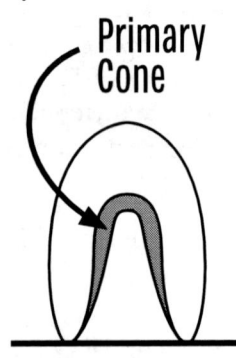

Primary Cone

One of the most useful characteristics of burning Propane is that it burns exceptionally clean emitting minimum pollutants and simple water vapor. The correct fuel/air mixture will result in a distinct cone with a light blue flame pattern. You may see some orange, which is acceptable, but the blue flame and a distinct cone pattern must be dominant--even all the way around the burner. The presence of a yellow flame or a fuzzy flame pattern indicates that the fuel mixture is incorrect. This condition could be the result of: 1) improper gas pressure, 2) improper stove burner adjustment, or 3) debris or foreign material blocking air flow into the burner area. The services of a trained technician are called for to resolve the issue.

The pilot light on my water heater will not stay lit more than a few seconds. What is wrong?
Any appliance that utilizes a pilot light also has a safety pilot valve controlled by a thermocouple. The job of the thermocouple is to detect the presence of the pilot flame. If it is not present (or hot enough) for any reason, then the safety pilot valve shuts the whole system down. When the system will not stay lit for more than a few seconds or extinguishes immediately upon releasing the button, the thermocouple has either malfunctioned or is not getting hot enough. The first possibility requires replacement of the thermocouple, while cleaning and repositioning the thermocouple in the flame pattern of the pilot light might aid the latter condition. In either case, the trained technician is your best bet.

Why do the windows in my RV collect condensation when we cook or bake in cold weather?
When Propane burns, it consumes oxygen from the air and produces carbon monoxide along with large amounts of water vapor. The water vapor is what is collecting on the cold glass when you are cooking in the RV. The fact that oxygen in the air is being depleted, along with the fact that carbon monoxide is being produced, requires that replacement air be made available. Most RVers recognize that this is the same as in their homes except that the volume of air available in an RV is much smaller. Thus, it is a matter of degree. It is common sense to open either a window or roof vent to replace the air (oxygen) being consumed and to exhaust the carbon monoxide produced by the combustion process. Actually, a power vent in conjunction with an open window is the best solution. This will assure that the air is adequately replaced and will minimize the condensation of moisture on the windows.

The flame pattern on the burners of my stove appears not to be connected to the burner itself.
Your description of the visible flame actually beginning above the burner could be an indication that the gas pressure is too high for some reason. A misadjusted air shutter at the burner may also cause this condition. You need to have the Propane system checked as soon as possible as this can be a very dangerous condition.

The electrical ignition device for my range has stopped working. Can I ignore this condition and just use a match to light the burners until I can obtain a replacement unit?

The electrical ignition device or piezo-ignition device for Propane appliances are convenience items only. They are placed there to aid the RVer by making the job easier. As such, there is no problem operating the appliance by lighting it with a match or "gas match" device.

I know that the LPG system probably should be checked annually for preventive maintenance, but how do I know that I am not getting ripped off with needless service?

Great question! First, please be assured that this is an essential service to ensure safe and worry-free operation of vital systems in your RV. Picking a good service facility is probably the most important aspect of actually getting the quality service that you deserve and pay for. The facility should utilize trained technicians such as those certified by RVIA--the Recreation Vehicle Industry Association. The facility need not be elaborate, but it must contain adequate space to perform quality work and have the essential supplies and equipment to do the job. The actual service of the LPG system should include, at minimum, the following:

- A thorough visual inspection of the LPG tank or cylinders, the regulator and all hoses and pipes that are readily visible.

- The gas-operating pressure and a lock-up test of the LP gas regulator should be conducted.

- A leak test of the tank valves, regulator and all visible piping should be conducted. There are various ways to conduct this test, including a liquid leak check solution, a bubble leak test, an electronic leak test, or by a pressure drop-type test.

- Each LPG appliance should be functionally tested and adjusted for proper operation. Repair of any abnormalities should be completed before releasing the RV for service.

As you can see, a complete and proper LPG preventive maintenance program should ensure safe and worry-free operation during your subsequent travels.

Would an RV Propane leak detector be a good investment?

Actually, there are a couple of LPG system leak detectors available that are both affordable and do a good job of monitoring the LPG system for leaks on an ongoing basis. Just how important are these systems? The answer to that question has to go back to the individual RVer and his sensitivity to such issues. The annual preventive maintenance program described above is adequate in the vast majority of cases to identify, diagnose and correct potential LPG problems. The real question becomes: At what price is peace of mind important to you? In addition to system LPG leakage testers, there are hand-held probes that sense Propane in a specific area. These devices are quite affordable, but are generally used to troubleshoot a leakage problem after an RVer detects it.

RESERVED FOR YOUR NOTES.

BOOK 5: ELECTRICAL SAFETY

CONTENTS

Author's Foreword 85
What's It All About? 85

RV ELECTRICAL SAFETY — 86
Understanding the Importance of Electrical Safety 86
Effects of 60Hz Alternating Current on the Human Body 87
RV Electrical Systems Overview 88
The RV 12 Volt DC Electrical System 88
The RV 120 Volt AC Electrical System 91
The RV Battery System 94
Summary 94

AUTHOR'S FOREWORD

The very complexity of our RVs presents one of the more demanding and frustrating aspects we will incur in our RVing lives. The multiple electrical systems in our RVs are essential in order to accomplish the various tasks that we require and complete them safely. Electrical safety demands more from an RVer than knowing enough not to stick a finger or other object into an electrical socket or other electrical device. The electrical system(s) is one of those areas in which familiarity will yield great dividends in terms of peace of mind and will provide many benefits throughout the period of time in which we operate and live in our RVs.

> "Electrical safety demands more from an RVer than knowing enough not to stick a finger or other object into an electrical socket or other electrical device."

WHAT'S IT ALL ABOUT?

RVing opens up vast and diverse vistas to millions of us every year. The lifestyle presents options ranging from weekend tailgate parties, to extended vacations, to international travel, to "snow birding," to a full-timing life onboard your RV.

To a large degree, the amazing flexibility of the RV itself is responsible for the remarkable growth of RVing by attracting many newcomers to the lifestyle. However, the RV's flexibility does not come without a price in terms of complexity of the vehicle itself. Consider for a moment that an RV must provide not only all of the systems contained in a luxury automobile, all the storage and hauling capability of a large truck, but also all of the systems and utilitarian value of our homes. All of this must be capable of driving down the highways and back roads of the country day after day without excessive difficulty or cost in the hands of what amounts to nonprofessional owners/operators/drivers.

Nowhere in our RV is that inherent flexibility more apparent than it is in the electrical systems of the RV. The word "systems" is totally appropriate in this context because today's RVs contain two distinct types of electrical systems. Further, each is capable of operating from a multitude of sources, depending upon what resources are available to us in any given moment or location. While all of this demands some pretty sophisticated engineering, construction and packaging on the part of the RV manufacturer, it must not demand too much effort or understanding from the users of the system. Users need only comprehend what basic systems are in place, learn the proper operation of the electrical systems, know what the correct result of their actions should be, and keep a good healthy respect for the safety aspects of dealing with electricity. This book has been written with that premise as its basis. It is not our intent to make you an electrical engineer or a professional maintenance person but only to instill in you the understanding about what is involved in living with your RV's electrical system(s) safely.

RV ELECTRICAL SAFETY
UNDERSTANDING THE IMPORTANCE OF ELECTRICAL SAFETY

Electrical energy in any form can be dangerous. It is equally important to know how to avoid an electrical accident and what action to take in case an electrical accident does occur.

Most accidents and injuries arise from contact with electrical current and are a result of lack of understanding or negligence on the part of the person injured.

The human body is a relatively good conductor of electrical energy. Therefore, when a person comes into direct contact with electricity, current will flow through the body to the point of ground. Electricity will always follow the path of least resistance to a ground. In this case, we are referring to an electrical ground that is not necessarily the physical ground (earth). As electricity seeks a ground, it possesses considerable energy. That power can be used to provide useful work (such as running a fan or light) or it can be destructive (such as a short circuit or shock). Electricity must be controlled in order to be useful in our lives. An excellent example of uncontrolled electricity is lightning, which kills more than 1,000 individuals each year.

Generally, RVs contain both a 120 VAC (120 volt alternating current) system to operate some of the household devices and a 12 VDC (12 volt direct current) system to provide your automotive needs. Typical devices connected to 120 VAC systems include lights, air conditioners, fans, converters or inverters and water heaters. The 12 VDC system is considered to be the primary power system in the RV, and it is commonly used to provide power for the water pump, lights, and fans in the living area of the RV along with all the requirements of the RV's engine, instruments, lights, fans, radio and accessories. All of these uses for electricity are called "loads" and represent useful work or functions that we require. Note that a "load" is an electrical path to ground, but it is controlled, thereby providing a safe path to ground while using the flowing electricity to complete a task (work).

The first property of electricity that we need to understand is that electrical current will always seek the path of least resistance to earth ground.

Harmful electricity (electrical shock) can cause serious injury or death as it pursues the path of least resistance to ground. If you are the path of least resistance, the consequences are potentially serious. The difference between an unpleasant shock and fatal electrocution depends upon many factors, including the type of electricity present, the path the electrical current travels through your body, how you contact the live circuit, how well insulated you are from earth's ground and your overall health. It is best to treat all types and amounts of electricity with a healthy respect. Should your RV electrical system require repair or maintenance and you are concerned about working safely with electricity, it is highly recommended that you consult a trained professional to do the job. The effects of alternating current on the human body are detailed on the following chart.

EFFECTS OF 60HZ ALTERNATING CURRENT ON THE HUMAN BODY

Current in Milliamps	Effect
1 milliamp (ma)	Not discernable - no effects
2 ma	Tingling sensation
5 m	Painful shock
10 ma	Localized muscle contractions sufficient to cause locking onto the circuit for 2.5% of people
15 ma	Localized muscle contractions sufficient to cause locking onto the circuit for 50% of people
30 ma	Breathing impaired - may cause unconsciousness
50 - 100 ma	Possible fibrillation of heart muscle
100 - 200 ma	Certain fibrillation of heart muscle
200+ ma	Severe burns and muscle contractions - heart may stop beating
Over 2 amps (2000 ma)	Irreparable damage to body tissue

Electrical Shock:
Burn Symptoms and Treatment

The possibility of life-threatening electrical injury exists wherever there is electric power or lightning involved. The amount and type of current, the duration, the area of exposure and the pathway of the current through the body determines the degree of damage. Should the current pass through the heart or brain stem, death may occur immediately. Current passing through skeletal muscles may cause muscle contractions severe enough to result in bone breakage or may prevent the victim from releasing from the electrical source. Direct current (DC) is less dangerous than alternating current (AC) in most cases.

Electrical burns are of three distinct types: flash (arcing) type burns; flame (clothing) burns; and the direct heating effect of tissues by the electric current. Electric shock may produce:

- loss of consciousness that may be short-lived
- dazed, confused behavior
- burns on the skin
- rapid, shallow breathing
- muscular pain, fatigue, headache, and nervous irritability

What You Should Do

Make sure the victim is clear of the source of electric current before attempting treatment of any kind. Turn OFF the electricity at the source or roll the victim from the wire or power source with a wooden implement such as a broomstick, or one made of another nonconductive material such as dry cloth, plastic or cardboard. Call EMS immediately. Check the victim's airway, breathing and circulation (ABCs of emergency care). If necessary, begin CPR. Continue CPR and monitor ABCs until help arrives. It may be necessary to treat an electric shock victim for shock. If the victim revives, place him or her in the recovery position and continue to monitor the ABCs until help arrives.

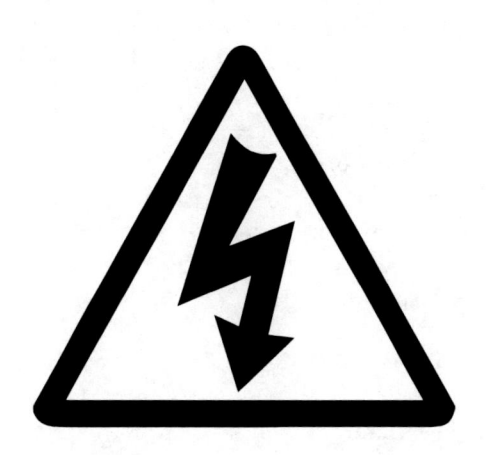

RV ELECTRICAL SYSTEMS OVERVIEW

Electricity contains much potential energy that, if controlled and directed, can perform considerable useful work. Yet electricity may be uncontrolled, and in this state represents a severe safety hazard.

Recreation vehicles typically employ two different types of electrical systems to provide for the electrical needs of the RV while traveling the highways and while parked. The complex electrical system(s) in our RVs is designed to control and to harness the power of electricity for our benefit. When controlled in this manner electricity obeys very specific laws of nature. The most useful of these laws is the power equation, which is $P = I \times E$. Stated another way it means that P (power in watts) is equal to the product of E (voltage) and I (amperage). We can use this formula to size and properly construct our RV for safe and reliable electrical performance. For instance, let us consider that we have a portable 1200-watt electric heater and a new dash radio (protected by a 3-amp fuse) that we plan to use in our RV.

First, let us consider an electric heater. We know that its rating is 1200 watts and it operates on 120 VAC power. We can determine the amperage by using the formula $I = P/E$ or 1200 watts/120 VAC, which yields 10 amps of current. This load is perfectly acceptable for the wiring and 20-amp circuits in our RV--no problem.

Now we will consider the radio. Here we know the operating voltage is 12 VDC and that a 3-amp fuse protects the system. To determine the power consumed by the radio, we use the formula $P = I \times E$ or 3×12, establishing that the radio will consume a maximum of 36 watts. This will help us size the extra batteries or solar system that we plan to add to the RV. This very useful formula is referred to as the Watt's Triangle.

Watt's Triangle (Ohm's Law)

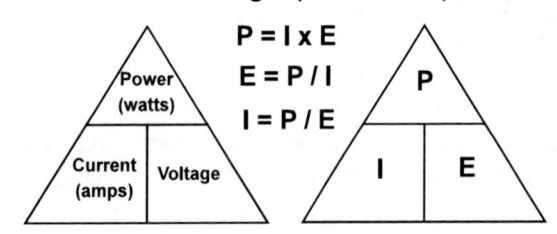

$$P = I \times E$$
$$E = P / I$$
$$I = P / E$$

THE RV 12 VOLT DC ELECTRICAL SYSTEM

The 12 VDC RV System and Components

DC Power: The first type of electrical power system is low-voltage direct current (DC). Direct current in recreation vehicles consists primarily of 12 volts, with some larger coaches and buses employing 24 volts or a combination of 12 and 24 volt systems. The direct current used for these systems normally comes from one of five sources on an RV:

- Engine alternator
- Power converter/inverter
- Battery bank
- Solar panel
- Wind generator

In its minimal configuration, the 12 VDC system will have a battery, a charging device and the wiring and components required to connect these items to function as a system. To be complete, the 12 VDC system requires several components to provide a functional power delivery system capable of meeting our RV requirements. In addition, there are many--typically hundreds--of additional 12 VDC components (loads) that control, monitor or utilize this system as a source of power.

Basic 12 Volt System

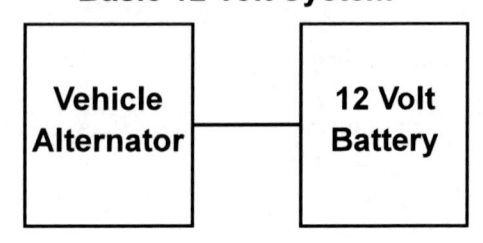

Vehicle Alternator — 12 Volt Battery

The battery has been with us almost since the beginning of automotive endeavors and has evolved to a high degree, yet remains the same basic device as originally designed. The battery is a simple insulated box containing a series of plates that are alternately connected to posts at either end. These are the positive and negative terminals for the battery. The plates of the battery are made from various materials with most having a high content of lead. The entire box is then filled with water/sulfuric acid; hence, the term lead-acid battery. A battery has the ability to store chemical energy and to release it on demand as electrical energy. This simple device utilizes electricity to create a chemical reaction within the battery to store energy and then later reverse that process to return electrical energy when there is a requirement for it. Today there are other types of batteries used in the RV world, including the gel cell battery and the absorbed glass mat (AGM) designs which have gained popularity in the RVing world primarily due to the convenience provided RVers since they require virtually no maintenance. Batteries are often used in multiples for RV applications that require more power for self-containment. By design, the RV battery will produce approximately the 12.6 VDC that powers the typical low-voltage RV power system.

The charging system (source), as noted above, can be from one of several components or from more than one depending upon availability. Virtually every RV 12 VDC system has an engine-driven alternator that serves as its primary DC voltage source. This may be located on the RV engine or on the engine of the towing truck for trailer applications. The alternator in its basic form is simply a magnet that rotates within a series of wires. In the process, useful electrical energy is created, which, in turn may be used to operate a 12 VDC device or fed to the battery to be stored for future usage. The alternator creates the 12 VDC power to keep the battery fully charged when the engine of the RV is operating. To accomplish this, it will produce DC power at a slightly elevated voltage, approximately 13.8 volts when operating to push that energy into the battery. Remember that electrical energy flows only with a push that is created by a voltage differential; thus, the 13.8 VDC of the alternator will flow electrical energy into the battery that operates at only 12.6 VDC.

In our basic 12 VDC system, there are two wires used to complete the circuits within the RV. Generally, the "negative ground" of the battery (black) is wired directly to the chassis of the RV, effectively making the entire metal structure of the RV a source of negative battery potential. The "positive lead" of the battery (red) is then used to complete the various circuits (loads) as required. Thus, the whole system may be referred to as a single-wire system, obviously because only a single wire must be run to any device that is mounted directly on the metal structure of the RV. If the device is not mounted on a conductive material, two wires will be required.

What we have just described is a complete 12 VDC power system, although it is not a very useful one. We can now tap into this system to obtain power to operate lights, fans, entertainment systems, operate our ignition system as we drive, etc. While we drive, the alternator will produce the necessary power for the applications (loads) in use and to charge the battery. When we park, the alternator is taken out of the loop and the battery must now provide all the

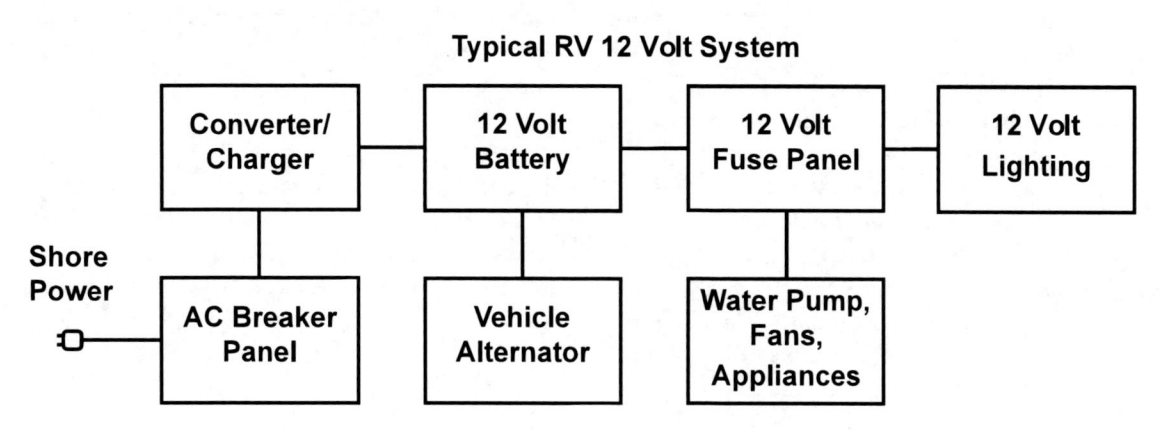

Typical RV 12 Volt System

12 VDC power that we require until it is depleted. At that point, we must find an alternative source of power. This is where the other 12 VDC sources noted earlier come into play. We can plug into shore power and let our converter or inverter provide the required DC power or perhaps our solar panels or wind generator will meet our ongoing requirements for DC power. It is possible to utilize more than one source of DC power without harm to either the source or the loads operating on the combined system, providing all sources are properly regulated.

DC Electrical System Overview
Nearly all of the safety rules that apply to AC current also apply to DC systems. The primary difference is that the voltages present in a typical DC system are approximately one-tenth that of a household AC circuit and that batteries (which remain with the RV at all times) are added to the system as a source of DC power. Therefore, many of the safety rules pertaining to DC electrical systems deal with battery issues.

Unlike most other electrical components in your RV, batteries (liquid lead acid-type) may require regular periodic maintenance. Batteries are one of the simplest yet least understood elements of your RV electrical system, thus, there are many precautions necessary when working with batteries to be discussed later.

Simply stated, a battery is an electrical storage device. As noted earlier, a battery stores chemical energy and is capable of releasing it as electrical energy upon demand. To accomplish this, nearly all batteries used in RV applications contain sulphuric acid as a component of their electrolyte solution; therefore, they present specific safety hazards that must be considered.

Corrosive, flammable hydrogen and oxygen gases are produced during normal battery operation. This gas can create an explosion if flames or sparks are present in close proximity to the battery.

While the risk of severe electrical shock is not as great with low voltage DC electrical circuits, it is still possible to sustain significant injury, including electrical burns if proper safety procedures are not followed. DC electrical systems operate on a lower voltage than AC, but, as a direct result, they also carry higher relative current (amperage). Conductors can fail or break down, creating a fire and burn hazard when higher than normal current overheats them. This makes it imperative to use an appropriately rated fuse or circuit breaker to protect the 12 VDC circuit. This safety device prevents them from overheating and creating a risk of fire.

Common Sense DC Safety Rules
- Always disconnect DC power when working on the low-voltage DC electrical system. When in doubt, it is safest to disconnect the entire system by pulling the negative (ground) battery cable and disconnecting shore power.

- Always disable the converter and solar panels (if present) in your RV before working on the batteries or DC electrical circuits. Even with the batteries disconnected, the solar panels or converter may be capable of producing DC power and energizing the circuit you are working on. Consult your owner's manuals for specific instructions on disabling or disconnecting these devices.

- Some RVs have a master shut-off switch to shut down DC power while others may not. If your RV is not equipped with a DC disconnect switch, you must disconnect the DC ground (negative) conductor from the circuit in order to disable DC power. Do not break a live circuit at the battery terminals due to the risk of arcing in the presence of hydrogen gas. Instead, disconnect the DC ground conductor at the chassis ground connection, which should be far enough away from the battery to minimize the possibility of an arc causing a safety hazard.

- Note that some master switch systems are only a partial shut-off. Be certain that you understand what circuits are shut off with the master switch. These same precautions should also be followed when using a battery charger or when attempting to use battery "jumper cables."

- Before working on or touching a 12 VDC power source, use a test probe or meter to verify that the circuit you are working on is not energized.

- When working on or near circuits that must be energized, use only properly insulated tools and great caution. Routinely inspect tools and test instrument probes to insure they are not damaged, becoming a shock hazard.

- Always replace fuses or circuit breakers with identical components that carry the same rating. To use a higher-rated component might momentarily solve a problem, but it might also allow more current to flow in the circuit than the wiring is capable of handling, leading to a fire hazard. Over time and with repeated usage, circuit breakers can weaken, resulting in more and more false trippings. Replacing consistently tripped breakers should be one of your first trouble-shooting procedures.

THE RV 120 VOLT AC ELECTRICAL SYSTEM

120 VAC RV System & Components
AC Power: The second type of electrical power commonly used on an RV is the one most of us are more familiar with since it is the same type of power we have in our homes. We refer to this power as alternating current (AC). In the United States, residential alternating current is supplied at a nominal 120 volts, 60 Hz (cycles per second). Typically, three different sources may provide alternating current for an RV:

- Shore power

- Generator

- Inverter

The 120 VAC power system used in our RVs also requires several components to make it a functional system. Note that in contrast to 12 VDC power, there is no direct way to store 120 VAC power. Therefore, in the case of a 120 VAC system, we require a constant source of electricity; that may be shore power or may be provided by one of the other onboard systems noted earlier. In either case, the AC power is fed into a distribution system (panel) that, in turn, is wired to the familiar household power outlets throughout the RV.

In the case of a 120 VAC system, there are three wires utilized throughout the RV. The source of 120 VAC power will have a power lead (black), a ground lead (green) and a neutral lead (white) that must be maintained throughout the RV. The source power receptacle will have its ground lead (green) attached to ground (earth). Onboard the RV, the green lead is also grounded to the chassis and ultimately to earth through the tires, etc. for the safety of the occupants. It is vital that this wiring procedure be followed at all times for safety. Once the power source is hooked up, the power will be directed to a distribution panel, which will contain either fuses or circuit breakers (for each circuit) to protect the wiring integrity in the case of a short or other fault. From the distribution panel, wires and outlets are provided permitting the RVer to attach his appliances, etc. just as he would at home. If the RV is equipped to generate its own source of AC power (generator or inverter), then the system will also contain an isolation device commonly referred to as a transfer switch. This device is intended to prevent more than one source of AC power from being connected to the RV at the same time. The transfer switch design can be fully manual (a switch or plug in) or fully automatic which provides the ultimate in convenience as this RV device senses what power is available and switches itself in a prescribed fashion. This completes the basic RV 120 VAC electrical system. As with the 12 VDC system, many devices (loads) can be attached to this basic system.

Basic 120 Volt System

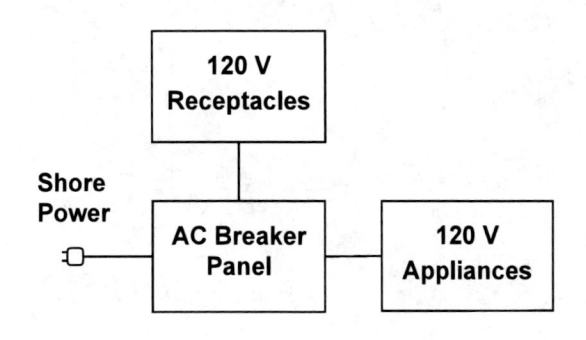

RV 120 Volt System

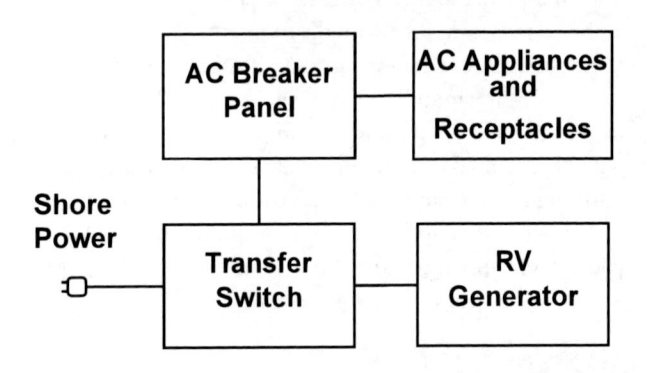

```
┌──────────────┐   ┌──────────────┐
│  AC Breaker  │───│ AC Appliances│
│    Panel     │   │     and      │
│              │   │  Receptacles │
└──────┬───────┘   └──────────────┘
       │
┌──────┴───────┐   ┌──────────────┐
│   Transfer   │───│     RV       │
│    Switch    │   │  Generator   │
└──────────────┘   └──────────────┘
```
Shore Power →

The electrical system(s) on your RV is among the most highly regulated. In general, it is fully covered by codes and standards for recreation vehicles in ANSI A119.2 (standard on recreation vehicles) and in the National Electrical Code Section 551 for electrical requirements.

When You Plug Into Shore Power
One of the most dangerous activities for the RVer when dealing with 120 VAC comes during the few moments when you actually connect your RV to the shore power system. Consistently following good practices during this procedure will eliminate most of the risks involved, but, because we are dealing with an unknown (shore power), we should not let our guard down even for a moment. Remain alert and be cautious as you complete each step. By doing so, you are preventing a potentially serious shock hazard and protecting your RV from the damaging effects of an improper electrical hookup.

Prior to plugging your RV into a shore power outlet, use a small polarity tester to ascertain the proper wiring of the park electrical system (it is necessary to have the breaker turned ON for this test). The polarity checker will indicate by a varying light pattern that the power source is OK or faulty. These devices are readily available at home improvement stores for a few dollars and will go a long way toward saving you from a serious shock threat or from damage to the electrical components of your RV. It may be necessary to use an adapter to fit the 30-amp or 50-amp receptacle of the park system to the 20-amp plug of the tester. If the power is not acceptable or cannot be repaired by the park operator, move on, as it is not safe to stay plugged in at this location.

Before plugging your RV into shore power (and when unplugging prior to leaving), always make sure the breaker at the pole is in the OFF position. Only then should you plug in your shore cord and turn the breaker ON. This procedural step assures that live current is not present at the shore power outlet when you are connecting your shore cord. Without this simple step, should you have any AC device ON, there would be an immediate draw on the system creating a spark as the plug is put into the receptacle. This is more obvious when we recognize that devices such as a converter, inverter or refrigerator are always ON, adding to this concern. An electric spark of this type can cause severe electrical burns. It may also cause a power surge within the RV, potentially damaging the electronics and/ or computers in your RV. Another harmful result of this is to pit and char the plugs, resulting in wear and increased resistance, thereby shortening the power cord's life.

Use caution when connecting to shore power. Make certain that you are standing on dry ground when connecting to shore power. Wet grass or damp ground and bare feet are more conductive and can significantly increase the risk of electrical shock. Recall the rule regarding the electrical "path of least

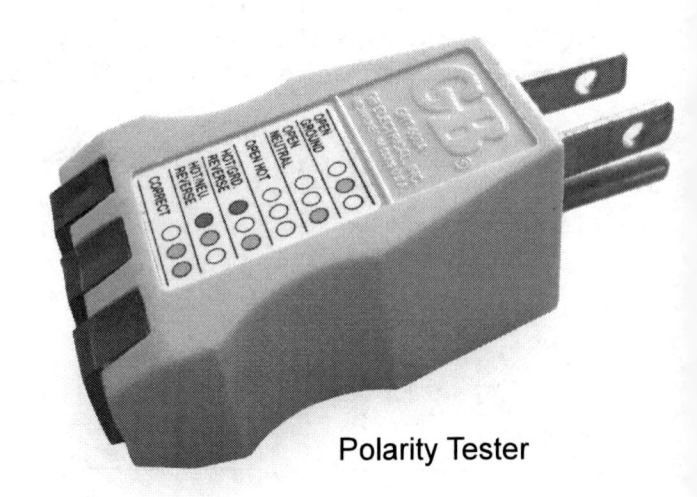

Polarity Tester

resistance." If necessary, carry a block of wood or a rubber mat to stand on when you must handle the shore power cord in damp conditions.

Inspect your shore cord and plug every time you use it to make sure there is no wear or damage that could result in exposed conductors or poor connections. Check the condition of the prongs of your power cord. If they are pitted or charred, consider replacing the cord or, at minimum, clean the prongs to bright copper condition. Immediately repair or replace any damaged power cords.

Common Sense AC Safety Rules

- When you must work with electricity, always make certain to shut off electrical power. It is best to turn off the main breaker in the AC distribution panel and to disconnect shore power at the source. Post a sign on or near the shore cord connection and distribution panel to warn others that you are working on the electrical system. This step is intended to prevent someone else from plugging in the power cord or turning the system ON.

- Before working on or touching a 120 VAC power source, use a test probe or meter to verify that the circuit you are working on is not energized.

- If your RV is equipped with a generator that has an automatic start feature, be sure to disable the auto start feature before working on the coach's electrical system or the generator. Consult the generator's operating instructions or turn off the main breakers on the generator to be certain.

- RVs equipped with an inverter may energize some circuits by the inverter, even with the generator output disabled and shore power disconnected. Be certain to disable the inverter's AC output by turning OFF the main breaker in the inverter sub-panel or by disconnecting the DC input to the inverter. Consult your inverter owner's manual for specific instructions on disabling inverter output.

- When working on or near circuits that must be energized, use only properly insulated tools and great caution. Routinely inspect tools and test instrument probes to insure they are not damaged, thereby providing a shock hazard.

- In the event it is necessary to probe live circuits with a meter or other test equipment, it is suggested that you keep one hand behind your back or in a pocket. The rationale in this recommendation is that by using only one hand to hold test probes, the chance of electrical current passing through your heart is minimized.

- When working on the RV electrical system from outside the coach, avoid using aluminum ladders and touching other metal objects such as metal pipes or poles that create a low resistance path to ground. Recall that the normal electrical ground path goes through the tires that are not as conductive as is the human body. Touching a low resistance path to ground could make YOU the path of least resistance.

- When replacing breakers or fuses, always use breakers rated appropriately for the conductor (wire size) that they are intended to protect. If you are uncertain of the correct breaker size, consult a qualified electrician. Over time and with repeated usage, circuit breakers can weaken, resulting in more and more false tripping. Replacing consistently tripped breakers should be one of your first trouble-shooting procedures.

- When repairing or replacing any 120 VAC component or conductors (wire) in your RV, use an identical item to assure that it has adequate capability.

- Do not arbitrarily replace breakers with a higher amperage rating to cure a frequent false tripping problem. To do so might create an overloaded wire, presenting an overheating or fire hazard. It is better to find the actual cause of the repeatedly blown circuit breaker and repair it as required.

THE RV BATTERY SYSTEM

RV Battery Safety Concerns

The most common RV battery type, the lead-acid battery, requires a certain amount of maintenance. Batteries should be checked regularly for proper fluid level. Batteries contain sulfuric acid making your routine maintenance activities somewhat hazardous. For this reason, there are numerous safety precautions to be followed.

The actual time between checking and servicing the batteries will vary depending upon the conditions in which they are used and how they are charged and recharged. If you use your batteries "hard," such as when doing a lot of dry camping, they should be checked more frequently. When servicing is required, you should use only distilled water to replenish what liquid is lost.

- Remove all metal jewelry (rings, watches, bracelets, necklaces, etc.) before working with DC current and batteries. A battery short circuit created by such items can produce enough current to melt metallic jewelry and cause severe burns.

- Because batteries present a severe hazard potential (electrical, chemical and physical) it is recommended that someone should assist you or at minimum be within range of your voice to come to your aid when you work near batteries.

- Always wear safety goggles (to protect your eyes) and proper protective clothing. Avoid touching your eyes while working near batteries.

- In case of accidental contact with battery acid, wash immediately with soap and water. In case of acid contact with your eyes, flush with clean water for a minimum of 15 minutes and seek medical attention immediately.

- When disconnecting or removing batteries, always disconnect the negative conductor (black) first, then the positive conductor (red). Reconnect the positive conductor (red) first, then the negative conductor (black).

- Be extremely cautious when using metal tools around batteries. Short-circuiting a battery with a metal tool will result in a large spark and may cause an explosion of the battery as well as personal injury. It is a good safety precaution to use only insulated tools or to cover all but the very working end of your tools with an insulating material such as electrical tape.

- When adding water or electrolyte to a battery, use only nonmetallic containers and funnels to prevent the possibility of arcing.

- Do not overfill batteries. The result will be excessive gassing and corrosion in the area of the batteries.

- Corrosive, flammable hydrogen and oxygen gases are produced during normal battery operation. This gas can create an explosion if flames or sparks are present. Never smoke while working near batteries.

- Regularly inspect all DC connections, especially at the battery terminals, to insure that they are tight and free of corrosion.

- Always allow adequate ventilation when charging or using a battery in a confined space.

- Never attempt to charge a damaged or frozen battery.

- Always have baking soda and clean water available to neutralize acid spills or leakage.

SUMMARY

RVs have two separate, but interdependent, electrical systems. You don't need to be an electrician to operate these systems successfully. Understanding what each system does for you and how they relate to each other will be sufficient for most RVers. Safety is always of paramount importance when maintaining batteries and generators and when using electrical appliances and devices.

BOOK 6: SAFE DRIVING

CONTENTS

Author's Foreword 97
What's it all About? 97

RV DRIVER CONSIDERATIONS — 98
RVing and the Mature (Aging) Driver 98
Who Should Drive the RV 99
Preparing the RV for Travel 100

LEARNING TO DRIVE THE RV — 102
Becoming an RV Driver 102
Additional RV Driving Considerations 105

SHARING THE ROAD WITH OTHERS — 108
Understanding Truckers 108
Road Rage 110

DRIVING THE RV — 112
Two-Lane Traffic 112
Multiple-Lane Traffic 112
RV-Specific Driving Situations 113
Defensive Driving Tips 114
Mountain Driving 115
Additional Safety Tips 116
Road Signs, Signals, and Highway Markings 117

ADVERSE DRIVING CONDITIONS — 118
Slide Prevention and Recovery 120

TRAFFIC INCIDENTS — 121

RV-SPECIFIC EQUIPMENT OPERATION — 122
Auxiliary Engine Braking Systems 122
Summary 124

AUTHOR'S FOREWORD

As we progress through *The RVer's Ultimate Survival Guide,* we have fully considered the mechanical issues facing us and will now move on to the "on the road" subjects. As you will hear over and over, the basic realities that separate RVs from the automobiles that most of us drive is the fact that they are larger, heavier and longer. All of this adds up to the realization that we must drive defensively and with a full recognition of the limitations of our vehicles. We must also drive smarter. Now some of this may be intuitive to a number of us, but much of it is not. The focus of this book is to identify RV-specific problems and provide proven ways to handle them.

> "As you will hear over and over, the basic realities that separate RVs from the automobiles that most of us drive is the fact that they are larger, heavier and longer."

WHAT'S IT ALL ABOUT?

For potential RVers and many of those already involved in the RV lifestyle, the sheer thought of driving a vehicle as large as a "house" around the country is often intimidating, to say the least. For many, nothing in their backgrounds has prepared them for the moment when they must guide their large RV onto the highway, through construction, or into a tight campground for the very first time. In other cases, perhaps only one family member drives the RV due to a fear of the unknown and the unfamiliar. For many RVers, the opportunity to brush up on their driving skills or to learn new ones is a very appealing thought. Others only complete a driving course to gain an additional discount on their insurance. Yet the lure of the RV lifestyle continues to prompt tens of thousands of normal everyday citizens to put aside their driving fears and face those issues head on in an RV.

This book contains a large quantity of information on this critical aspect of RVing and presents it in a concise fashion. The information presented here has been compiled by RVers with a large amount of personal road experience in RVs and other large vehicles. They have identified the succinct issues and have put them into print to help make your life on the road safer.

RV DRIVER CONSIDERATIONS
RVING AND THE MATURE (AGING) DRIVER

The recreational vehicle (RV) presents a mobile living experience that more people are discovering. The fact that increasing numbers of older persons are becoming RVers is understandable because often only then do life and circumstances afford them the opportunity to do so. Trailers, motorhomes, pop-up trailers, slide-in campers and even van conversions all offer a great way to enjoy our leisure time. The maturity of the average RVer can be a strong ally in this arena.

The safe operation of an RV by older drivers is a special concern for a number of reasons. Aging can affect vision and reaction time behind the wheel of passenger cars and RVs alike. RVs place demands on the driver beyond those of a passenger car, making any deterioration more of a limitation. Awareness of one's abilities becomes a critical issue.

A lifetime of driving experience (generally in passenger cars) also provides invaluable expertise that usually serves older drivers well. That experience, however, can result in established driving habits (good and bad) that are deeply ingrained. RVs handle differently from cars and require more time to brake and room to maneuver safely than do automobiles. RVs also handle differently in relation to the driving environment, presenting special considerations. Bridge heights and weight limits, gas station canopies and dips in the road can all become concerns for the first time in a lifetime of driving. Our vehicle's space requirements are much greater, meaning that even lane changes will require additional space for safe execution. It is true that all of this will again become almost second nature with practice. You never want to become lax or complacent when driving an RV, but a feeling of comfort will come with time, adding to your enjoyment of the RV lifestyle.

For more on the subject of aging and how it might affect our RV driving, consider that for most of us traveling by RV is a recreational activity. We are either retired or vacationing, and many of us are enjoying the year-round or full-time RVing lifestyle. That means we are usually not racing to beat deadlines and are not in as great a hurry as we were previously. Our more leisurely pace gives us the option of traveling during periods of low traffic. We can plan our overnight stops to avoid traffic and schedule shorter days when necessary, leaving after rush-hour traffic in the morning and stopping before the afternoon traffic begins. As we grow older, our reactions become slower. It may take longer to recognize dangerous situations and respond to them appropriately. We also do not see as well as we used to. As a result we must focus more on our driving and learn to recognize signs by their shapes and colors. Also, as a result of our aging, we may not hear as well as we used to. To offset that reality, many mature drivers focus (use all of their ability to concentrate) in order to eliminate internal and external distractions.

A final age-related consideration is that taking medication while operating an RV may affect alertness and ability to concentrate. A cautious RVer should check with a doctor or pharmacist to see how any prescribed medications might affect driving. When all factors are fully considered, the aging driver issue is probably not the primary consideration in our determination of whether or not to pursue the RV lifestyle.

When To Give Up Driving The RV
Probably one of the most difficult decisions an RVer faces is determining the appropriate time to quit driving our RVs. It is possible that you can reduce the size and/or width of your RV and safely continue driving as an interim measure, however, the time will ultimately come when any RV is too much to handle safely. It may still be possible to drive your automobile, but the RV is just too challenging and has the potential to do too much damage to others. This concern is not exclusively a result of driving the RV but also includes the RV's housekeeping requirements and the setup/teardown chores as well. Ask yourself the following questions to help determine if it's time to quit driving your RV.

- Have you been having small accidents? Are the scrapes and dings on your vehicle the result of your driving?

- Have you caught yourself making errors in judgment? Have you found yourself not knowing where you are, where you are going or how to get to your destination?

- Do you lose patience in situations that are out of your control or have you found yourself the focus of more incidents of "road rage"?

- Do those who have traveled with you for some time seem to be more fearful or hesitant than normal?

- Do turning and backing pose a particular problem for you? Do you find that the RV's setup/teardown chores must be put off because they are more than you can handle at the moment?

If the answer is "yes" to any of these questions, you should give careful consideration to hanging up the spurs. Your safety and that of your loved ones are at stake. This may be a very difficult decision indeed, but one that you should make yourself rather than have it forced upon you. Remember also that this does not necessarily mean the end to your RVing. It is only necessary to find alternative ways to get there.

WHO SHOULD DRIVE THE RV

There is something very comforting about traveling with one's home--actually hauling or towing it along while exploring the incredible diversity and beauty of the countryside. It is an exhilarating experience that more and more people are enjoying. There is a strong feeling of self-sufficiency in RVing, similar to what pioneers must have felt in their covered wagons, often described as the first RVs. While hardly traveling in luxury, the pioneer moving to new homesteads carried their home and possessions with them as do today's RVs. They must have enjoyed the feeling of independence, the ability to camp for the night anywhere and the ability to withstand whatever nature dished out. There are several reasons for all adults in the RV to learn to drive and operate the RV beyond just getting from one spot to another.

All RV spouses and passengers are encouraged to become proficient operators of the RV, and this is becoming a common occurrence. Undoubtedly, women are equally capable of operating big rigs as men--the traditional operators. Look no further than the trucking industry or the RV next to you for examples. Following are several reasons why passengers may want to become proficient in the operation of their RVs.

An Exciting Experience

Driving an RV can be an exciting experience. Proficient handling of a large vehicle brings with it an indescribable satisfaction. Often a former full-time passenger will bubble over with enthusiasm after only a brief time behind the wheel of an RV. Remember also that the time will come when you may want to continue this lifestyle when your partner can no longer drive. Now is the time to prepare for that eventuality.

Emergency Situations

Most passengers need the ability to take over should the primary driver become incapacitated. In driving classes, the question is often asked, "If my spouse collapses while at the wheel, what should I do to take over?" attesting to the fact that this is a real concern. We never know when such a horrible reality might present itself. The effort should be to seek to establish control of the steering wheel by grabbing hold and removing the hands of the disabled operator. Once steering control has been assumed, physically remove the driver's foot from the accelerator pedal. The next step is to bring the vehicle to a safe stop by applying pressure to the brake pedal, downshifting the transmission or using the auxiliary braking device--whatever is most accessible. Do NOT turn off the ignition key. That will cause the power steering and power brakes to become inoperative, making the vehicle very difficult or impossible to control and bring to a safe stop. Once the vehicle is safely stopped, you can take action to assist the operator. Actually, the RV makes the described process much easier than might be possible in most automobiles. This is because of the extra space between the seats and in the cockpit area. Note that if the situation is already hopeless when first detected, it may only be possible to remain belted in the passenger seat and "ride out" the imminent crash.

Relieving the Primary Driver
Everyone onboard the RV should be qualified to drive to give the primary operator breaks throughout the driving day. Doing so will greatly enhance safety and enjoyment of any trip. After two or three hours behind the wheel, drivers become less attentive due to the discomfort of sitting in one spot for an extended period of time and the concentration required. Having a qualified co-driver can give the primary driver a much-needed break. In most cases, your partner will welcome a co-driver's assistance as this permits him/her to enjoy the beauty of the countryside rather than just pass through it.

PREPARING THE RV FOR TRAVEL

Proper weight distribution is essential when loading your RV. This topic is fully discussed in Book 1. Careful attention to this very important topic will assure that your RV travels are safer and more enjoyable. An improperly loaded RV will handle and perform poorly, making driving a real chore. It is not uncommon to observe an RVer pulling into a campground in the afternoon or evening literally "white-knuckled" from the stress of the drive. This should not be the case. Modern RVs are well-engineered vehicles that drive easily when they are operated within established limits. In contrast, ignore those limits and the RV can turn into an ill-tempered beast taking away some of the fun. Much of your consideration regarding this issue comes when you select and purchase the perfect RV for your requirements. After that fact, the use of a quality predeparture checklist created for your specifics will assure that you have paid adequate attention to the pre-travel details.

Predeparture Checks
- Make sure you have your vehicle registration and proof of insurance with you in your vehicle. Keep the RV title and an itemized inventory of your RV's contents in a safe place away from the RV. Full-time RVers should invest in a quality fireproof safe and have it installed securely in the RV to carry those critical papers and other valuables. Even then, a full listing of the personal items on board should be generated and left in a secure location such as with family, friends or in a safe deposit box.

- Inspect carefully the total RV for fluid leaks. Look for liquids on the ground and for seepage on all visible lines and fittings. Check the ground under the place where the RV is stored to be certain that any liquids observed there did not come from your RV.

- Verify that all tires have the proper inflation and have no visible defects. This topic is fully discussed in Book 2. While traveling, it is necessary to constantly verify that the tires remain properly inflated.

- Walk around the RV looking for stationary objects that could impede your departure. This is also the time to plan your departure route and to brief anyone who is going to assist you. It is best to plan your departure route so that you will not have to back out, since this is the most hazardous driving exposure.

- Go fully through the RV to stow all loose items, close and lock all doors and compartments, and lock the refrigerator and oven. Turn off the propane if this is your preferred way to travel for safety (as recommended by most RV experts). See a full discussion in Book 4.

- For vehicles equipped with air brakes, check the air pressure warning system (gauge, light or horn) by using the brake pedal to pump the air pressure down sufficiently to check the low-air warning. If the air pressure has bled down while parked, verify that the warning system operates correctly as the pressure comes up. Do not attempt to move the RV until the air pressure is above the required minimum.

- Make certain that all lines and hoses are disconnected and properly stowed and that the TV antenna is down. Any other property used when the RV was set up should be picked up and stowed. Note that large diesel engines require a very high amperage flow to the starter (800-1000 amps) when starting during cold weather; thus, many RVers prefer to leave the RV plugged into shore power, allowing the converter to assist the batteries in starting the rig. Once running, the electric supply line can then be disconnected and stowed.

- Make a safety check of your tow vehicle and towing apparatus. This topic is fully covered in Book 7.

- Truck trailer combinations must check that all hitch/5th wheel connections and safety devices are fully in place and secure. This topic is fully discussed in Book 7.

- Remove any wheel chocks, if they are used, including those commonly used between tandem axle trailer tires. After the vehicle has been moved a small distance, it will be possible to pick up and stow any wheel-leveling blocks that have been used.

- Start the vehicle engine. Verify that oil pressure is established quickly.

- From behind the wheel, with the engine running, check all gauges for normal operation and readings, particularly the air gauge if your vehicle is so equipped. Cold engine starts will generally show a lower than normal temperature and often a higher than normal oil pressure; this is normal. Continue to monitor the gauges as you drive to verify that they settle at their normal position. After a brief wait (one-two minutes) a fast idle speed can be used to build air pressure if desired.

- Take just a few moments when you first get behind the wheel to get comfortable, particularly if it has been some time since your last RV trip. Adjust the seat, position the mirrors as necessary (this may take some assistance for towing mirrors used for trucks and trailers) and familiarize yourself with the essential controls and instruments. Go through the motions for the cruise control, headlights (including dimmer), wipers and window washers and radio if that is a driver's duty in your RV. Of course, it is also necessary to fasten the seatbelt prior to pulling out.

- Monitor the towed vehicle in your rearview mirror or rear vision camera as you first pull out to see if the wheels are turning (brakes released) and to determine if the front wheels of the car follow the direction of the tow vehicle (steering wheel lock released). Many RVers station the co-driver to stand alongside the tow car to check this visually while the driver pulls forward and through an initial turn. The passenger can also verify that the tow bar locks have properly snapped into the correct travel position from this vantage point.

This typical checklist sample is comprised of generic items which may or may not apply to your specific RV. It is suggested that you take the time to create one made for your particular requirements and that you use it routinely.

Camping and RV Checklists
www.escapees.com/checklists

LEARNING TO DRIVE THE RV
BECOMING AN RV DRIVER

As we begin this section, we will assume that you are already a competent licensed driver who merely wishes to transition into the RV driver's seat. The first step in this process is to believe in your own ability to drive a large vehicle. Self-confidence is a major contributor to a successful transition into the driver's seat. With that conviction, a good place to get started is to visit with the local department of motor vehicles (DMV) to pick up whatever materials they have available covering the subject of RVs and other large vehicles. It is also a good time to verify the laws of your state in regard to RVs.

With that cursory information digested, now is the time to get behind the wheel. Sit in the driver's seat while the vehicle is parked. Adjust the seat and the mirrors so that you can adapt to the view from that perspective. What you will generally find is that the RV, because of its height and large windshield, affords an excellent view of the road in front but quite limited vision to the sides and the rear. This is the reason for the multitude (and large size) of mirrors on RVs compared to automobiles. Mirrors are the great equalizer making up for our somewhat limited direct vision. The next observation you will discover is that the vehicle's width (particularly motorhomes) will become very apparent and must be dealt with mentally. The length of the vehicle is obviously present as well, but it is behind you and is somewhat out of your mind, but the width is right there with you every moment, and you will have to fit it onto the highway. Beyond that, everything is more or less familiar. Take as much time as needed to get comfortable with these new surroundings. If possible, spend time sitting immediately behind the driver as the vehicle is going down the road. This will demonstrate the driver's view out the windshield and in the rearview mirrors as well as the normal readings of the instruments. This is also the time to observe the controls utilized in driving the RV. Really, it is not much different from our automobiles except for RV specifics such as the auxiliary braking devices, trailer brakes, ICC light controls and greater instrumentation.

Once you are familiar and comfortable with the RV cockpit, it is time to take your RV to a large parking lot when few other vehicles are present. Learn vehicle placement—how the vehicle sits in a traffic lane. Check out the view in the mirrors. Notice where lane markers appear in the mirror when the RV is positioned a foot or two away from them. Note that most roads establish a 12-foot lane width, which will put an eight or eight and one-half (8-8½) foot RV approximately two feet from either side. The object of this practice is to determine exactly what visual cues you will have when the RV is correctly positioned on the roadway. Note all of the visual cues, including the outside mirrors, inside mirror, rear-view camera and the location of the roadway shoulder and centerlines in the front windshield. In other words, this is the view you will see as you properly position the RV for traveling down the road.

The most apparent difference new drivers quickly recognize is the need to use side-mounted mirrors for any side and rear vision. Backing a vehicle using only rearview mirrors may initially appear difficult, but a little practice is usually all it takes to become proficient. The best place to practice is in an empty parking lot. With a truck/trailer, backing requires more practice than a motorhome alone. It should be noted that a motorhome with a tow car cannot be backed at all.

Adjust your flat side-mounted mirrors so you can barely see the side of your RV. This reduces the size of your blind spot. Use a supplemental convex mirror adjusted to include the blind spots, especially those along the side close to the front tire. Keep in mind that objects viewed in a convex mirror will appear farther away than they actually are. Make sure mirrors are adequate in size and that they are positioned properly for best vision. Mirrors obviously are important for more than just backing. RV drivers must learn to check traffic conditions to the side and rear frequently, even when cruising the open highway, to avoid surprises. Truckers are taught to check mirrors every 30 seconds or less in congested areas. Although that sounds like a chore, it soon becomes automatic and not distracting. The reason we do this is to provide an early detection of a hazardous situation approaching from the rear or alongside.

Size Does Matter

Relating well to images in the RV's mirrors is a good sign that the driver has adequate perspective on the size of the vehicle. Without this perspective the RVer tends to turn too tightly, run over curbs, sideswipe stationary objects, encounter overhead structures and crowd other traffic.

> **During the maiden voyage, gaining a good perspective on size is much easier and more relaxing in an empty parking lot or lightly used residential street. In situations where traffic is not a real concern, maneuvers can be practiced while closely watching the distance to the edge of the pavement, curbs, ditches, poles and other obstacles.**

With experience you will become a full-fledged driver. The best advice is to take it easy and go through steps slowly as your confidence builds. Continue with the parking lot routine as long as necessary and only then progress to lightly traveled surface roads, etc. When seeking areas to practice, be aware that some city and secondary roads are actually more difficult for large oversized vehicles than are major state or interstate routes. There may be substandard roads, construction, protrusions, dips and bumps, four-way stops or open intersections, all of which can be a challenge for the RVer. Following are some additional tips to consider before you hit the road.

Driver Positioning

The recommended hand positions for a steering wheel equipped with an airbag are one hand at the four o'clock position and the other at the eight o'clock position. These locations give the driver full control yet still afford protection (from the expanding airbag) in the event of airbag deployment.

The recommended hand position for a steering wheel without an airbag is the ten o'clock and two o'clock points on the wheel as has been recommended for many years. These positions offer the driver the maximum of vehicle control. When turning corners, use the push-pull method with your hands on the steering wheel. Move the appropriate hand to the twelve o'clock position and pull downward while pushing up with the other hand.

The best seating position is as high as possible and 12 inches or more from the steering wheel. This provides full control during vehicle maneuvering and prevents injury in case of an airbag deployment. Always wear your seatbelt while operating the vehicle. Your chances of surviving a collision are much better if you are wearing a seatbelt.

Vehicle Positioning

Position your vehicle in your lane so other drivers clearly see it. In particular, this means to avoid traveling in the others' blind spots. When you must travel through the blind spot of another operator, do so as quickly as possible. Observe the "No-Zones" applicable to tractor-trailers (see later discussion) and recognize that every automobile has some blind spot that is to be avoided. In heavy stop-and-go-type traffic, it is not possible to totally avoid traveling in these locations. Thus, an added awareness of the other vehicle's movements is required.

Awareness of Your Surroundings (Five Keys to Safety)

Professional truck drivers are taught a proven set of techniques that has enhanced trucking safety over the years. RVers can also benefit from the same techniques--all intended to focus the driver's attention on his positional awareness.

- Aim High in Steering: Using the technique of routinely looking some distance down the road will provide a forewarning of the traffic and problems that may be developing ahead. This is aided by the high line of sight provided by the height of the RV. Failure to look far enough ahead is frequently the direct cause of emergency braking situations. Seek to look ahead 15-20 seconds. As your speed increases it is necessary to look farther down the road to retain the same forewarning.

- **Get the Big Picture:** It is always good advice to get the big picture, especially in a driving situation. We are not alone on the road. There are always situations developing around us that could take us by surprise and involve us in an instant if we remain unaware.

- **Keep Your Eyes Moving:** Drivers must remain fully aware at all times. The driver's scan should include the road ahead, the instruments, the mirrors and all the rest of your cockpit situation. Your scan should include a general look at everything that might affect you. Scan often. A complete scan every 30-60 seconds is generally recommended.

- **Leave Yourself an Out:** Our situational awareness allows us to maintain options to avoid what might develop in our path. Our planned "out" may be the shoulder, center divider, braking or some other means of avoiding whatever might develop. Our "out" must be dynamic and ever changing. In some truly difficult conditions, the only "out" might be to stop for the day to let the condition clear. RVers are fortunate in these situations as we are fully prepared to wait out almost anything.

- **Make Sure They See You:** Common sense dictates that you make yourself as big and obvious as possible. It is documented that what is seen can often be avoided by other drivers. As large as the RV is, we can make it stand out even further by the use of lights, avoiding blind spots and completing maneuvers such as passing as rapidly as possible.

New Driver Prerequisites

- Learn the walk-around inspection described in the Predeparture Checklist.

- Learn the normal (running) position of the gauges on the dash. Your first indication of trouble often appears in the gauges.

- Learn the meanings of GVWR, UVW, NCC, CCC, SCWR and GCWR. See Book 1 for this information.

- Place a permanent label indicating the height of the vehicle on the dash near the speedometer. That way, when you encounter fueling facilities or low bridges, you will not have to try to recall just how much clearance you require.

Prepare to enjoy your new experience!
Now is the time to move to an interstate highway without much traffic. Start by driving only limited distances--say between adjoining rest areas or approximately 100 miles each time. In most cases you will not have to make a full turn--only gradual turns as you enter and leave the interstate and an occasional lane change. Drive at least five mph slower than traffic or at a speed that is totally comfortable to avoid passing anyone initially. Become familiar with your placement in the lane by looking in the mirrors. Try to maintain a comparable space between the center of the road lane marker and the white line on the right side of the road. Observe a spot on the windshield to mark your location in the lane, but do not focus on it. Doing so will draw your attention away from driving and can create a safety hazard. Focus on the differences noted between the RV and other vehicles with which you are familiar. For instance, the slower acceleration in merging situations, the slowing down and down shifting on hills, and the slow or impossible ability to pass other vehicles all serve to remind us that we are actually driving our house down the road and that we must take that into account.

As we progress, ask the primary driver to sit behind you if possible--not in the passenger seat. The new perspective from the passenger seat may cause the primary driver to react to situations that are not, in fact, emergencies. Drive routinely (not with long periods between sessions) to maintain and build on your driving proficiency. Accumulate several hundred miles before you make a decision as to how much driving you really want to do. As your experience increases, broaden your exposure by trying new driving experiences. For instance, make the exit from the expressway and into a town to seek out a fuel stop or dining opportunity. Take the state route between towns, rather than the highway interstate route, to assess this type driving and the RV's ability there. These variations will allow you to practice an ever-wider range of driving experiences. The assessing of the parking facilities available in town to avoid getting trapped where there is no exit for large vehicles is another learning experience that you can only learn by doing. As all drivers of large vehicles recognize, it is sometimes necessary to park at a remote location or bypass the business altogether when adequate parking facilities just do not exist. Making that call is a sign of good judgment and a full appreciation of your vehicle's limitations.

When it comes to learning to operate a truck/trailer combination, the task is often easier because both partners already have some experience driving the tow truck. In that situation, the primary adjustment is understanding the length of the combination when maneuvering, turning corners, passing and parking. Practice by taking the combination vehicle to a parking lot and trying to stop with the rear bumper of the trailer on a line drawn in the parking lot. See Book 7 for a full discussion of towing issues.

ADDITIONAL RV DRIVING CONSIDERATIONS

RV Heights

RVs are much taller than passenger cars, demanding that operators quickly become aware of road height restrictions of service station canopies, bridges and low-hanging tree branches. Prior to beginning your travels, determine the maximum height of the RV and mark it clearly somewhere on the RV dashboard. Learn to pay attention to road signs specifying low bridges or obstructions. In general, you can relax on primary interstates and highways because of clear standardized markings. If construction or other temporary changes mandate a height restriction, they are generally well identified. However, on state, county, city roads and private property the warnings regarding height limitations are inconsistent or missing altogether. Of particular concern, the RVer must be doubly cautious when traveling outside the USA because height limitations are posted in meters, not feet and inches. For example, while approaching a bridge at 60 MPH (96.56 KPH) is not the best time to convert your RV's height of 12 feet 6 inches into 3.81 meters.

Maneuvering the RV
The additional weight, size and high center of gravity make the RV far less agile than the typical passenger car. Combine that with the reality that an RV operates at 100% of its GVWR (maximum legal total weight) 100% of the time, and you begin to realize just why the RV does not perform like a sports car when maneuvering. What might be a safe lane change in a passenger car may be downright dangerous (and very uncomfortable) in an RV. This requires the RV driver to think farther ahead and plan any required moves. Avoid abrupt maneuvering and fast turns. When it is essential, such as in campground-parking situations, slow to a crawl and utilize whatever outside guidance is available. One of the most important safety practices required of the RV driver is to perform all directional changes slowly. On multi-lane highways, for example, a lane change may be into the path of an undetected car or motorcycle in the next lane (your blind spot). A rapid lane change might result in an accident, but a very deliberate, well-signaled lane change might permit the other driver to give a blast on his horn or take evasive action. It is imperative to be thinking of what lies ahead and what is likely to happen--also known as defensive driving.

Emergency maneuvers sometimes get RV owners into trouble because they are not sufficiently familiar with the handling characteristics of their rigs and their own limits. The best solution in this case is to explore the limits of handling under controlled conditions well before you are called upon to use this skill. On a wide, isolated road with good visibility in both directions and no other traffic, practice a few rapid lane changes while staying well within the bounds of safety. Gradually increase the pace of the lane changes until you get an idea of the vehicle's capabilities and your own skill. Too many drivers have no idea of these limits until they are faced with a real emergency evasive maneuver, then over-steering the vehicle and possibly losing control is a common result.

Stopping the RV
Similar to the maneuvering issues noted above, the added weight of the RV, combined with the high center of gravity and truck-type tires, all combine to limit the stopping ability of the RV. Truck-trailer combinations and motorhome owners who tow cars must be particularly aware of the hazards of brake fade. Brake fade is overheating of brake lining surfaces to the point where friction is greatly diminished or lost. The result is a brake pedal that is firm to the foot but produces little or no stopping action. The proper use of brakes can help prevent fade. Brake fade normally occurs while traveling downhill grades that require frequent brake application to hold speed to a desired level. It should be noted that an ultra-cautious driver might actually create more problems as he/she seeks to remain at a conservative downhill speed. In an RV, the brakes can become overheated after several applications and will require an extensive period of time to cool adequately and regain their stopping capability. If an emergency occurs while overheated, it may be impossible to stop and an accident could result. To avoid this, use lower gears, auxiliary stopping devices and the engine to retard vehicle speed to the point where only minimal brake applications are necessary for speed control. If the combined weight of the tow truck/trailer or motorhome and towed car are so great that downhill speed increases even when the lowest gear is used, it may be necessary to pull over to the side of the road frequently to allow for brake cooling. Under extreme conditions, it may be necessary to have the co-pilot drive the tow car to the bottom of the grade. Keeping a good distance between vehicles reduces the need to use brakes and will help prevent rear-end collisions.

It is recommended that operators test the braking of their rigs under gradually more severe conditions while in a safe area to get an idea of stopping distances and of the effect of hard braking on vehicle handling. An RV that tends to lean excessively on curves and corners will lean even more dramatically under hard braking required to avoid an obstacle in the road.

Braking Distance
Many factors affect the vehicle's ability to come to a stop. The size and weight are the biggest factors. In general, the heavier the vehicle, the longer it takes to stop. Other important factors in determining braking distance are the tires, condition of the brake components, engine type and the usage of auxiliary stopping devices.

**Braking Reality for RVs
(Ignoring Driver Reaction Time)**
- At 60 mph, it takes the average new car from 120-130 feet to stop.

- At 60 mph, it takes a motorhome by itself nearly 200 feet to stop.

- Modern tow trucks are capable of stopping performance from 60 mph in the 150-170 feet range when not towing.

- At 60 mph, it takes a motorhome with a tow car, but without a supplemental braking system, well in excess of 200 feet to stop.

- Truck/trailer combinations require stopping distances of over 200 feet when towing.

- Exact stopping distance is a very complicated issue with many variables to consider. The trend is clear, and the fact remains that RVs will not stop as fast as the traffic around them. When towing anything the stopping distance will greatly increase. When we consider that any collision from behind is generally the fault of the following driver, we must conclude that RVs are very vulnerable to liability, and we must take full advantage of all possible stopping assistance. See Book 1 and Book 7 for a lot more discussion on this topic.

Braking on Slippery Roads

Antilock braking systems are very effective in slippery road conditions, but the condition of the roadway still limits your ability to stop quickly. You should try to avoid a false sense of security from your ABS braking system.

The brakes on trailers and 5th wheel trailers may be applied independently of the tow vehicle to assist in maintaining control on slippery roads. Note that truck-trailer combinations, even if the truck is equipped with ABS, can still experience wheel lockup and a jackknife situation on the trailer because the ABS does not benefit the trailer. The force of the trailer pushing from behind can still force the rear of the truck (which has more stopping power) to slide sideways. When towing a trailer on very slippery roads, it is advisable to activate the trailer brakes manually before engaging the brake pedal of the truck.

Following Distance

For your own safety and protection, it is recommended that you maintain a four- to six-second interval ahead of your RV when driving. At higher speeds the actual distance must increase. It is not always possible to keep four seconds between your vehicle and others such as in high-density traffic. Under these conditions, if you leave even one car length, another vehicle will fill it forcing you to drop farther back. Remember that, with your RV's greater weight, it simply takes longer to stop.

Covering the Brakes

One proven technique for minimizing the stopping distance penalty of RVs is by covering the brakes--a procedure taught in the Motorcycle Safety Foundation defensive driving course. Here, as you approach a situation that makes you uneasy, place your foot above the brake pedal without actually touching it. This action reduces your reaction time if your anticipation proves correct and you need to apply the brakes quickly.

Braking with Antilock Braking Systems (ABS)

ABS is a significant advance in our RVing safety. When used correctly, the ABS will consistently provide the shortest possible stopping distance for the conditions available at the time. ABS does two things: it allows minimum stopping distance by keeping the wheels from locking or sliding, and it gives you steering control while in a panic-stop condition. ABS only works when you apply maximum pressure to the brake pedal and keep it firmly applied until you stop or pass the danger. Pumping the brake pedal prevents the ABS from achieving this. The noise associated with the ABS system and the pulsing or sensation felt through the brake pedal may cause some driver concern. If your automobile is so equipped, take it out and practice a simulated emergency. You should not attempt this with the motorhome because the violent stop may spill the contents of cabinets and drawers. Get used to the noise and the feel of the brake pedal in a safe environment in order to feel comfortable when you face an emergency.

SHARING THE ROAD WITH OTHERS

Regardless of the enticing thought of traveling the highways without other people, traffic and aggravations, this is not the real world. The reality is that we must share the road with others. They have reasons for being there that are as important to them as are our reasons. This nation's highways are used for interstate transportation of goods, and are responsible for delivering the bulk of the products and goods upon which we rely. As a result, much of the usage of the highways falls under the heading of commercial trucking. As an industry, commercial trucking pays more than its fair share of the cost of the highway system and probably utilizes the roads more aggressively than others. There has been increasing animosity between RV operators and truck drivers as the number of RVers grows. By understanding the essence of a trucker's job, learning how to communicate with them on the road, and being truck smart, we can help to improve relations.

UNDERSTANDING TRUCKERS

As with other highway users, the overwhelming majority of truckers are courteous, careful and highly skilled. They are professionals whose "office" happens to be the road. Truckers have a very difficult job as they have responsibility to get a large vehicle with a heavy load to a destination within a tight deadline. Most are paid by the mile or by a percentage of the freight hauled, so time becomes money to them. As traffic congestion increases and other drivers become more aggressive (such as at commute time), a trucker's job becomes even more difficult. Considering their many hours on the road and the sometimes impossible schedules, the trucking industry has a remarkably good safety record. Do not assume the responsibility to enforce speed limits on truckers. It is best to allow them to pass easily and to continue safely on their way. The commercial driver license required by truckers has strong penalties associated with excessive speed, recklessness and overloading, so most guard it carefully.

The "No-Zone"
Another important aspect of driving is to be aware of the "no-zones." Following are descriptions of these no-zones and how the DOT recommends avoiding them.

Side "No-Zones":
Do not hang out on either side of trucks. There are large blind spots on both sides. If you cannot see the driver's face in his/her side-view mirror, the driver cannot see you. If that driver needs to change lanes for any reason, you could be in big trouble.

Rear "No-Zones":
Avoid tailgating a truck. Unlike cars, trucks have huge no-zones directly behind them. The truck driver cannot see your vehicle back there, and you cannot see what's going on ahead of you. If the truck driver brakes suddenly, there is no place for you to go.

Front "No-Zones":
Pass safely and quickly. Do not cut in front of a truck too soon after passing. Trucks and buses require nearly twice the time and distance to stop as cars. Look for the entire front of the truck in your rearview mirror before pulling in front, and then do not slow down.

Back-Up "No-Zone":
Never cross behind a truck that is backing. Many motorists and pedestrians are injured or killed each year because they ignored trucks that are backing up. Truck drivers do not have a rearview mirror and may not see you cutting in behind them.

Wide Right Turns:
Avoid the "squeeze play." Truck drivers need to swing wide to the left in order to safely complete a right turn. They cannot see cars squeezing in between them and the curb. Watch for their blinkers and give them room to negotiate the turn.

Trucker Communication
Truck drivers often communicate by flashing their lights. As one truck passes another, the vehicle being passed will flash his headlights to signal to the passing driver that the passing move is complete and the trucker is clear to pull back into the lane. If the truck's headlights are already on, the driver might turn them off briefly to give the same signal. Generally, truckers will extend the same courtesy to RVers as they pass. Remember to observe the truck as you are passing it to determine if the headlights are on so you will not misinterpret the headlight signal. With the high-powered trucks on the road today, it is often the truck that is passing. The RV driver should extend the same "passing complete--OK to pull in" signal to the trucker. Once the passing vehicle has started to move back into the lane, the passing driver will usually acknowledge help by flashing either the clearance lights on the back of the trailer or four-way or emergency flashers.

Headlights may also be used to signal OK when another vehicle is entering an expressway. If a trucker encounters a vehicle entering the expressway, the driver on the roadway may briefly turn on the headlights, signaling the other driver that he will create space for the merging vehicle. A trucker may also use this signal on a multi-lane highway when the adjoining lane traffic needs to pull over to pass or clear traffic. Once both vehicles are past the slower vehicle, the assisted driver returns to the right lane and allows the first truck to pass. At night, the driver in the overtaking vehicle may momentarily turn off the headlights to avoid possible confusion with a passing indication.

RVers can follow the same procedures as truckers. Some vehicles equipped with daytime running lights have a switch that enables the driver to momentarily turn them off. With lights that cannot be turned off, drivers can use their high beams for a few seconds to avoid confusion with the passing indication. Do not signal with headlights if it is locally illegal to do so; i.e., in metropolitan areas with a lot of traffic, or if you are uncomfortable doing it.

The CB radio is also a helpful communication tool as most truckers monitor the CB for information, communication and entertainment.

Working with Truckers
There are lots of little things we can do to ease the burden of sharing the road and to help our commercial companions on the road.

Hills
When you are passed on an interstate, it is common for the truck to be at or near full power. This will result in the truck slowing at the next hill. Looking at the big picture, it should be apparent that while you might catch and pass the truck on the hill, it would certainly pass again on the far side, creating dangerous repeated passing situations. It is recommended that you disengage your cruise control and follow the truck up to the crest of the hill where it will once again disappear into the distance.

Rest Areas
Rest areas are another of the highway's features that must be shared. It is important to note that RVs have a distinct advantage here over both trucks and automobiles as we carry our own facilities where they do not. Often rest areas are filled with RVs crowded around the rest rooms while the occupants may be having lunch, taking a break and not using the public

facilities. Often the trucker has to park a great distance from the facility or not at all. A more considerate procedure is to stop in the parking spots or along the side or at the end of the rest area away from the marked lanes. Overnight stops should be handled in the same manner.

Fueling
Whether you use the truck pumps or RV islands at fuel stops to fill your vehicle, courtesy dictates that when finished you pull forward far enough to open up the fuel lane for another vehicle to begin before you go inside to pay your bill.

ROAD RAGE

What Is Road Rage?
A driver's exaggerated emotional response to an action by another driver is defined as "road rage." Road rage is often triggered by a small inconsiderate act of a driver, who often is not aware of what has been done. The road rage reaction is never justified. However, in these days of unrelenting frustration caused by increasing volumes of traffic, it is not uncommon. During 1998 authorities recorded more than one million cases of road rage. Many more cases went unreported. It is easy to see that road rage is an enormous problem and one that should be thought through.

Causes of Road Rage
It is commonly believed that the main cause of road rage is overcrowding of the roadways. In the past decade, the number of vehicles has increased by over 11%, the number of total miles driven has increased by 35%, but the available roads increased by only 1%. The problem of road rage is at its worse in urban areas where stress levels are higher, and demands on individuals are very high, further adding to the problem. Stress is known to create anxiety, which can lead to short tempers and may feed the road rage problem.

Road rage is causing more deadly accidents every year.
Number of fatal accidents involving aggressive driving or road rage on the part of the driver

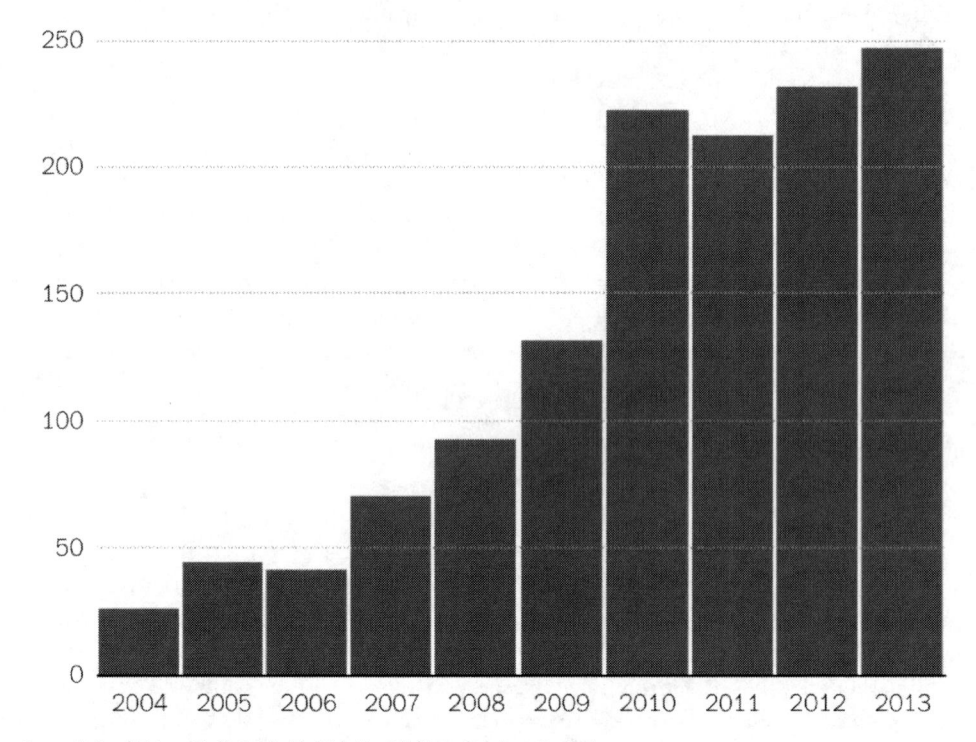

Source: National Highway Traffic Safety Administration Fatality Analysis Reporting System.

Avoiding Road Rage

- Avoid displaying aggression to other drivers when they do something wrong or inconsiderate.

- Drive purposefully to avoid any action causing another driver to apply his brakes. Drive smoothly and consistently.

- In an RV, stay out of the express lanes (left lane) except to pass. Note that in some states and on some interstates RVs are confined to the right lanes. Return to the right lane as soon as you have completed passing, signaling your intent before all moves.

- Plan your passing maneuvers to be completed as rapidly as possible by overriding the cruise control, thereby shortening passing time.

- Plan your passing maneuver to have comfortable clearance as you pull out and return to the original lane. Every driver has a "comfort area" around his/her vehicle. When you infringe on someone's comfort zone, they may react defensively.

- When unsure or hesitant about safely completing a passing maneuver or lane change, do not attempt it. Patience is our best friend in this matter.

- Signal your intentions every time you change lanes or direction.

- It is never a good idea to attempt to enforce the speed limits or other traffic laws on other drivers. Leave that to law officers.

- Drive in a manner so as not to impede traffic. If you notice traffic building behind you on a two-lane highway, pull over and let them by. On mountain grades, there may be pullouts just for this purpose. Some states have a law, that if six vehicles are lined up behind you, you must pull over to let them pass. Check your rearview mirrors frequently.

- A less-traveled and generally more scenic route is recommended if you are planning to drive under the speed limit. When in heavy traffic, you should try to move with the traffic flow.

- Never cross multiple lanes at one time. Each lane change should be a separate planned event with the proper signal. It is not possible to get a complete view of conditions beside and behind you for that kind of maneuver, and other drivers have no way of knowing your intentions.

- As traffic backs up approaching a lane reduction, do not continue to the head of the line and force your way in. The other drivers have been waiting their turn in line and you should do likewise. They will legitimately be irritated if you don't. You may have noticed trucks blocking the lane to prevent others from doing it, however, that is never recommended.

- If someone comes alongside you shouting or signaling disapproval for any reason, avoid eye contact, slow down and let him continue on his way.

- Traveling in a motorhome caravan entails some additional concerns. Always allow enough distance between your vehicles for people to maneuver around you. This will require at least six to eight vehicle lengths between you. Likewise, be sure to discuss with the caravan leader your desire to travel with the flow of traffic to avoid angering other motorists, especially on two-lane roads where passing opportunities are few.

Overreacting

To avoid a road rage response in you, it is necessary to understand yourself fully and to control the issues that stimulate such a reaction. Once you are aware of how you react to things, it is possible to learn to control that reaction. Learning to react to the action that triggered your emotion, and not to the person who did it, will lead to cooling down quickly permitting you to refocus on driving. To illustrate this point, don't attempt to "punish" an errant driver when he infringes upon your personal "comfort zone." It is much better to merely back off a little farther from the traffic ahead and to slow down a bit, allowing more aggressive drivers to pass easily.

DRIVING THE RV
TWO-LANE TRAFFIC

Speed Control

Maintain a steady, consistent speed that is close to the speed limit. If your vehicle is not equipped with daytime running lights, use your headlights to make yourself more visible to oncoming traffic. Accidents often happen because a vehicle--even one as large as an RV--is not seen. This is especially true in passing situations and can result in a head-on collision.

Passing Situations

Passing with a long RV--especially pulling another vehicle--can be a slow process. If you must pass, fully consider the extended time it will take to get around the vehicle in front of you and do not take a chance. If it is necessary to pass, the best procedure is to drop back and begin accelerating in order to be at passing speed when it is clear to pass. This process permits you to get around the other vehicle in the shortest possible time. If you have vision or depth perception problems or are uncertain that there is adequate distance to complete the pass, do not attempt it. Pass only when there is no approaching traffic or wait for a formal passing zone ahead.

MULTIPLE-LANE TRAFFIC

Entering Expressways

Upon entering the on-ramp, find a gap in traffic and time your accelerations to enter the roadway at that point. Use the length of the on-ramp to build up speed permitting you to move into the gap at approximately the same speed as the flow of traffic. Merging can be a challenge with an RV due to the extra length and slower acceleration, requiring careful planning. Remember, that in a merging situation, the through traffic is entitled to that lane.

Exiting Expressways

Move into the far right lane well in advance of your exit. Doing this avoids a desperate last-minute attempt to find a gap in traffic in the exit lane. With a large RV, the posted exit speed for the off-ramp sometimes dictates that you begin decelerating before leaving the expressway. Use the posted exit speed as a guide remembering that an RV may require a lower speed for safety and comfort.

> It is not uncommon for the right lane to disappear at an exit (exit-only lane). RVers who commonly travel in the right lane should watch the signs and traffic lane markings to be prepared by moving over one lane well in advance.

Expressways in Metropolitan Areas

Where traffic is heavy, the center lane may be the best choice for the RV. However, you must be prepared to travel at the speed of traffic in that lane. Sometimes, trucks and RVs are limited to the right lane(s). When traveling in the right lane, it is important to hold your speed constant to allow entering motorists to adjust their speed to the speed of traffic. You would impede traffic more by slowing down than by remaining constant. If the lane to your immediate left is clear, you may move into it temporarily to allow ramp traffic access.

Encountering a Stopped Vehicle

The presence of a vehicle stopped by the side of the road should alert the RV driver to be prepared for almost anything. There is just no way to know for certain exactly what might happen. Someone could open the door and get out, or come around from the other side, or the vehicle could suddenly pull out into traffic without warning. Truckers are trained to be prepared for any possibility and to give stopped vehicles a wide berth. If traffic permits, it is always better to move to another lane until you have passed the stopped vehicle.

RV-SPECIFIC DRIVING SITUATIONS

Blowouts

A tire blowout is an alarming experience in any vehicle. In an RV the thought can be doubly terrifying. If you experience a blowout or rapid air loss on either axle, the Michelin Tire Company recommends briefly pushing the accelerator to the floor to regain control through momentum in the direction you are traveling then gently decelerating. If you are on an expressway, gradually move into the right lane or shoulder. Immediately turn on your four-way emergency flashers to warn traffic around you that something is wrong. Do not apply the brakes immediately as this could lead to a complete loss of control.

A front axle blowout may be felt in the steering wheel, while a rear axle blowout, is felt through the driver's seat. For a front axle blowout use any auxiliary braking device available. It will help to slow the vehicle down without applying the brakes. If a blowout occurs on the rear axle, do not use your auxiliary braking devices. It will produce the same effect as applying the brakes, which might result in the tire coming off the rim. Allow the vehicle to slow down, without applying the brakes, to 10 or 15 mph before pulling off the road surface.

With a 5th wheel or travel trailer, it is common to have a tire failure on the trailer and not feel it. Keep a vigilant eye in your rearview mirror for any sign of smoke or debris behind the trailer. Much more on this important topic appears in Book 2.

Turns

All turns in an RV, either a motorhome or a truck/trailer, require swinging wider than would be required in an automobile. Wide turns increase your chances of an accident, as there may be another vehicle in your blind spot, or the wide turn may confuse those behind you regarding your intentions. The law requires you to turn into the first available traffic lane and, once you have completed the turn, to verify that your turn signal was canceled.

Delay the start of a right turn to avoid striking curbs, signs or stationary objects on the right. You may also cover your right turn by moving left far enough to complete the right turn without providing enough room for someone to pull alongside. It is still necessary to watch the right mirror because pedestrians or bicycles might approach you on that side.

When operating an RV, it is very important to understand the effect the long overhang (body extension beyond the wheels front and rear) will have when turning the RV. In any turn, the rear overhang moves initially opposite to the turn. Do not initiate a turn when the opposite side is close to any obstruction, including traffic in the adjoining lane, because the overhang will swing into that lane as you make your turn. The front overhang may also infringe upon the area opposite the turn and must be considered when turning. Remember also that in a van or bus-type vehicle, the steering wheels are actually located behind the driver, requiring you to delay the start of the turn. It is suggested that drivers visualize the rear wheels as the pivot point for making turns, since they must clear any objects as they follow through the turn. Travel trailers and 5th wheels generally are capable of making shorter, sharper turns. Therefore, you can go farther into the intersection before starting the turn. As a general consideration, the longer the wheelbase (distance between the front and rear wheels), the larger the turning radius of the vehicle and the less maneuverable it will be.

Due to the length of your vehicle's wheelbase, the rear wheels do not follow in the same path as the front wheels. They will cut a reduced radius as they turn. This explains why you must delay the start of the turn to avoid hitting the curb with your rear wheels. Automobiles towed behind motorhomes will generally track fully behind the RV because they are narrower initially. Thus, they should present no problem in turns. However, if the towed vehicle is the same width (or wider) than the tow vehicle (motorhomes with trailers or truck/trailers), then the trailer will cut a much-reduced radius when turning and must be fully considered when planning and executing the turn.

DEFENSIVE DRIVING TIPS

- Drive with your lights on to be seen.

- Approach all intersections cautiously, anticipating late through traffic.

- Maintain at least four to six vehicle lengths between you and the vehicle ahead.

- Avoid traffic bunch-ups by slowing slightly, allowing traffic to clear.

- Use your turn signals well in advance and verify canceling after usage.

- Keep your brakes cool by utilizing smooth driving techniques.

- Watch for drivers merging from the right without looking.

- Try to anticipate and be prepared for drivers crossing several lanes as they near an exit.

- Stay out of the fast lane on expressways.

- Install supplemental brakes on any towed vehicle to regain stopping performance of the towed vehicle.

- Check your mirrors frequently as part of your driver's scan.

- Use an assistant when backing or maneuvering in tight situations.

- Make all turns in large RVs slowly and deliberately.

- Take a break, switch drivers or stop for the day when tired.

- Position your vehicle to allow others to see around you on two-lane roads.

- Drive a couple of miles per hour slower than the speed of traffic.

Wheels Leaving the Roadway

In the rare occurrence when the right-hand wheels of the RV leave the roadway, it is imperative not to overreact and jerk the steering wheel trying to return the wheels back to the roadway. At typical highway speeds, a loss of control could result. The correct procedure to return your vehicle to the roadway is to slow the vehicle carefully while maintaining the steering wheel in a straight-ahead position. Slow down enough to re-enter the roadway without swerving. The size and severity of the step between the main roadway and the shoulder will determine at what speed you should attempt to re-enter the roadway.

Backing Up

The essential first step for successfully backing an RV is to confirm visually that there are no overhangs, low branches, or obstacles protruding from the ground before you begin. Many hazards are not visible from inside the RV. The best solution to backing a recreational vehicle is to go slow.

Backing in, Not Out

In most situations it is easier for an RV to back into an area than it is to back out. This will subsequently allow you to pull forward as you leave, giving a direct view of traffic conditions and negating the need for guidance.

When backing in, quickly seek to align the RV with the orientation of the parking space by initially backing up to that location, which permits you then to back straight into the parking space. Following this procedure, your only remaining concern is how far to back up. When backing a travel or 5th wheel trailer and gripping the steering wheel at the top it is necessary to turn the steering wheel in the opposite direction you want the rear of the trailer to move. If this is confusing, some instructors teach drivers to position their hands at the bottom of the steering wheel. This will then require you to turn the wheel in the same direction you wish the trailer to move. Whatever your strategy is, keep it consistent and review the steps required in your mind prior to initiating the backing maneuver. The vehicle's rear wheels are the pivot point when backing.

Using an assistant to help you back up is recommended, but do not rely totally on them. The driver is still the responsible party. Establish hand signals well in advance to assure that they are well understood. Two-way radios are also helpful and may avoid misinterpreting hand gestures. Since the ultimate responsibility lies with the driver whenever there is any question, get out and look things over.

Many RVs are equipped with a back-up camera which can be very helpful during backing situations. Back-up cameras generally offer a good view directly behind the vehicle but may distort the distance to an object.

MOUNTAIN DRIVING

Early in the learning process, all drivers need to determine what is the maximum vehicle speed of your RV for each transmission gear. To determine maximum gear speeds, accelerate at full throttle on level ground and note the speeds at which the transmission shifts. A tachometer is not essential to this process, but, if the vehicle is so equipped, you will find that the transmission shifts at more or less the same engine speed throughout the process. Never allow the vehicle speed to exceed this rpm. Maximum gear speed is important because the transmission (automatic only) will generally upshift uncontrolled to a higher gear if that speed is exceeded. Manufacturers do this to keep you from damaging your engine or transmission; however, your ability to control your vehicle speed may be jeopardized as a result.

Ascending Mountains

You will want to climb a long, steep grade at a little less than full throttle and monitor the temperature gauges (engine/transmission) closely during the ascent. Prior to beginning any significant climb, disengage overdrive and be prepared to manually drop another gear or two if the engine or the transmission shows any sign of overheating. On a diesel engine, the turbo boost and pyrometer gauge (not necessarily the throttle position) will indicate how hard the engine is working. A little under the maximum is where you want to be. It is also best to keep most engines near the peak horsepower rpm. This will vary significantly; thus, you will need to determine the specific rpm for your engine from the operator's manual. The proper gear selection combines horsepower and a relatively high engine rpm to help the fan move more air across the radiator.

Descending Mountains

Most diesel engines operate in the 2,000-3,000 rpm range maximum, while gasoline engine vehicles may operate between 4,000 and 5,000 rpm.

The general technique utilized to descend a long, steep hill is to attempt to maintain speed control with the use of lower gears and auxiliary stopping devices to the degree that speed increases slowly. Note that the engine and auxiliary stopping devices work most effectively at higher rpm, so your desired speed and gear should place the engine rpm at approximately 80% of the established maximum. When the speed (and rpm) does increase to near the maximum, then the brakes are used to decelerate the vehicle to slightly below the initial desired value. This procedure will get you safely to the bottom of the hill and preserve the brakes to the maximum amount possible. Never apply light brake pressure all the way down the hill for speed control as this will create excessively hot brakes, which may become ineffective and unavailable for use in an emergency situation.

A frequently asked question is, "What gear should I use to descend a grade?" As a rule of thumb, diesel engines may require a downshift of one or two gears to safely descend, while gasoline engine vehicles can usually descend a grade in the same gear that you use to climb it. In any case, if your vehicle speed or rpm level increases rapidly, you are in the wrong gear.

Remember that the GCWR of the tow vehicle was established based on the assumption that anything towed will have its own functional braking system. The additional weight of a towed vehicle without brakes will cause you to use more brakes than normal. They may prove to be totally inadequate during mountain driving. If the grade is particularly long and steep and you do not have supplemental brakes on the towed car, it might be better to disconnect and have your travel partner drive it down the mountain.

ADDITIONAL SAFETY TIPS

Determining What Is Ahead
As a conscientious driver, mentally review what conditions might be encountered as you progress down the road. A common driver's concerns might be what percent is the approaching grade? Are there any low-speed curves or switchbacks to slow my progress anywhere on the hill? Are there bridge heights or weight limits that I need to be concerned with? The answers for these, and a multitude of additional helpful tips, are contained in the book, *Mountain Directory for Truck, RV and Motorhome Drivers*. This invaluable document is available at Camping World or through RV magazine ads and is produced in both East and West Coast versions. It is best to review this information the night before you travel, and keep the book handy while you travel for the copilot to review as needed.

Cruise Control Operation
The cruise control is a wonderful device that can help you maintain a steady, consistent speed when road conditions permit. However, cruise control is less effective, and even dangerous, to use in heavy traffic or in other situations that require the driver to make frequent speed adjustments. Cruise control should never be used in wet or slick road conditions.

Night Driving
Verify the proper functioning of all the RV's exterior lights prior to each morning's departure. It is especially important to check the lights on tow vehicles as well. If traveling into the night, stop prior to sunset to check lights again. It is also desirable to verify sidelights and tow car lighting by checking in the side mirrors. The effectiveness of your lights and your ability to see ahead is greatly reduced if your light lenses are dirty or obscured. Consider replacing your regular headlights with halogen bulbs. Halogen lights are brighter and enable you to see farther, though they also tend to have a narrower field of view. Halogen lights may also blind oncoming drivers sooner, so you should switch to low beams a little quicker than with standard bulbs, and be sure to keep headlights in proper adjustment.

Driving at night becomes more difficult with age because we require approximately double the light to see clearly as compared to a 20-year-old. Seniors also have a lower tolerance for high-contrast lights such as headlights and stoplights. As a result, we find our senses somewhat uncomfortable at night as we are more easily blinded by surrounding traffic. This is the primary reason that many RVers avoid night driving altogether despite the fact that we can somewhat control the nighttime environment.

The generally accepted rule is that you must dim your lights about 500 feet from an approaching vehicle and when following within 250 feet behind another vehicle. It is also recommended that the interior lights of your RV be set as low as possible to best allow for driving activities. Interior lights should also be carefully shielded to prevent reflections from the windshield, side windows and instrument panel. All of this will enhance your vision of driving situations outside the RV.

If an oncoming driver's lights blind you, avoid looking directly at them. Instead, direct your vision toward the right edge of the road. Flash your high beams once to alert the oncoming driver, unless this practice is prohibited by law. If the driver does not respond, assume that the lights are extra-bright or improperly adjusted and nothing further can be done. Do not retaliate by switching to your high beams. That could trigger an accident or a road rage response from the other driver.

Emergency Signals or Flashers
Use your flashers whenever you are stopped near moving traffic or when you are in a lane of traffic proceeding slowly up a grade. You have all seen situations where traffic was stopped on the roadway for a construction project and a truck was just ahead of you with his flashers going. He was communicating that something you cannot see forced him to slow down or stop.

Emergency Flares and Triangles

Emergency flares are used to warn other motorists that your vehicle is disabled and stopped on or near the traffic lane. In two-way traffic situations, one flare should be placed 10 feet in front of your vehicle. Two other flares or triangles should be placed 100 feet in front and 100 feet behind your vehicle. On four-lane roads, one flare or signal should be 10 feet behind, with the others placed farther behind in 100-foot increments. At night, if you have no lights on the vehicle and your vehicle is either on or very near the road surface, one of the flares should be placed near the back end of the vehicle. Emergency flares or traffic signals are to be used for temporary lane blockages only. Move your vehicle from danger as soon as it is possible and safe to do so. In the meantime, you should wait for assistance a safe distance away from the disabled RV.

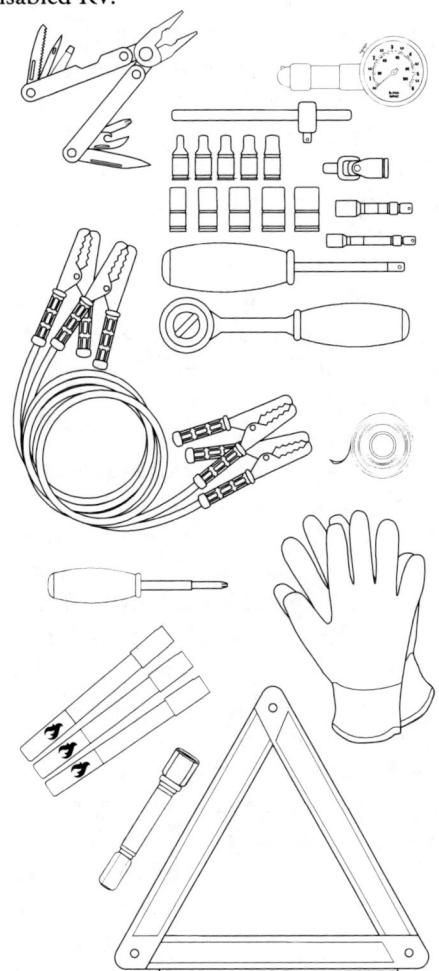

Items to Include in Your Tool Kit

ROAD SIGNS, SIGNALS AND HIGHWAY MARKINGS

Road signs communicate what you should expect. You should learn to recognize road signs by their shape and color. The Department of Motor Vehicles or Department of Transportation will provide a driver's handbook listing all signs that are, by design, universal. Signs, signals and highway markings are used alone and in combination to control traffic and make safe driving easier. Signs have three purposes: they regulate, warn and inform. The shapes and colors of highway signs have special meanings intended to assist you in understanding their message quickly.

STANDARD COLORS:

Red - no, do not, or stop

Green - direction or guidance

Yellow or yellow-green - general warning

White - regulatory, law or rule

Orange - road construction or repair warning

Blue - driver services, such as food and lodging

Brown - recreation and scenic areas information

STANDARD SHAPES:

Octagon (8 sides) - STOP

Diamond - warning

Rectangle - traffic regulations or directions to drivers

Inverted triangle - yield right-of-way

Pennant - no passing

Pentagon (5 sides) - school zones and school crossings

Circle - railroad crossing ahead

Cross buck (X) - actual railroad crossing

Shield - route marker

ADVERSE DRIVING CONDITIONS

Our desires notwithstanding, it is not always bright and sunny blue with light breezes for our RV travels. Adverse weather and driving conditions do occur, and we must be prepared to deal with them properly by reducing speed, turning on headlights or increasing our following distance. We may have to utilize all the tricks we have learned by making slow, gradual movements with the steering wheel, the brakes and the accelerator while avoiding heavy braking. Under adverse conditions, abrupt actions can cause us to lose control very quickly.

With an RV, it is probably better to stay put until conditions improve enough to allow you to make the trip safely. The RV owner should take comfort that, in extremely bad conditions, it is possible to pull over and wait out a storm in relative comfort.

In addition to flexibility in when we travel and when we do not, RVs often have superior traction compared to an automobile because of the large amount of weight concentrated over the rear (driving) axle. Although the traction may be better, a motorhome that becomes stuck is more difficult (expensive) to free than is a passenger car. The radio (weather radio in particular) is a valuable tool for traveling RVers when subject to inclement weather. Broadcasts that warn of traffic snarls, accidents, road construction or any other incident that slows traffic should be taken seriously. If the traffic flow ahead is impeded, an alternate route may be possible even if the trip is lengthened. While most passenger cars can handle adverse weather, the large profile of a recreation vehicle creates special handling requirements during wind, snow, fog and heavy rains.

Wind
Wind is the most serious weather condition affecting RV drivers, particularly those who are skittish or concerned with handling larger rigs. Lighter motorhomes and trucks pulling trailers also have another type of wind to contend with. That is the wind pushed in front of a tractor-trailer as it passes, pushing you to the side and back again. You can reduce this effect by positioning your RV in the far right portion of the roadway as the tractor-trailer approaches and avoid overreacting with steering wheel corrections. A greater distance between vehicles will reduce the effect of this type of wind.

Crosswinds pose the greatest handling difficulty, while headwinds require a heavier throttle to maintain usual speeds. All RVers enjoy the benefits of a tail wind, but they never seem to be as common as the other wind types for some mysterious reason. The strong gusts of crosswinds can push a large motorhome or truck/trailer into the other lane if the driver is not paying full attention. As your RV passes into and out of highway overpasses or cuts in the hills, the sudden change in crosswinds will be most noticeable and difficult to control. This is especially true of travel trailers. In most cases, reducing speed is the RVer's best defense against strong winds. Trailers can gain some control by activating the electric brakes manually to help stabilize a swaying trailer when it is momentarily bad. Using a quality, properly adjusted sway control device at the hitch is also effective and inexpensive insurance. See Book 7 for more discussion. While it is possible to control an RV while traveling in dangerously strong winds, the safest and most comfortable thing to do is to pull over and wait it out. Some states post signs on roads warning that high winds are common. The highway patrol may close sections of roads to RVs or other high profile vehicles for the same reason. It is a good idea to call ahead for local information. Wind seems to have a varying effect on individual operators and generally requires adjustments for safety. Reducing speed and turning the steering wheel slightly into the wind will allow the RV to track straight down the road, correcting only minutely in reaction to momentary wind gusts. Pay special attention when approaching underpasses or hills where it can feel as though the wind direction shifts 180 degrees. The tendency in this situation is to overcompensate by turning the wheel too far in the opposite direction. Overcorrecting can lead to whipsawing down the road chasing the wheel in both directions. Learn to make smaller adjustments and complete them more gradually. Turn lights on in windy situations to make yourself more visible.

Rain

Many states have laws that require you to turn your headlights on if your windshield wipers are operating. Regardless of the law, this is a good practice. You must also provide more space between you and the vehicle ahead when traveling in rainy weather because of the reduced visibility. Note that the road is especially dangerous in the first 15 minutes of a rain because water mixes with oils on the roadbed creating a very slippery condition. An added danger is that rain may settle into depressions in the roadway. As your RV crosses standing water, the tires may rise up onto the surface of the water. This phenomenon is called hydroplaning. Hydroplaning will occur at various times depending upon many factors, including the condition of the tire's tread pattern (design and wear), depth of water and speed. When hydroplaning, the vehicle has virtually no steering or stopping ability. Avoid standing water whenever possible and cross any that is encountered as slowly as possible. The most important thing to recall when traveling in rain is that the wet roadway increases braking distance by 50% or more and that your visibility decreases greatly.

Fog, Dust, Smoke, and Haze

The reduced visibility brought about by fog, dust, smoke and haze requires a reduced speed and an increased following distance. Again, lights must be used for greater visibility. While driving at night in these conditions, low beams may give you better road visibility and yellow (fog) lights may penetrate fog better. Obscured visibility situations such as these are responsible for the worst traffic accidents on record. The loss of hundreds of vehicles and many lives each year has occurred when drivers drove into low visibility without reducing speed essential to driving safely. Monitoring channel 19 (varies in some locales) on the CB may provide some warning of conditions that require your corrective action. If you learn of the conditions before entering the obscured vision area, pull off in a clear area long enough to allow the condition to dissipate before moving on.

Snow, Sleet and Hail

Although many RVers tend to head south in the winter, some enjoy and seek out snow activity. Recognize that tires selected for most RVs are chosen for their weight-carrying ability, ride comfort and quietness, not for their traction qualities. Thus, RVs have limited traction when on slippery surfaces. If this is your desired RV usage pattern, traction-type tires should be obtained. Carry chains when traveling in snow country and know how to put them on. Many RVs cannot accommodate chains due to limited wheel well clearances. Check this out in advance of the need. Trailer RVs are not as common for use in snow country, but if chains are necessary, they must be placed on at least one axle of the trailer for stopping ability. Motorhomes with dual rear wheels require chains for one tire on each side. Snow, sleet and hail reduce visibility and create slippery roadways. Reduce your speed and increase your following distance according to the conditions. Turn on lights to make yourself more visible. If driving at night, determine if running on low beams gives you more visibility.

Ice

Ice presents a unique set of problems. It has a dramatic effect on your tire's ability to provide traction or to adhere to the road. Decrease speed dramatically and make large increases in your following distance. If there is any alternative, an RV should not be on the road during icing conditions. Generally, it does not take too long to wait until the danger of icing goes away due to sunshine or de-icing chemicals. Waiting it out is definitely the best choice of action.

Wet Brakes

Rain, snow, sleet, hail, ice or even slush can splash and build up on brakes and reduce your braking ability. This condition is most common in vehicles equipped with drum brakes. Disc brakes, by design, disperse water more quickly but are still subject to corrosion on the caliper slides, which may create a dragging condition, resulting in rapid wear of linings or rendering the brakes totally inoperative.

When operating in adverse conditions, you should test your brakes occasionally by applying normal pressure to see how they respond. If you find your braking ability is reduced, continue down the road while applying a light pressure on the pedal for a brief period. This will heat the brakes just enough to rid them of the moisture and permit them to operate normally. If they still do not work properly, repeat this procedure cautiously a couple of times. If they remain ineffective, it is time to stop and investigate the cause for this condition.

SLIDE PREVENTION AND RECOVERY

Without a doubt, a slide of any kind in your RV would be a terrifying experience. There is no question that, under normal weather and road conditions, a slide would be very rare, and the correction of a slide by an inexperienced driver would be even more unlikely. Yet the possibility of a slide does exist and will be briefly discussed here for familiarity and possible application for other vehicles and other circumstances. Slides can be classified into four types:

A locked wheel slide
A condition in which the wheels of the RV are locked due to excessive braking causing the RV to lose control and continue to slide in the direction of travel. One of the purposes (and advantages) of ABS is to prevent the locking of wheels during braking, making this type of slide impossible. For non-ABS equipped RVs, the operator merely needs to release the brake pedal sufficiently to allow the tires to turn and regain control. Panic braking is the most common cause of this condition and can be prevented by planning and looking ahead for the big picture.

A rear-end slide
This type of slide can occur in a turn when too much power is applied to the rear wheels. The result is that you may lose forward and lateral traction. A second type of power slide occurs with trucks/trailers when a heavy trailer pushes the rear of the tow truck outward during a turn--generally during heavy braking. The result is a "jackknife" of the rig. Slower cornering speeds and minimal braking during cornering can avoid this type of slide. A contributing cause could be inadequate trailer braking due to maladjustment or malfunction of the trailer braking system.

A power slide
Applying too much power and causing the rear (drive) wheels to spin is a power slide. Few motorhomes and truck/trailer combinations have adequate power to accomplish this when loaded except when traction conditions are very poor. However, a tow truck without the trailer and load is very capable of sliding the tires. A few vehicles utilize an electronic traction control mechanism to avoid this condition. All RVers can easily avoid this condition by driving smoothly and avoiding "jack-rabbit" starts.

A momentum slide
With a momentum slide, the vehicle pushes straight ahead even as the driver is turning the wheel correctly. Race cars would call this condition "extreme under steer." This slide occurs when the turn demands more lateral force than the tires are capable of providing under the conditions. Simply put, this is a case where the driver attempts to turn while traveling at too high speed. Slowing to a speed appropriate for the conditions present is the only preventive measure for this type of slide.

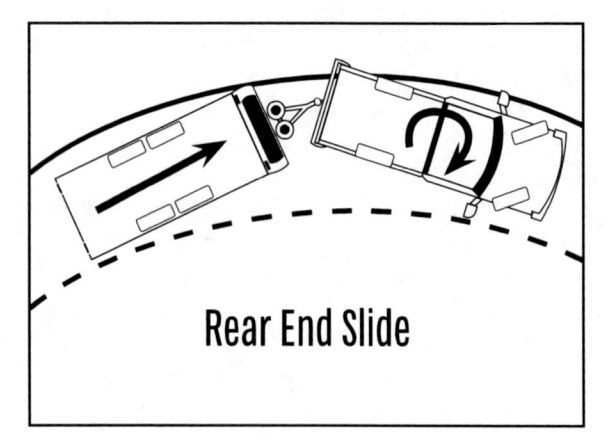

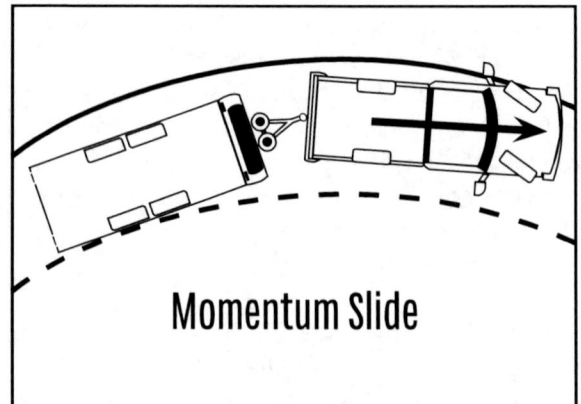

Rear End Slide

Momentum Slide

TRAFFIC INCIDENTS

Traffic Accidents and Other Happenings

Traffic accidents are the most common emergencies that RVers will encounter in their travels. Good defensive driving techniques will help us avoid becoming involved in an existing accident. The most important technique for avoiding a traffic accident is not to follow too close. Maintaining our distance (comfort zone) gives us time to react and avoid the incident. During any evasive maneuvering, we must also watch our backs and try to provide warning to drivers behind us, giving them time and distance to complete similar evasive maneuvers. In any highway situation in which an emergency maneuver is necessary, we must think first of our own safety by avoiding the accident. However, once that is assured, our thought process should turn to our relationship with other traffic. Drivers are accustomed to responding to brake lights and emergency flashers which are designed to alert other drivers to danger. Use them as soon as you have time to activate the flashers. Keep in mind that emergency flashers on most vehicles do not work while the brake pedal is depressed (brake lights are activated).

Avenues of Escape

When an accident avoidance situation is stable, turn your attention as soon as possible to identifying the "avenues of escape" available to you. Defensive drivers routinely prepare for this as they drive by maintaining a "comfort zone" around the RV. Quickly glance to the road shoulder to see if it is clear and firm enough to support the weight of your RV. Even if it is inadequate, it may be the best option. It is better to be mired in mud than to be involved in an accident. Ideally, the shoulder should be wide enough to avoid going into a ditch or ravine that may present an even worse consequence than that which you are trying to escape.

Mechanical troubles, such as an engine that unexpectedly quits, can cause emergency situations as well. If this happens to your RV, you need to find a safe place to stop before your forward speed dissipates. On a multi-lane expressway surrounded by other traffic, use emergency flashers as quickly as possible and move gradually in the direction of the shoulder. Steering rapidly to the shoulder through other traffic is a highly risky procedure requiring split-second decisions as to what is the best procedure.

Emergency Signaling Devices

When required to move across lanes through traffic because of a disabled engine, flat tire or other mechanical problem, arm signals can be very effective additions to the vehicle's turn signals. Your passenger may have to use arm signals as well to let drivers on the right side notice the emergency situation more quickly. Immediately upon reaching the side of the road, turn on the emergency flashers. Set out flares or other emergency signaling devices to warn oncoming traffic. The emergency signaling devices are even more important if you are unable to pull completely away from the flow of traffic or if you're just over the crest of a hill or around a curve. If possible, have someone stand at the crest of the hill (or curve) to warn traffic until a safe situation is created. In the event of a flat tire, it is often possible to drive slowly to an exit or safer area. If it is one of the duals, see Book 2 for details on tire limitations. It may be better to risk damage to the wheel (RV) than to stop in a very hazardous location on the roadway. Make certain that anyone who attempts to change the tire is not exposed to traffic, and clear the traffic lane as soon as possible. It may be safer to call for professional assistance.

Becoming stuck in a traffic lane is one of the most hazardous situations of your life whether it is a high-traffic condition or on a seldom-used road section where other drivers may be less attentive. Obviously, maintaining your vehicle routinely, practicing preventive maintenance (in advance of a need) and operating within all applicable manufacturers' limitations will go a long way toward preventing the unanticipated mechanical breakdown in the first place.

RV-SPECIFIC EQUIPMENT OPERATION

Normal Ranges for Dash Gauges
The following are average normal operating readings for the dash gauges of diesel and gasoline engine RVs. Not all RVs will be equipped with all gauges. Some of those functions may be warning lights or gauges calibrated only green/yellow/red. Anytime a gauge reading moves out of the normal operating range (for your vehicle) or a red warning light comes on, you should investigate to determine if there is a problem.

Normal Operating Ranges for Diesel Engine RVs
- Engine water temperature, 170-210 degrees--a movement of 20-30 degrees when climbing or descending a hill would be normal.

- Transmission temperature, 180-210 degrees--a movement of 20-50 degrees when pulling hard would be normal, and a much higher reading when a "transmission" retarder is used would be normal.

- Amperage gauge, 10-60 amps--the initial reading immediately after engine start or after dry-camping will be much higher (the alternator's rated amperage) tapering to this value over a period of time.

- Volt meter, 12-14.6 volts

- Oil pressure, 20-80 psi--at operating rpm

- Air pressure for suspension and brakes, 100-130 psi

Normal Operating Ranges for Gasoline Engine RVs
- Engine water temperature, 180-210 degrees--a movement of 20-30 degrees when climbing or descending a hill would be normal.

- Transmission temperature, 180-210 degrees--a movement of 20-50 degrees when pulling hard would be normal.

- Amperage gauge, 10-60 amps--the initial reading immediately after starting or after dry-camping will be much higher (the alternator's rated amperage) tapering to this value over a period of time.

- Volt meter, 12-14.6 volts

- Oil pressure, 20-80 psi--at operating rpm

AUXILIARY ENGINE BRAKING SYSTEMS

Diesel Engines
Virtually no experienced RVer has ever made the comment that his or her rig has too much braking capability. More commonly, they lament that they would really like to have more. Due to their design, diesel engines provide very little compression braking to assist in stopping. If your RVing lifestyle frequently takes you into mountainous or hilly terrain or you tow routinely, it is highly recommended that you purchase some form of auxiliary braking system. It is less expensive to order the coach with the braking device installed at the factory, but a quality retrofit is functionally equal to the factory-installed units.

There are several types of auxiliary braking devices available. The most popular ones are the exhaust brake, the engine brake, the transmission brake or retarder and the driveline retarder. The vast majority of RVs with auxiliary braking devices use the exhaust brake or engine brake because it is very cost effective.

The Exhaust Brake
Sometimes called a retarder, the exhaust brake is normally found on RVs equipped with diesel engines. This quiet braking aid operates by activating (closing) a shutter valve in the exhaust system just behind the turbo charger. The closed valve causes a buildup

of pressure in the exhaust system, turbo and into the combustion chamber of the engine. The pressure buildup there creates braking horsepower that is used to slow the vehicle down. With a transmission that offers mechanical lockup, the system is quite efficient. This means that almost the same horsepower that is used to keep your vehicle in motion can be used to help slow you down. The maximum efficiency is reached at the maximum engine rpm. This device can be wired through the transmission and activated with either a hand on/off switch or by a foot switch mounted on the floor. If the vehicle is equipped with the Allison World transmission, it can be programmed to pre-select any gear you wish. Most are programmed at the chassis manufacturer to pre-select fourth through second gears, so the transmission will automatically downshift through the gears taking maximum advantage of this device. This feature may also be deactivated so that you can manually downshift with the exhaust retarder turned on.

On slippery roads, exercise care to keep the wheels from locking at transmission downshift. If you are adding an aftermarket unit, check with the manufacturer of the RV or engine before installing this device. Some manufacturers have specific restrictions or limitations on the use of exhaust retarders.

The Engine Brake
Commonly referred to as a "Jake brake," the engine brake is used on many larger diesel engines in motorhomes and large trucks. This brake is a little more expensive and cannot be used on every engine because of limited space inside the valve covers. The principle of this device is the use of a combination of air pressure and oil pressure to cycle valve closing, resulting in a buildup of pressure within the cylinder, creating a braking force. An engine brake is almost 100% efficient in the conversion of engine horsepower to braking horsepower.

The engine brake also gives you the option of engaging only half the cylinders for reduced braking action. This device is much more likely than the exhaust brake to cause wheel lockup on slippery roads and creates a loud raspy noise when used. Some cities and localities have imposed limits on the use of engine brakes at certain hours of the day.

Transmission Retarder
Another efficient means of slowing a vehicle down is the use of a transmission retarder. In this system, a specially equipped transmission utilizes the transmission fluid to convert the RV's energy (speed) into heat to assist the vehicle in slowing. The process can be controlled in one of two ways: with a small stick mounted in the driver's area that can be moved to variable positions, or it may be engaged automatically when the brakes are applied and the system is turned on. The transmission is also downshifted to help this device operate more efficiently. The transmission retarder avoids any engine load or damage, but the transmission fluid can be quickly overheated with heavy usage. This device may also lock up the rear wheels on slippery road surfaces.

Driveline Retarder
The most efficient, and probably most expensive, means of slowing a vehicle is a driveline retarder. When engaged, the electromagnet around the drive shaft creates an opposing magnetic field around the drive shaft that causes the drive shaft to resist turning, thereby slowing the coach. The driveline retarder is engaged by pulling down on a stick similar to the transmission retarder. Driveline retarders can also cause the rear wheels to lock up in heavy applications, particularly in conjunction with a transmission downshift.

Gasoline Engines
Vehicles powered by gasoline engines have an advantage over those powered by diesel in that they create substantial backpressure, which allows the engine to work against itself when the accelerator is released. The result is considerable stopping power causing the vehicle to slow. Where added stopping power is desired, there are only two choices available. One is an exhaust brake very similar to the diesel engine exhaust brake, and the other is a driveline retarder. Neither device is totally satisfactory and has had only limited acceptance compared to the diesel devices. The exhaust brake creates minimal added braking force and has created some engine problems. The driveline retarder is quite effective; however, its detractions are that it is very heavy and very expensive for what is generally a more cost-sensitive market.

SUMMARY

There is little doubt that safely operating any vehicle (especially an RV) is probably the most demanding task that we must routinely perform in order to enjoy our chosen lifestyle. While driving may be second nature for many of us due to a lifetime of practice, it still commands our constant attention and the complete focus of our thoughts to accomplish it comfortably and safely. *The RVer's Ultimate Survival Guide*--Book 6 has provided you with much of what is important in that pursuit. All that remains is to be ever vigilant in your day-to day driving activities and to maintain your focus on the task at hand.

BOOK 7: TOWING SAFETY

CONTENTS

Author's Foreword 127
What's It All About? 127

MOTORHOMES USED AS TOW VEHICLES   128
Towing with a Motorhome 128
Tow Dolly 130
Tow Bars 131
Towed Car Braking System 135
Tow Bar Safety Tips 137

TOWING AN RV TRAILER   138
Towing a Recreation Vehicle Trailer 138
Medium-Duty Trucks 140
Recreation Vehicle Trailers 142
Braking Systems 143
Travel Trailer (Ball-Type) Hitches 144
Hooking Up Conventional Trailers 146
Hooking Up a 5th Wheel Trailer 146
5th Wheel Recreational Vehicle Trailers 147
Safety Tips & Considerations for RV Trailers 148
Summary 148

AUTHOR'S FOREWORD

As *The RVer's Ultimate Survival Guide* progresses through the various topics facing us on the road, we move forward into Book 7, which covers towing issues. Today, virtually all RVers are towing something. It may be a dingy, a trailer or some other plaything behind a motorhome or a travel or fifth wheel trailer. Because of this reality and the fact that towed vehicles are getting bigger and bigger and even multiplying (double trailers), we have devoted this book to a full discussion of issues that arise when we elect to tow anything.

WHAT'S IT ALL ABOUT?

In this book we would like to share some safety issues that everyone who tows should be concerned with. That concern is not only for your own safety, but also for that of everyone on the road and for those parked near you at the campground.

Consider that towing legally and towing safely are not always the same. Even though you may have all the towing equipment required by state or federal laws, it is not necessarily everything you need to travel safely while towing. You also require an understanding of a number of technical terms that you will encounter as you read your operator manuals along with some basic towing information. We suggest that you read and understand Book 1 before you read this book.

This manual is not a substitute for the technical information found in vehicle manufacturer's owner's manuals and the towing guides. Its purpose is to give you some basic information about issues you need to consider and the equipment you require to ensure your safety and peace of mind. Peace of mind is that vague physiological quality that permits us to relax and truly enjoy the RVing lifestyle.

> "Today, virtually all RVers are towing something."

Today, for reasons as diverse as RVers themselves, many RVers find themselves towing something behind their RVs. Whether it is a tow car or cargo trailer, in the case of a motorhome or a trailer for those using trailer-type RVs, most RVers need to understand fully what is involved in towing safely. That knowledge extends to the equipment required, the proper usage of the towing equipment and the driving considerations incumbent when driving a longer, heavier vehicle.

MOTORHOMES USED AS TOW VEHICLES
TOWING WITH A MOTORHOME

It is essential for your safety that you operate your motorhome and towed vehicle within all the manufacturer's established ratings and limitations. Be certain to obtain and retain (as a permanent record) all applicable manufacturers' documents relating to your RV and its towing limitations. See Book 1 for a complete and detailed discussion of the terms and acronyms used in those documents.

Most chassis manufacturers publish specific limits regarding the weight of any towed unit, what equipment is required for safe towing and what assumptions were utilized to establish those limits. For example, the "Ford RV & Trailer Towing Guide" states that: "Towing vehicle's braking system is rated for operation at GVWR, not GCWR. Separate functional brake systems should be used for safe control of towed vehicles or trailers weighing more than 1,500 pounds when loaded." Generally, the only place to locate such important safety information is in the manufacturer's "towing guide." Note that towing guides are model-specific, which means that a new guide is prepared each year updating the information as required. Generally, the previous year's information is not available after the model year is complete. Your only chance to get this valuable information is when you purchase your vehicle.

When selecting and purchasing towing equipment for a motorhome, you have basically three (3) options: a transport unit (trailer), a tow dolly, or a tow bar. While all these options may provide the same basic function (towing an automobile behind the motorhome), they still differ significantly in many critical areas and need to be considered separately.

Driving a Motorhome While Towing
This book provides a great amount of detail and information relative to driving and controlling your motorhome as well as many of the factors that may affect your driving performance. This book only attempts to identify and discuss the differences you will encounter when you tow a second vehicle behind your motorhome. The differences you will encounter come from basically two obvious issues: your motorhome is now substantially longer and heavier. These factors have a lot to do with how you will control your vehicle(s) and how it will react to the road and driving conditions.

The first area of concern is length. You must now drive with greater care, always remembering that your vehicle is now about 25 feet longer, that it will cut a tighter corner radius (corner) when you turn sharply and that other drivers may not fully comprehend the full length of your combined vehicles. Because of this greater length, you will need to pass other vehicles with care, and you will require extra distance to compensate for the trailer length and slower acceleration due to the greater total mass.

The second issue is the greater weight of the combined vehicles. You will now have to maintain greater clearance between you and the vehicle in front of you since the stopping distance of your combined rig is greatly increased when towing. Since it is very difficult to maintain adequate distance between your vehicle and the one in front of you due to other cars "filling the gap," it may be necessary for you to actually watch the road over the top of intervening cars to provide adequate warning of a problem that will force you to stop. Hills will now present a greater challenge. It may be necessary to climb (and descend) hills in a lower gear to avoid over-stressing your engine and driveline. Your acceleration will be impaired along with your stopping distance, and your fuel consumption will go up. Many RVers brag, "They don't even know that the car is back there." Possibly there is some truth to that because the modern motorhome does tow extremely well with no obvious negative reactions. However, your motorhome certainly does know that a car is back there. Whenever you add 15-20% additional mass to the motorhome, it must control that weight when maneuvering as well as accelerating and stopping it. There is a measurable negative effect.

Should you drop a wheel of the motorhome or towed vehicle off the road, avoid the tendency to react rapidly and excessively. It is much better to regain your composure and vehicle control first, then slow down and finally return slowly onto the roadway after verifying that the lane is clear. Refer to Book 6.

In a large motorhome, you are physically a long way from your towed vehicle. This distance effectively isolates you from what is happening "way back there." For this reason, you must check your mirrors frequently to keep track of the towed vehicle and the traffic around you. It may be necessary to utilize mirror extensions in order to see the towed vehicle. This is particularly true if you are towing with a wide-body motorhome. If you have a rearview camera, always use it while towing. If you do not have a rearview camera, consider the usage of a wide-angle viewer that can be attached to the rear window of the motorhome to provide a constant view of the tow vehicle.

At all times while towing, avoid rapid turning maneuvers. Slow and easy is the best rule when towing. This rule of thumb is doubly important when road traction is poor such as during rain or snow. The towed vehicle attempts to follow the motorhome at all times; however, due to the long rear end overhang of the motorhome, the reaction of a tow car or trailer to a turn is more extreme. This creates a significant force on the rear of the motorhome, which reacts through the long lever (overhang) as a major side load on the rear tires. Under extreme conditions or when traction of the tires is poor the result could be a lateral (side) skidding of the motorhome.

Transport Unit or Trailer
When using a transport unit or trailer (all four wheels of your towed vehicle will be carried off the ground), you will also require the following equipment to tow it safely. Legally, you need lighting for the rear of the unit, safety chains, and mirrors on both sides and, if the trailer weighs over 1,500 (typically) lbs., you will be required by most state laws to have a braking system and a breakaway safety device. The following tips will ensure your safety before, during, and after towing. You will also have to verify that the motorhome hitch is adequate to handle your tow load and that the ball is the correct size for the coupler on your trailer. Refer to Book 1.

Safety Tips & Considerations for Car Trailers
- When hooking up and unhooking a trailer, be sure to place blocks under both the front and rear of the trailer wheels so the trailer is unable to move on its own. You want to avoid endangering anyone in the area, or yourself, by a runaway trailer.

- Have someone guide you while backing and hooking up. Verify what hand signals will be used in this process. The use of small handheld CB radios (or family radio transceivers-FRS) will make the job much easier and safer.

- Check your safety chains to be sure they are properly attached. They should be crossed in an X pattern between the tow vehicle and the trailer without dragging the ground even while turning. This allows the trailer to corner properly and will help the trailer to follow the tow vehicle should your hitch fail.

- Attach the electrical cable and check the function of all taillights, brake and turn signals (front and rear) on both vehicles.

- Inspect your hitch and trailer tongue/coupler for cracked welds, worn or missing pins and that all hardware is present and properly secured.

- Check your trailer tires for proper inflation. Note that the motorhome tires will also be carrying a greater load and may require additional air pressure to support the load. Refer to Book 2.

- Consider the use of a load equalizing-type hitch. This may be required if the the extra load causes the rear of the motorhome to sag excessively, or if the tongue weight of the trailer drives the rear axle (GAWR) or tires to exceed their ratings.

- Never attempt to load or unload a trailer or tow dolly that is not securely hitched to a tow vehicle.

- Never unhitch a trailer or tow dolly that is loaded. The trailer jack may collapse on the trailer or the tow dolly tongue may fly up when the coupler is released.

- Consider the usage of an electronic tire pressure monitoring system for the towed car. Such systems can greatly increase your safety by giving an early alert to a tire problem. Often the driver is very isolated from the towed car, preventing first-hand knowledge of what is occurring behind. Refer to Book 2.

TOW DOLLY

Most of the above trailer tips also apply if you tow an automobile with a tow dolly (2 wheels down). Similarly, the law still requires safety cables, lights for the tow dolly and mirrors on both sides of the tow vehicle. Braking systems are available for some dollies. Check with the dolly manufacturer. Note that lights are also required on the towed vehicle that is on the dolly. Many RVers use a light bar secured to the roof or trunk of the towed vehicle, or they "hard wire" the towed car lights into those of the tow vehicle. Always tow your vehicle with the front wheels on the dolly. This keeps the "toe in" on the towed vehicle from causing the vehicle to sway or whip. It also keeps the majority of the weight over the dolly's axle for safety purposes. Note the following precautions when towing on a dolly:

Safety Tips & Considerations for Tow Dollies

- You cannot safely back up a loaded tow dolly. It may jackknife and cause damage to both the towed vehicle and the tow dolly.

- If a loaded tow dolly depresses the rear of the towing vehicle more than three to four inches, it is recommended that you install air shocks or helper springs on the towing vehicle for added stability and to retain proper headlight alignment.

- Tow dollies reduce the cargo capacity of the towing vehicle by the tongue weight, which is normally about 75-125 lbs., depending on the towed vehicle.

- Check the weight capacities of trailers and tow dollies (and their axles) to be certain they will handle the vehicle you want to carry.

- Proper transmission gear selection is important. Always check the manufacturer's recommendations.

- Be sure tilt-bed dollies and trailers are securely locked in the towing position after loading so they cannot tilt while towing.

- Tow dollies generally utilize nylon straps to secure the car to the dolly. Over time, these straps may fray and deteriorate. Replace them with material and hardware rated for the specific application.

TOW BARS

Towing with a tow bar is significantly different from towing with any type of trailer or dolly. When a tow bar is used, the vehicle being towed remains firmly on the ground, and there is little or no weight added to the towing motorhome. In addition, there is no trailer or dolly to store, and, depending on what type of tow bar you choose, there may not be any storage requirement at all. The additional convenience afforded by a tow bar accounts for the fact that the use of a tow bar is overwhelmingly the RVer's favorite means of towing a car. The legal issues of towing with a tow bar are the same as the other two methods. Lights, safety cables and mirrors on both sides are a requirement. Brake requirements, however, vary from state to state and province to province if traveling in Canada. Some will enforce trailer laws on towed vehicles, while others do not. Towing a vehicle with a tow bar is uniquely different from towing on a trailer or dolly in that the car often seems to disappear completely behind the motorhome. This reality exists because there is no added width to the towed car when using a tow bar in contrast to the width added with either a trailer or dolly. This means that the RVer will have to be certain that he/she can see the towed car while in transit. The result is that motorhomes may require larger or more mirrors, a rearview camera, a wide-angle viewer in the rear window and considerable driver care.

Another significant area of difference is that the tow bar does not provide any method of braking the towed car. After reading this far in *The RVer's Ultimate Survival Guide,* you have learned that, just like money, you can never have too much braking power to enhance your personal safety and assure your peace of mind while RVing. When tow bars first became readily available and somewhat common, there were few available ways of adding brakes to the towed automobile. Today the reality is totally different since there are now 15-20 tow car-braking systems affordably priced and readily available to the RVer. Today every responsible, serious RVer should conscientiously consider having a supplemental towed car braking system installed.

Tow Bars With Attitude!

Towing automobiles has evolved not only into a nearly universal procedure for motorhomes but also one that is for the most part, trouble-free. That statement is valid only when we follow the manufacturer's recommendations regarding tow bar installation and usage and the motorhome manufacturer's towing guidelines. However, RVers still find ways to get into towing difficulty or incur potential safety problems. How often have you witnessed a tow bar installed at an acute angle between the motorhome and tow car? As you can see by the photo below, it is not uncommon. There are a lot of reasons why it is necessary to keep your tow bar level (no more than a 3-4 inch rise to the motorhome, never down). Those reasons have to do primarily with geometry, physics and other scientific principles fully considered by the manufacturer when they recommend that you install the tow bar virtually level. One ramification of an improperly installed tow bar that is not commonly recognized is that the tow bar angle greatly

Unsafe Tow Bar Angle

increases during severe braking due to the rise in the rear of the motorhome and dive of the nose of the tow car. These result in a significant lifting force applied to the rear of the motorhome, which greatly decreases the stopping power of the combined vehicles. So, just when you need it most (emergency conditions) you decrease your vehicles ability to stop safely. This effect is particularly problematic during poor traction conditions such as rain, ice or snow. This detrimental effect is minimized but not eliminated by the usage of tow car brakes and by keeping the tow car size to a minimum; but why would any RVer be willing to give up any stopping power? Refer to Book 1 and Book 6 for further information on this topic.

Tow Bar Types
There are two basic types of tow bars commonly available, both of which are suitable for towing your automobile: rigid A-frame tow bars; and self-aligning models. The self-aligning type tow bars also come in two unique versions: car-mounted and motorhome mounted. Considerations associated with the type of tow bar you choose are as follows:

A-frame Tow Bars:
Hookup of an A-frame tow bar is often a two-person job. You must position the towed vehicle in the exact spot that will allow you to lower the tow bar's coupler onto the ball of the tow vehicle. While many RVers get along just fine with this design, others find them to be a lesson in frustration. Some RVers leave the A-frame type tow bar attached to the tow car even while driving around town. While this may appear to be a simple solution, it is unsightly to many, may obstruct your view while driving, and, most important, it presents a real safety hazard. Should the tow bar pivot forward and contact the ground, the car may be catapulted into the air, inflicting considerable damage and/or injury. The careful RVer must be doubly cautious to assure that the bar is locked in the upright position and then secured with a second, redundant, lock, chain, or safety device of some type.

Car Mounted:
This type tow bar adds considerable weight (50-70 pounds) to the front of your towed vehicle during normal driving, which can adversely affect handling and the front-end suspension geometry. It can also be damaged, along with your bumper or frame, by hitting a pole or

Rigid A-Frame Tow Bar

Motorhome Mounted Tow Bar

obstruction in a parking lot, or by other drivers (who may not perceive the extension of your vehicle) parking in front of your car. In some designs, protrusions on the front of the tow car remain even if the tow bar itself is removed for storage. Thus, they can be hazardous to one's legs as they walk around the automobile.

Motorhome Mounted:
These popular and versatile types of tow bars are available in lightweight aluminum versions as well as heavier steel models. These tow bars are convenient to hook up and store in place when the car is disconnected. They do not encumber the front of the towed car when not towing and generally utilize relatively small attachment points on the car, maintaining a cleaner appearance.

An essential item for towing with a tow bar is the base plate, which bolts to the front of your towed vehicle, providing an attachment point(s) for the tow bar. Base plates are custom designed for each specific towed vehicle. Check with your dealer or manufacturer for the correct equipment. Periodically check the welds and bolts to ensure there are no cracked welds or loose bolts.

Typical Drop Receiver

To provide the safest possible towing experience, you may also require a dropped (or raised) receiver to adjust the height of your motorhome's hitch to match the towed car's base plate. The two should be within four inches of level, meaning the car can be up to four inches below the motorhome but never higher. At other levels, during a rapid braking situation, the towed vehicle could possibly be forced over or under the tow bar into your motorhome. This may result in vehicle damage and/or reduced braking performance of the motorhome if the towed car rides under the motorhome, lifting the rear suspension.

Tow Bar Ratings
One of the most important decisions the RVer must make, once he or she determines to tow a car, is what tow bar to purchase. The first and most important consideration is the weight of the vehicle you are planning to tow. The vehicle to be towed, fully equipped for towing and loaded with fuel, etc., should weigh no more than 1) the maximum weight limit of the receiver hitch on the rear of the motorhome 2) the maximum weight rating of the draw bar and tow ball (if used) and 3) the difference between the fully loaded motorhome and the GCWR of the motorhome. Tow bars are available in the following standardized ratings:

- Class I   up to 2000 lbs.
- Class II   up to 3500 lbs.
- Class III   up to 5000 lbs.
- Class IV   up to 10,000 lbs.

The weight class (towing capability) of the tow bar you choose must include your towed vehicle as well as its contents, including a full tank of fuel. Note that many RVers are forced to use their towed car as a trailer in order to off-load weight from overloaded motorhomes, please refer to Book 1.

There is an increasing trend in RVing to tow larger and larger automobiles (and trucks), thus you should consider your future needs as well as your current requirements when purchasing a tow bar.

Towed Car Compatibility

Most front-wheel drive manual transmission vehicles can be towed with all four wheels on the ground with no additional modifications required. Most front-wheel drive automatic transmission vehicles will need a transmission lube pump or an axle disconnect in order to tow it four wheels down. Transmission lube pumps are designed to circulate the transmission fluid to keep the transmission lubricated to avoid transmission damage. Axle disconnects allow the wheels to rotate without driving the transaxle. Most rear-wheel drive vehicles require a transmission lube pump or a device to disconnect the drive shaft in order to tow four wheels down. To avoid much of this hassle, a common choice is a four-wheel drive vehicle with a manual transfer case. This type vehicle can generally be towed flat without the use of additional equipment. The market for an easily towable vehicle continues to grow (thanks to the rapidly increasing ranks of RVers) driving greater interest in such vehicles. Manufacturers producing such vehicles are often rewarded with considerable additional sales as a result. Always refer to your vehicle owner's manual for specific instructions and limitations. In addition, FMCA annually summarizes the tow capability of most vehicles in production and publishes the list in their magazine and on their website at www.motorhomemagazine.com.

Another issue you will want to determine is how well your towed car tracks behind your motorhome. The best way to check this aspect of towing safely is to have someone follow your tow car while closely observing the front wheels. If possible, this should be accomplished at slow speed on dirt or gravel as any problem will be much more obvious. The front wheels should closely and accurately follow the motorhome's movements. Note: due to the long overhang (distance behind the rear axle) of many motorhomes, the rear end (and tow car) will initially turn opposite the direction of the turn and then quickly follow the tow vehicle through the turn. If your towed vehicle does not track (follow) well, you should take it to an alignment shop and have it thoroughly checked. Have them reset the front-wheel caster to the maximum factory-recommended setting. This will reduce the wear on your vehicle (in particular, its tires) as well as improve your towing safety.

Power steering on a towed car (if equipped) acts as a damper for the front wheels when towing four wheels down. Manual steering vehicles do not have this dampening effect and can go into front-wheel oscillation (shimmy) when towed. This condition can vary from vehicle to vehicle, even those of the same model and year. A properly aligned front end and replacement of worn steering components will minimize this tendency. If you should experience this condition, have a good alignment shop check and repair the entire front end for wear and damage. If this does not cure the problem, then reset the front-wheel caster to the maximum factory-recommended setting. Some RVers use a bungee cord attached between the steering wheel and the floor to minimize a vehicle's tendency to shimmy. This should be a solution of last resort because virtually all automobiles can be towed flat without shimmy, providing everything is in good repair and set to factory specifications.

Do not back up when towing with a tow bar. When towing four wheels down, the caster built into the front wheels will cause the front wheels to turn fully and forcefully in one direction when backing. The caster is used to keep the steering wheels pointed forward and to help bring them back to center after cornering, much like a bicycle front wheel. This same tilt works in reverse when backing up, putting undue stress on your tires, rims, front suspension and the entire towing system. This may cause "scrubbed" tires or bent or broken tow bar components.

TOWED CAR BRAKING SYSTEMS

There are five basic categories of supplemental braking systems on the market today. These are the critical safety systems that activate the brakes on your towed car when you apply the brakes of your motorhome.

Surge or Mechanical Brake Systems:
Surge brake systems develop braking force by using the momentum of the towed car pushing toward the motorhome when it decelerates. This is a simple braking method that applies all four (4) brakes in proportion to the deceleration of the motorhome. The manner in which a surge system works assures that the towed car will never have to stop more than its own weight, protecting the automobile brakes from damage. As the car is slowed, the force applying the brakes is also diminished. The simplicity of this system extends to the fact that surge systems remain attached to the motorhome at all times, so no storage is required when not in use. Additional cars may be equipped with a braking system by simply purchasing and installing an additional brake actuation cable. Surge brake systems can provide a brake activating breakaway capability through the use of an additional cable pulling the brake pedal. These are commonly offered as an option to the basic system. Breakaway systems are very important for your safety and security.

Hydraulic Brake Systems:
A hydraulic braking system taps into the hydraulic brake lines of your tow vehicle and the towed car to apply the brakes of the towed car in the normal fashion, through the master cylinder, brake lines, etc. The hydraulic brake pressure comes from the tow vehicle and must pass through some device to isolate the two braking systems and to provide a fail-safe feature. Such systems may be plumbed to operate on either two or four wheels of the towed car and are generally proportional to the deceleration of the motorhome. Breakaway capability can be added to hydraulic braking systems, but, it may add considerable complexity to the system. A brake pressure source or accumulator must be provided along with a device to activate the system should the two vehicles separate.

Air Brake Systems:
Air-applied braking systems work with the air brakes on your motorhome in most cases, or they can operate from a separate source of air pressure (a compressor). In most cases, air systems utilize some type of air cylinder to actuate (press) the brake pedal in the towed automobile. The result is four-wheel brakes that operate as they normally do. The sensor type that determines the amount of air pressure applied varies by manufacturer. Some use no sensor at all, applying the brakes fully at each stop while others use some means to determine the deceleration rate of the motorhome and apply the towed car brakes proportionally. Breakaway protection for air brake systems requires either an accumulator or separate air pressure system to be available in the towed car and a device to activate it should the two vehicles separate while driving.

Vacuum Systems:
There are at least two types of vacuum-operated towed car braking systems. One creates its own vacuum with a vacuum pump powered by the towed car electrical system, while the other works with the vacuum system on your motorhome. The latter system is typically used on gasoline-powered motorhomes exclusively, because diesel engines do not normally provide a vacuum source. Vacuum-operated braking systems apply the brakes of the towed car by physically pulling the brake pedal toward the floor when brakes are called for. As with air-powered systems, there are different ways for the system to determine how much braking is to be applied, and some use no method to proportion the braking effort at all. Breakaway protection can be added to this type of braking system at the cost of some additional complexity. A source of vacuum (accumulator or pump) must be carried in the towed car along with a device to activate the system should the two vehicles ever separate while driving.

Portable Systems
These are portable devices that are placed on the driver's side floor and attached to the vehicle brake pedal. They are self-contained and require 12-volt power from the towed vehicle. Acceleration sensors inside the device control the application of the vehicle's brakes.

11 Considerations For Tow Brake Satisfaction

The selection of a proper tow brake system for your tow car is one of the most important issues facing RVers. The decision to purchase was only the first consideration. With that behind us, the next issue becomes "what system to purchase." Today there are 15-20 systems available to RVers, all of which offer differing features, complexity and ease of use, making the selection difficult. Each of the following 11 items is very important to the author. RVers wishing to purchase a quality system that will perform as expected for a lifetime, and at an affordable cost, are likely to consider the same points to be important.

- The brake system should not "tap" directly into the towed vehicle electrical system. To do so may jeopardize the integrity of the onboard computer or antilock brake system, if equipped. Most automobile manufacturers specifically discourage such action on the part of the owner. Warranties may be adversely affected by such modifications.

- The tow car brake system should not tap into the hydraulic brake system of the tow car. This may adversely affect the performance of the antilock brake system, if equipped, and could result in the loss of brakes altogether due to improper material or workmanship issues. Brakes are a certified safety system that must not be haphazardly modified during the installation of aftermarket components. Some automakers may allow this under very specific requirements.

- The brake system should operate all four brakes on the tow car. Some systems are two-wheel only greatly increasing the wear on the tow car brakes.

- The tow car brake system application should be proportional to the deceleration of the towing vehicle. Some systems apply the brakes fully regardless of the need determined by the tow vehicle.

- The tow car braking effort must be adjustable. Some systems apply the same braking force regardless of the vehicle on which it is installed. Adjustability gives the operator the opportunity to vary the braking effort depending upon the conditions at hand.

- The tow car braking system must be easy to install and remove. If it is not, the owner may use it once or twice and then leave it in the garage because the planned trip is too short to bother. A system left in the garage is of no benefit.

- The system should include breakaway protection as standard or optional equipment. This protection may be just as important as the braking system itself.

- The system should be simple. An overly complex system may not offer the reliability required.

- The tow car brake system should offer a cockpit indication that it is present and properly functioning.

- The tow car brake system should be easy to transfer from car to car and motorhome to motorhome.

- Purchase from a large reputable company. With many competing systems being developed for this relatively small market, it is likely that some manufacturers will drop out of the business, potentially leaving you with an "orphan" system.

VACUUM BRAKE SYSTEM

Image courtesy of Roadmaster.

PORTABLE BRAKE SYSTEM

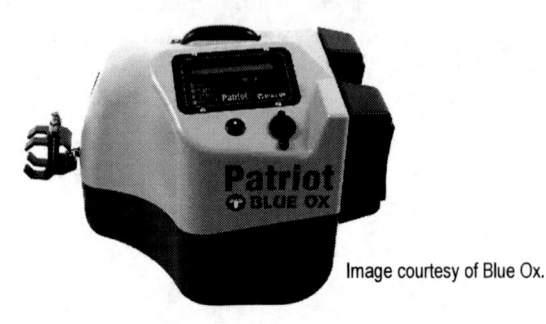

Image courtesy of Blue Ox.

TOW BAR SAFETY TIPS

- Inspect your towing system for loose bolts and worn parts. Repair or replace any questionable components before attempting to tow. Make certain that the ball is the correct size for the tow bar coupler you are using and that it is adjusted for a proper fit.

- Hook up while on a smooth, flat surface with the tow car straight behind the motorhome.

- After hooking up the tow bar, set the towed vehicle's steering, ignition key and transmission to the recommended tow positions. Generally, the transmission should be in neutral and the ignition key in the accessory position to unlock the steering wheel. If used, verify that the drive shaft is properly disconnected or that the lube pump is functioning. Note that some vehicles require that one or more circuits or fuses be disconnected or removed to tow the vehicle. CONSULT THE OWNER'S MANUAL FOR SPECIFICS!

- Check your parking brake to ensure it is disengaged.

- Latch the legs on a self-aligning tow bar by pushing the towed car back until they click into the locked position or by pulling the motorhome forward a few feet.

- Check your safety chains or cables to be sure they are properly attached.

- Attach the electrical cable and check the function of all taillights, brake and turn signals (front and rear) on both vehicles.

- Check the tire pressure on both vehicles. Refer to Book 2.

- Verify that the tow bar is parallel to the ground.

- The towing system is only as strong as its weakest component. Safety cables or chains must all be rated to support the total weight of all towed loads.

- Locate your spare key and lock the towed vehicle's doors.

- Check that all pins and locks on your towing equipment are present and properly snapped into place.

- Check your mirrors for proper adjustment so as to view your towed vehicle and to provide a full view of the traffic behind your rig.

- When convenient, have someone watch the towed car for the first few feet of travel. Any fault will be readily apparent to the observer.

- Never allow anyone to ride in the towed vehicle. This can be very dangerous, as well as possibly being illegal.

- The RVer must ensure that the ball and the coupler are the same size and are rated for the maximum weight of your towed car. Use only quality towing products purchased from reputable sources. There are many substandard components on the market (particularly tow balls), which look good but can fail during service. Make certain that they are adjusted for a proper fit. Secure and lock it in place with a padlock or a pin designed for this application to prevent the coupler lever from unlocking.

- Consider using an electronic tire pressure monitoring system for the towed car. Such systems can greatly increase your safety by giving an early alert to a tire problem. Often the driver is very isolated from the towed car, preventing first-hand knowledge of what is occurring behind. Refer to Book 2.

- Each time you stop, check the tow bar, baseplate and cables to make sure they are still properly attached and in good condition. Check the tires of the towed vehicle to make sure they are not going flat. If you are using a dolly or trailer, check the wheels to make sure they are not hot to the touch. If the wheels are hot, it may indicate a brake or bearing problem.

- Between trips, clean the tow bar and cables to keep them in good condition. Check the manufacturer's instructions for recommended maintenance.

TOWING AN RV TRAILER
TOWING A RECREATION VEHICLE TRAILER

Many RVers choose to enjoy the RV lifestyle in a recreation vehicle trailer. Often this decision is made based on the current ownership of a suitable truck for towing the trailer, or it may be the desire to have additional living area or a vehicle that can be left in one location for a long period of time. Whatever the reason for their selection, trailers remain the most common form of RVing. The trailers commonly used for RVing range from the smallest pop-up camper or single-axle camping units suitable for towing by even the smallest automobile, continuing all the way up to 40' four-slide-out 5th wheel trailers offering all the convenience and luxury anyone could possibility require. The common denominator that each trailer RVer faces is that they all have to obtain the required towing equipment, learn the proper usage of this equipment and practice the safe driving procedures necessary to travel safely. This portion of Book 7 is intended to identify the important issues and to guide an RVer down the safe path leading to a safe RVing experience with a trailer.

Selecting a Towing Vehicle
SUVs, pickup trucks, medium duty trucks, vans, minivans and passenger cars can all be equipped to tow a trailer. However, the selection of an appropriate towing vehicle and the proper equipment to tow a trailer safely, depends on the type of trailer and its size, weight and configuration.

Many tow vehicle manufacturers offer towing packages that delineate and provide the minimum equipment necessary to tow differing types of trailers, depending upon their fully loaded weight, size and configuration. A typical towing package may include a heavy-duty radiator, special battery, flasher system, alternator, suspension and brakes, as well as an engine-oil cooler, transmission-oil cooler, wiring harness, towing-specific axle ratio and special wheels and tires.

When choosing the tow vehicle that best meets your needs, ensure that its tow rating is adequate to safely tow, maneuver AND STOP your trailer with the full tanks, cargo and passenger load that you will carry. Note that financial (cost) was not on the list of primary considerations. Most RVers have financial limitations, but they should never allow them to come before the physical (safety) issues.

Obviously, some vehicles are better suited to tow than others. This is equally true for "ball hitch" (conventional travel trailers) or for 5th wheel trailers. In general, a tow vehicle with a longer wheelbase and shorter rear overhang is going to provide greater towing stability (down the road). A tow vehicle with a higher center of gravity such as a 4x4, will be less stable laterally (turning) than a vehicle not so equipped. In contrast, a shorter wheelbase will be more maneuverable in the cities and campgrounds, and the 4x4 will give you greater security when traveling on smaller or unimproved roads. The length of the truck bed is of concern because 5th wheel trailers use this area for turning clearance. Short-bed trucks may not provide adequate clearance or may require the use of a special slide-back-type hitch to enhance tight maneuvering. One important consideration for 5th wheel-type tow vehicles is bed height. Because of the height of the truck bed, it may be necessary to raise the trailer to achieve correct trailer ride height. If this critical trailer towing requirement is not met, the result will be the rear axle of the trailer will be

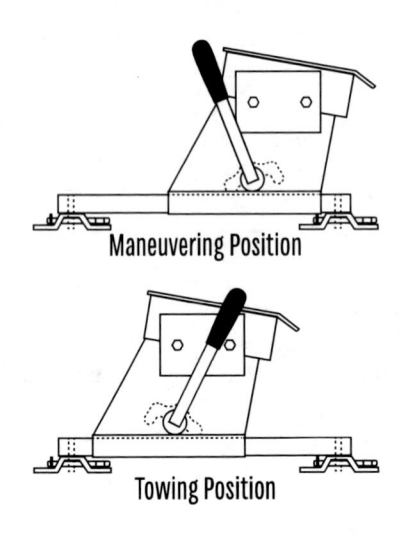

Maneuvering Position

Towing Position

TRAILER TOWING SELECTOR

F-250/F-350/F-450 SUPER DUTY® PICKUPS CONVENTIONAL TOWING [1]

Maximum Loaded Trailer Weight (lbs.)

Engine	Automatic Transmission Axle Ratio	GCWR (lbs.)	REGULAR CAB F-250 SRW 4x2	F-250 SRW 4x4	F-350 SRW 4x2	F-350 SRW 4x4	F-350 DRW 4x2	F-350 DRW 4x4	SUPERCAB F-250 SRW 4x2	F-250 SRW 4x4	F-350 SRW 4x2	F-350 SRW 4x4	F-350 DRW 4x2	F-350 DRW 4x4	CREW CAB F-250 SRW 4x2	F-250 SRW 4x4	F-350 SRW 4x2	F-350 SRW 4x4	F-350 DRW 4x2	F-350 DRW 4x4	F-450 DRW 4x4
6.2L SOHC V8 FFV	3.73	19,200	12,500	12,500	12,500	12,500	–	–	12,500	12,400	12,500	12,300	–	–	12,500	12,200	12,500	12,100	–	–	–
		19,800	–	–	–	–	13,200	12,700	–	–	–	–	12,800	12,400	–	–	–	–	12,500	12,100	–
	4.30	22,200	12,500	12,500	12,500	12,500	–	–	12,500	12,500	12,500	12,500	–	–	12,500	12,500	12,500	12,500	–	–	–
		22,800	–	–	–	–	16,100	15,700	–	–	–	–	15,700	15,300	–	–	–	–	15,500	15,100	–
6.7L V8 Turbo Diesel	3.31	23,500	12,500	12,500	12,500	12,500	–	–	14,000	14,000	14,000	14,000	–	–	14,000	14,000	14,000	14,000	–	–	–
	3.55	23,500	12,500	12,500	12,500	12,500	–	–	14,000	14,000	14,000	14,000	–	–	14,000	14,000	14,000	14,000	–	–	–
	3.73	32,100	–	–	–	–	19,000	19,000	–	–	–	–	19,000	19,000	–	–	–	–	19,000	19,000	–
		32,100(2)	–	–	–	–	19,000	19,000	–	–	–	–	19,000	19,000	–	–	–	–	19,000	19,000	–
	4.30	35,000(3)	–	–	–	–	–	–	–	–	–	–	–	–	–	–	–	–	–	19,000	–
		40,400	–	–	–	–	–	–	–	–	–	–	–	–	–	–	–	–	–	–	19,000(6)

F-250/F-350/F-450 SUPER DUTY PICKUPS 5th-WHEEL/GOOSENECK TOWING

Engine	Axle Ratio	GCWR																			
6.2L SOHC V8 FFV	3.73	19,200	12,900	12,500	12,900	12,500	–	–	12,700	12,300	12,600	12,200	–	–	12,400	12,100	12,400	12,000	–	–	–
		19,800	–	–	–	–	13,100	12,600	–	–	–	–	12,700	12,200	–	–	–	–	12,400	12,000	–
	4.30	22,200	15,900	15,500	15,900	15,500	–	–	15,700	15,300	15,600	15,200	–	–	15,400	15,100	15,400	15,000	–	–	–
		22,800	–	–	–	–	16,100	15,600	–	–	–	–	15,700	15,200	–	–	–	–	15,400	15,000	–
6.7L V8 Turbo Diesel	3.31	23,500	16,600	16,200	16,500	16,100	–	–	16,300	15,900	16,200	15,900	–	–	16,100	15,100	16,000	15,700	–	–	–
	3.55	23,500	16,600	16,200	16,500	16,100	–	–	16,300	15,900	16,200	15,900	–	–	16,100	15,100	16,000	15,700	–	–	–
	3.73	32,100	–	–	–	–	24,700	24,300	–	–	–	–	24,200	23,800	–	–	–	–	24,000	23,500	–
		32,100(2)	–	–	–	–	25,300	24,900	–	–	–	–	24,800	24,400	–	–	–	–	24,600	24,200	–
	4.30	35,000(3)	–	–	–	–	–	–	–	–	–	–	–	–	–	–	–	–	–	26,500(4)	–
		40,400	–	–	–	–	–	–	–	–	–	–	–	–	–	–	–	–	–	–	26,500(4)(6)
			–	–	–	–	–	–	–	–	–	–	–	–	–	–	–	–	–	–	31,200(5)(6)

(1) Maximum loaded trailer weight requires weight-distributing hitch. See page 28 for additional information. (2) Pickup Box Delete Option. (3) Available with High-Capacity Trailer Tow Package only. (4) 5th-wheel towing capacity limited by availability of 26.5K hitch. (5) Gooseneck towing capacity. (6) F-450 calculated with SAE J2807 method.

Notes:
- This information also applies to models with Pickup Box Delete Option (66D).
- Trailer tongue (trailer king pin for 5th-wheel towing) load weight should be 10-15% (15-25% for 5th-wheel towing) of total loaded trailer weight. Make sure vehicle payload (reduce by option weight) will accommodate trailer tongue (trailer king pin for 5th-wheel towing) load weight and weight of passengers and cargo added to towing vehicle. Addition of trailer tongue (trailer king pin for 5th-wheel towing) load weight and weight of passengers and cargo must not cause vehicle weights to exceed rear GAWR or GVWR. These ratings can be found on the vehicle Safety Compliance Certification Label.

Sample data chart is excerpted from the Ford Motor Company® 2016 RV & Trailer Towing Guide©. This is typical of the information produced by vehicle manufacturers. We selected this document to illustrate the importance of reading and understanding the vehicle manufacturer's ratings and limitations placed on their vehicles when used for towing an RV. Note: "towing guides" are generally only produced during the current model year. It is important to obtain a copy and retain it as a permanent record.

forced to carry excessive load, often resulting in an overloaded axle or tire. Refer to Book 1.

Be cautious about making your purchase decision based on "opinions" of those who should be or want to be "experts." This may include truck salesmen that may exaggerate how much their truck can "pull." What about stopping? What about the ability to handle an evasive maneuver when someone pulls out in front of you?

Make your purchase decision based on FACTS to avoid what is often an expensive mistake!

Virtually all tow vehicle manufacturers publish a "Towing Guide" for their specific vehicles. The towing guide provides the critical information needed to properly match a tow vehicle to a trailer. In addition to operating the tow vehicle within its established Gross Vehicle Weight Rating (GVWR) and Gross Combined Weight Rating (GCWR) (see Book 1), the "Maximum Loaded Trailer Weight" must also be observed for safety.

Most towing guides are established based on a basic truck having minimum equipment with only a driver (no passenger) and no cargo. To the RVer, this means that there is no hitch in the bed, no extra fuel tanks, no toolboxes, no wheel chocks, no luxury options, and no passenger, etc. all of which can easily reduce published towing capacity by 1,000 to 1,500 pounds or more.

As a typical example of a "towing guide," we have reproduced a page from the *2016 RV & Trailer Towing Guide* as published by Ford (see previous page). This document establishes the GCWR and the maximum loaded trailer weight rating for all combinations of truck type, engine, transmission and rear axle ratio. Note that in all cases the actual weight that can be towed by a typically configured truck will be 1,000 to 1,500 pounds less than shown on the chart. Further, note the following statement quoted from the 2016 RV Towing Guide:

> Trailer tongue (trailer king pin for 5th-wheel towing) load weight should be 10-15% (15-25% for 5th-wheel towing) of total loaded trailer weight. Make sure vehicle payload (reduce by option weight) will accommodate trailer tongue (trailer king pin for 5th-wheel towing), load weight and weight of passengers, and cargo added to towing vehicle. Addition of trailer tongue (trailer king pin for 5th-wheel towing) load weight and weight of passengers and cargo must not cause vehicle weights to exceed rear GAWR or GVWR. These ratings can be found on the vehicle Safety Compliance Certification Label.

There is a wide range of suitable tow vehicles designed and equipped specifically for towing RV trailers. These vehicles are capable of legally and safely handling trailers ranging from 500 pounds to in excess of 40,000 pounds. A little research will generally identify just which vehicle will meet your specific requirements.

MEDIUM-DUTY TRUCKS

One of the most common mistakes made by RVers is the assumption that a one-ton dually pickup truck can pull any RV trailer out there. Truck dealers and people who do not understand vehicle limitations often reinforce this misconception and recommend (sell) the uninformed buyer a totally inadequate truck. It is quite true that you will see others (many) on the road doing just this. Just like your mother used to tell you, "Just because everyone is doing it doesn't make it right." To get a feel for the magnitude of this problem, refer to Book 1.

FACT: there are many 5th wheel trailers on the market with a GVWR greater than the maximum tow rating of most one-ton dually pickup trucks. Thus, anyone who is serious about their personal safety and the safety of those around them should consider a medium duty truck if they are in the market for one of the larger 5th wheel-type trailers that are available today. Many of the largest 5th wheel-type trailers being built today are targeted at those RVers with a "Medium Duty Tow Truck." Medium-duty trucks can be rated to haul trailers up to 40,000 pounds.

Common myths about medium duty trucks that should be considered with an open mind:

MDTs are too big!
The actual body dimensions of most of these trucks are only slightly larger than a one-ton pickup. The size difference is primarily in the height. Ask anyone who has one and you will quickly learn that size is not an issue. In fact, it is a positive attribute. You sit higher, enabling a clearer view of the road ahead, especially in traffic, providing you with more time to make decisions.

I'll never be able to park it at the market or the post office!
Most medium duty trucks have a turning radius smaller than or comparable to a pickup truck or full-size passenger car. They are very easy to maneuver, and, yes, they do fit into most parking spots!

MDTs are too expensive!
At a cost of about twice a typical tow-capable pickup truck, they may appear to be expensive. However, consider that it is a vehicle designed for rough commercial service. A medium-duty truck is likely to outlast a pickup several times over while enjoying reduced day-to-day maintenance. Further, the resale value of a medium-duty truck is typically much more favorable than a pickup. Many medium-duty truck owners will reiterate that it is actually less expensive to purchase and operate a medium duty truck hauler. Many RVers have owned and operated a medium-duty truck hauler for years and then fully recouped their entire original investment when they sold it.

Medium-duty trucks are being used and enjoyed by more and more RV owners. Refer to Book 1 to identify the weight safety benefits of the medium duty truck tow vehicle. If your trailer size is marginal or demands a medium duty truck hauler, take some time and speak with several current owners for their opinion. Be sure to drive one as part of your investigation. These simple steps alone will answer many of your questions and concerns. Wouldn't you rather have a sizable safety margin (capability) remaining rather than being overloaded or marginal during your travels?

Trailer towing vehicles are working near their maximum capability all the time. For this reason, you must keep your tow vehicle in top driving condition. The vehicle maintenance schedule must be followed religiously as a minimum. If you operate under difficult conditions (mountain country, dirt roads, short hard hauls, etc.), exceed the manufacturer's recommendations by shortening the service intervals. Routinely check the air pressure in your tires, use quality shock absorbers; have the alignment checked regularly, and, as always, purchase the correct hitch for the weight you are towing. Regularly check all hitch hardware, including attachment fasteners. Tighten or replace them as required.

RVers' Ultimate Survival Guide

RECREATION VEHICLE TRAILERS

There are many similarities between towing a car with a motorhome and towing an RV trailer with a tow vehicle. The legal issues remain essentially the same: adequate mirrors, safety chains, proper lighting and trailer brakes if the trailer weighs over 1,000-1,500 lbs (typical state limits). The federal government regulates brakes for trailers, and manufacturers normally include these with their trailers. Brakes should be checked regularly to ensure a safe stop. Most trailer brakes are electrically actuated drum-type brakes. Trailer braking systems are fairly simple, effective and low cost for a vehicle (trailer) that has no other power source (hydraulic, vacuum or air). In general, just as with your car, use your engine to decelerate (particularly when traveling in mountainous areas) rather than your brakes whenever possible so as not to overheat them.

Driving a Truck/Trailer RV

Book 6 provides a great amount of detail and information relative to driving and controlling your RV, as well as many of the factors that may affect your driving performance. This book only attempts to identify and discuss the specific differences you will encounter when you tow a trailer-type RV. The primary issues to consider are obvious: your truck/trailer rig is now substantially longer and heavier. These factors have a lot to do with how you will control your vehicle(s) and how it will react to the road and driving conditions.

The first area of concern is length. You must now drive with greater care, always remembering that your vehicle is now 50-60 feet in overall length and will cut a tighter turning radius (corner) when you turn sharply, and other vehicles may not fully comprehend the full length of your combined vehicles. Because of this greater length, you will need to pass other vehicles with care. You will require extra distance to compensate for the trailer length and slower acceleration resulting from the greater total mass.

The second issue is the greater weight of the combined vehicles. You will now have to maintain greater clearance between your vehicle and the vehicle in front of you, as the stopping distance of your combined rig is greatly increased when towing. It is very difficult to maintain adequate distance between your vehicle and the one in front of you due to other cars "filling the gap." Thus, it may be necessary to actually watch the road over the intervening cars to provide adequate warning of a problem requiring you to get stopped. Hills will now present a greater challenge. It may be necessary to climb (and descend) hills in a lower gear to avoid over-stressing your engine and driveline. Your acceleration will be impaired along with your stopping distance, and your fuel consumption will go up. Many RVers brag, they "don't even know that the trailer is back there." There is some truth to that because the modern trucks do tow extremely well with no apparent or extreme negative reactions. However, your truck certainly does know that a trailer is back there. Whenever you add 100-200% additional load to the truck, it must control that mass when maneuvering, accelerating and stopping. It does have a measurable effect.

While driving, if you drop a wheel of the truck or trailer off the shoulder, avoid the tendency to react rapidly and excessively. It is essential to regain control first, slow down and finally turn slowly back onto the roadway after verifying that the lane is clear. Refer to Book 6. Watch for sudden changes in wind speeds. Be prepared to slow down to compensate for wind gusts and passing trucks and remain firmly straight ahead and fully in your own lane.

In large truck/trailer combinations, you are a long way from your trailer. This distance effectively isolates you from what is happening way back there. For this reason, you must check your mirrors frequently to keep track of the trailer and the traffic around you. Recognize that there are still areas that cannot be seen, and note that drivers often like to drive in that location. It may be necessary to utilize mirror extensions in order to see the trailer. This is particularly true if you are towing a wide-body trailer.

At all times while towing, avoid rapid turning maneuvers--slow and easy is the best rule when towing.

This rule of thumb is doubly important when road traction is poor such as during rain or snow. The trailer attempts to follow the truck at all times; however, the reaction of a trailer that may weigh more than the tow truck in a turn can be more extreme. This creates a significant side force on the rear of the truck. This action is more pronounced on conventional tongue-type trailers than for 5th wheel-type trailers due to the distance (lever) from the rear axle to the hitch ball. Under extreme conditions or when traction of the tires is poor, the result could be a lateral (side) skidding of the truck.

BRAKING SYSTEMS

Trailers have the option of three different styles of braking systems, and electric brakes are by far the most common. Most trailer manufacturers offer electric brake systems as standard equipment on their products. Some go the extra step and also offer "optional brake systems" for those customers valuing such systems. In any case, aftermarket manufacturers can retrofit alternative braking systems.

Electronically controlled electric brakes:
Electric brakes are actually electrically-actuated drum-type brake systems. Electric braking systems are fairly simple, effective and low cost for a vehicle (trailer) that has no other power source (hydraulic, vacuum or air). Electric brakes require a controlling device located in the tow vehicle that provides automatic or manual control of the trailer brakes. In addition, electric brakes require that a fairly large (10-gauge) wire be run between the controller and the trailer brakes and that a good ground be maintained between the two vehicles. The controller itself can use one of many types of technology to determine the deceleration of the tow vehicle and apply a proportional signal to the brakes to establish the required braking. All systems of this type have some means of adjusting the "balance," which essentially adjusts the controller for various mounting locations (position), and a "gain" control, which establishes how rapidly the power is applied to the brakes.

Hydraulic-controlled electric brakes:
This system is virtually identical to the above system except that the controller is hydraulically connected to the tow vehicle's brakes. The result is that it applies the trailer brakes in proportion to the amount of brake pedal pressure applied. Caution: hydraulic brake controllers must be connected directly to a tow vehicle's braking system. If the tow vehicle utilizes an antilock brake system, be certain that the brake controller is certified for use with antilock type brakes. In addition, anytime the brake system hydraulic lines are modified in any way, great caution must be exercised to avoid harming this critical safety component.

Surge-activated hydraulic brakes:
A master cylinder mounted on the trailer tongue operates a surge brake system. The actual wheel brakes may be either disc or drum-type designs, virtually identical in design and construction to modern automobile brakes. The forward momentum developed when the moving trailer mass pushes against the decelerating tow vehicle activates the master cylinder, which produces a hydraulic pressure that is applied to the trailer brakes. This is a simple braking method that applies the trailer brakes in proportion to the deceleration of the tow vehicle. The manner in which a surge system works assures that the trailer brakes will never have to stop more than the trailer's own weight, protecting them from overload and damage. As the trailer is slowed, the force applying the brakes is also diminished. This system remains attached to the trailer tongue at all times, so it is a simple matter to utilize different tow vehicles to pull the trailer if desired.

ELECTRIC BRAKE CONTROLLER

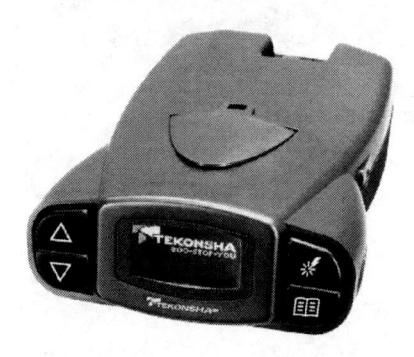

TRAVEL TRAILER (BALL TYPE) HITCHES

When towing a travel trailer, you will need to decide what type of hitch will best serve your unit, providing you the safest and most comfortable ride. There are two basic types of hitches to choose from: 1) conventional weight-carrying hitches; and 2) weight-distributing hitches. Whichever type you choose, the tongue weight should be approximately 10-12% of the trailer's actual gross weight. Higher weights will place greater demands on your tow vehicle and reduce towing performance. To figure hitch weight percentage, divide the measured hitch weight by the total weight of your trailer (including the hitch weight) and multiply by 100 to provide a percentage reading. For example, if the measured hitch weight is 500 lbs. and your trailer weighs 3,500 pounds, the hitch weight percentage would be 12.5%. Note that in some cases the hitch will have different ratings depending on whether it is used as a weight-carrying or weight-distributing type hitch. Read the entire manufacturer's literature very carefully. Hitches may be either bolted or welded to the vehicle frame. Care must be exercised when welding as there is a possibility that the heat from welding can weaken the attaching structure. An advantage of the bolt-on model is that it is easily removed for transfer to another vehicle. Be sure to observe any limitations established by the tow vehicle (chassis) manufacturer regarding drilling into structural components. Always use the proper grade attaching hardware, and torque all fasteners to specifications.

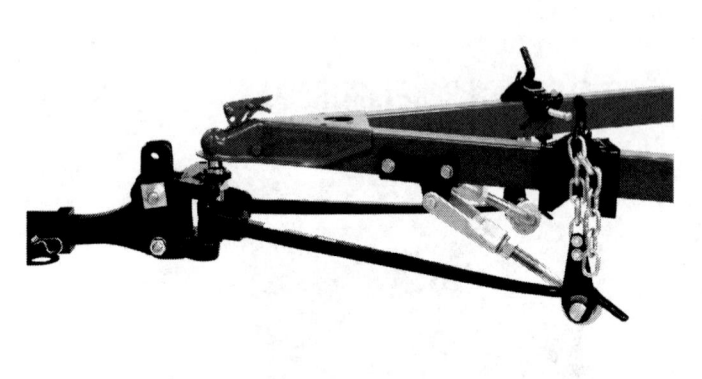

Photo courtesy of Cequent Towing Products.

Weight-Carrying:
Weight-carrying hitches are generally used for towing lighter trailers weighing a maximum of 3,500 lbs. With this type hitch, the tow vehicle's rear axle and tires must carry the normal weight of the truck and its contents, the trailer tongue weight, plus any weight that is shifted from the front axle to the rear due to the change in attitude of the vehicle. This may result in steering and braking difficulties as well as tire overloads if the weight is excessive. In addition, it may adversely affect headlight aiming. These limiting factors are normally easily resolved by switching to a weight-distributing hitch.

Weight-Distributing:
There are currently two basic types of weight-distributing hitches on the market today: with spring bars or without. The purpose of this type of hitch is to distribute the tongue weight of the trailer to both the front and rear of the tow vehicle. This is done to ensure a smoother, safer ride while avoiding the possibility of overloading the rear of the tow truck. Both systems are commonly used with a separate sway-control device.

Spring-Bar Models:
Spring bars are rated for weight capacity. Select spring bars that are rated for the actual tongue weight of the trailer, or slightly higher. The concept of this design is that when the spring bars are placed in tension, a portion of the tongue weight is shifted from the rear wheels of the tow vehicle to the front wheels, as well as aft on the trailer. If the bars are set with too much tension, they can cause a loss of rear wheel traction on wet or slippery surfaces, especially during braking, accompanied by a harsh ride. If torsion bars are set with too little tension, towing performance (stability) will likely be unsatisfactory. Note: Should you "jack-knife" your rig with the spring bars in place, the bars and brackets may distort and could possibly strike and damage your tow vehicle. The spring bars utilized for a large trailer can be very difficult to attach, with the result that many RVers do not compress them fully. The spring bars must be fully preloaded to provide the proper weight distribution. The procedure of using the tongue jack to raise the

trailer tongue (and rear of the truck) will ease the process of installing the spring bars. The use of a leverage bar will greatly assist the RVer in maintaining control while installing spring bars. Use caution during this entire procedure to prevent personal injury.

Non-Spring Bar Models:
This newer hitch design concept eliminates the use of the spring bars. In their place, it utilizes springs contained within the hitch system itself. In addition to distributing tongue weight, the spring action controls the upward and downward movement of the hitch, optimizes ride quality and decreases the tendency to jack-knife during an aggressive braking situation. After initial setup, you simply back into position and insert a pin to complete hookup making this type hitch very easy to use.

Hitch Adjustments:
Your travel trailer hitch has two basic adjustments to accommodate a variety of trailers and tow vehicles. The first is the height of the hitch. This is accomplished with the series of vertical holes where the two hitch pieces bolt together. This adjustment should be made initially to achieve an approximately a level trailer (with the spring bars installed) when fully loaded for travel. The second adjustment is the torsion bars (or spring towers) and is designed to transfer some of the tongue weight to the front axle of the tow vehicle. On some hitch designs, there is a third adjustment: the angle of the ball. This adjustment is designed to provide clearance for the coupler to move fully through its travel without binding on the ball shank. The angle adjustment is generally accomplished with a locking plate on one or both sides of the ball mount, which is keyed into one of several positions. Note that the two primary adjustments work together, so it may be necessary to "fine tune" them back and forth when first setting up your trailer for towing. As soon as possible, have the truck/trailer fully weighed wheel-by-wheel to assure that there is correct (even) distribution of weight between axles of the trailer and that there is proper weight transfer to the front wheels of the tow vehicle.

Sway Controls:
The use of a sway-control device is not a requirement for safe towing, but is a very common choice by RVers. A good sway-control system will make your travels much more pleasurable by minimizing the sway encountered when a truck passes, when crosswinds attack and if you happen to drop a wheel off the shoulder. If you choose to use a sway-control device, there are various types from which to choose.

Friction Activated:
Activated by the turning (sway) motion of the two vehicles, a friction bar will slide in and out of a tight-fitting (adjustable) friction surface. Whenever an angle (relative movement) occurs between the tow vehicle and the trailer, such as in turning, encountering a crosswind or swaying from varying road conditions, the movement of the trailer will be resisted by the internal friction of the sway bar. When using this type sway-control device, tighten the friction control until you notice that the tow vehicle will not quite straighten out after a sharp turn even at a slow speed. At that point, loosen the control slightly, and then fine-tune based on your towing preferences. Friction sway-control devices contain wearing components;, so they require ongoing adjustment to remain effective, as well as an occasional overhaul or replacement.

Cam Sway-Control Devices:
For larger trailers with heavy tongue weights, dual cam-sway controls are normally a better, more effective choice. The action of the cam is applied to the spring bars of the trailer to reduce sway and adjust weight distribution. To adjust this type of control, you will need to drive your tow vehicle and trailer directly at a fixed object, lining both vehicles up perfectly with no angle at the hitch. At this point, the sway control brackets should be centered over the friction cams. If not, loosen the hold-down bolts and move them forward or back as necessary. This sway control system does not rely on friction, so there is no wear or further adjustment required.

Electronic Sway-Control Systems:
Electronic sway-control systems electronically sense trailer sway and use the brake controller to apply trailer brakes asymmetrically to offset trailer sway. This is a very effective sway-control system at the expense of system complexity and a small amount of additional trailer brake wear.

An experienced RV dealer or hitch installer is one of your best resources to help you understand how to properly hook up and how to make required adjustments. Remember that fine-tuning of the hitch setup will be necessary based on the towing performance you experience on your first trips. There are many experienced RVers who are able and eager to help you with the learning process. Refer to Book 1 to determine how weight distribution is actually affected by your hitch setup.

Hooking Up Conventional Trailers

- When hooking up with spring-bar type weight distributing hitches, be aware that the spring tension is substantial and can cause serious injury if proper procedures are not followed. Place the spring bars into the operating position with a leverage bar, if required. Many RVers find it helpful first to use the hitch jack to raise the trailer tongue, minimizing the effort required to set the chain links into their cradle.
- Open the coupler and raise the trailer tongue to the level required by your tow vehicle. Set aside the electrical connection and breakaway cable to prevent damage.
- Get assistance to aid in positioning the tow vehicle. Have someone guide you while backing and hooking up. Verify what hand signals will be used in this process. The use of small handheld CB radios (or small family radio transceivers) makes the job much easier and safer.
- Slowly back the tow vehicle until the ball is directly under the trailer coupling.
- Lower the trailer coupler onto the ball by lowering the tongue jack. Secure and lock the coupler when the trailer weight rests fully on the tow vehicle.
- Fully raise the trailer tongue jack.
- Attach the electric cord and breakaway cable and safety chains. Test for proper operation of taillights, turn signals (front and rear) and brake lights.
- Remove wheel chocks or locks, and raise all corner jacks.
- Disconnect shore power, lower TV antenna and any other shore connections present.
- Check mirror adjustment and coverage area before driving.

Hooking Up a 5th Wheel Trailer

- When hooking up and unhooking your 5th wheel, be sure to place blocks under the front and rear of the trailer wheels so the trailer is unable to move on its own.
- Lower the tow vehicle's tailgate, if equipped.
- Raise the front of the trailer until the king pin box plate is slightly lower than the 5th wheel hitch plate. "High" hookup (having the king pin box plate above the hitch plate) can result in damage to the system and false hookups. Ideally, the trailer will be lifted slightly as you hook up.
- Remove the coupler lock pin.
- Back the tow vehicle slowly until the king pin rests in the coupler slot. The king pin will engage the latch plate, locking the hitch; you will hear this coupling audibly and should visually verify that it is locked in place.
- Set the parking brake on your tow vehicle.
- Check to ensure the king pin is locked in place.
- Replace the locking pin.
- Connect the breakaway system & electrical cables.
- Raise and secure the tailgate (if equipped).
- Remove the blocks or locks from the wheels.
- Raise the trailer jacks to their full-retracted position.
- Make sure your lights are working properly. Check the brake lights as well as the turn signals before towing.
- Disconnect shore power and any other shore connections, lower TV or satellite antenna and retract steps.
- Check mirror adjustment and coverage area before driving.

5TH WHEEL RECREATIONAL VEHICLE TRAILERS

As a general rule, 5th wheel trailers are considered more stable and easier to handle than conventional travel trailers because much of the trailer weight is carried directly by the tow vehicle's rear axle. The hitch itself (considered a weight-carrying hitch) is rigidly installed in the bed of a truck, slightly forward of the rear axle, and carries approximately 20-25% of the trailer weight. A "king pin" easily and firmly connects the two vehicles for towing. The hitches will either have the platform bolted directly to the tow vehicle frame, or they may be installed on rails allowing the hitch to be moved forward or backward in the bed of the truck. The rails are firmly bolted directly to the vehicle frame. When installing the hitch, consider the height of the trailer overhang section of the trailer. There should be a minimum of 5 ½" clearance in most cases. When choosing your tow vehicle, note that many short wheelbase vehicles may not permit the hitch to be installed in the ideal location due to limited cab clearance with the 5th wheel overhang when turning. If needed, you can purchase a 5th wheel hitch that unlocks and slides aft for tight turning maneuvers when you are at very low speed such as in a campground backing into a spot. Unlike all other methods of towing, safety chains are not required. 5th wheel trailers come equipped with wiring for lights and a brake actuating breakaway switch installed. There are several types of 5th wheel hitches commonly used in the RV industry today:

Standard Hitch:
The standard hitch design contains a platform that can tilt fore and aft only to accommodate rises and dips in the road and while unhooking and hooking up. This is the basic no-frills hitch design and is commonly used today.

Full-Floating Hitch:
The full-floating hitch design has gimbals (pivot points) that allow the platform to tilt not only fore and aft, but also from side-to-side. The benefit of this feature is that twisting forces are eliminated, reducing stress in the hitch and trailer tongue as the trailer rocks independently of the tow vehicle and vice versa.

Air Suspension:
Air suspension 5th wheel hitch designs typically place a full-floating platform onto a pivoting framework that is suspended on small airbags. The presence of the airbags cushions the vertical shock loads that are transmitted between the tow vehicle and trailer. The result is an enhancement of the ride quality for both vehicles and a minimizing of potential vehicle damage. Some large trailer manufacturers actually require an air suspension hitch when their trailers are towed with a medium duty truck. This is to prevent shock damage to the pin box and structural support of the trailer that can occur when large lightly loaded trucks are used as tow vehicles. To operate these systems requires a source of air pressure, adding to their cost when the tow truck is not already equipped with an onboard compressor. As an added benefit, the air suspension hitch can be easily adjusted for trailer ride height by simply adjusting the air pressure. Air suspension hitches are gaining popularity for large 5th wheel trailers and are now being manufactured for pickups as well as medium-duty trucks.

Hitch Adjustments:
Your 5th wheel hitch has two basic adjustments to accommodate a variety of trailers. The first is the positioning of the hitch in the bed of the tow truck. It should be located slightly ahead of the axle centerline to allow a very small amount of weight to be added to the front axle of the truck when towing. In most cases, it is not suggested that weight be removed from the front axle of the tow truck to assure proper steering control, braking power, front-end alignment and to keep the headlights oriented correctly. The second adjustment is height. The hitch and/or the pin box of the 5th wheel trailer may be adjustable. This adjustment should be made initially to achieve a level trailer when fully loaded for travel. When possible, have the trailer weighed wheel-by-wheel to assure that there is correct (even) distribution of weight between axles of the trailer. Note that, in some cases with a "high" tow truck, it may be necessary to raise the trailer on its suspension to achieve a level trailer attitude.

SAFETY TIPS & CONSIDERATIONS FOR RV TRAILERS

- When hooking up and unhooking your trailer, be sure to place blocks under both the front and rear of the trailer wheels so the trailer is unable to move on its own. You certainly do not want to endanger anyone or anything in the area by a runaway trailer.

- Have someone guide you while backing and hooking up. Verify what hand signals will be used in this process. The use of small handheld CB radios (or small family radio transceivers) makes the job much easier and safer.

- Check your safety chains to be sure they are properly attached. They should be crossed in an "X" pattern between the tow vehicle and the trailer without dragging the ground, even while turning. This allows the trailer to corner properly and will help the trailer to follow the tow vehicle should your hitch fail.

- Make certain that the ball is the correct size for the trailer coupler that you are using and that it is adjusted for a proper fit. Secure and lock it in place with a padlock or a pin designed for this application to prevent the coupler lever from unlocking.

- Attach the electrical cable and check the function of all taillights, brake and turn signals (front and rear) on both vehicles.

- Make sure your jack is fully raised.

- Inspect your hitch and trailer tongue area for cracked welds and damaged, missing or worn pins. Ensure that all hardware is properly secured.

- Check all connection points for rusting and weld cracks.

- Load your trailer carefully. Distribute the load as evenly as possible, retaining the original balance of the trailer.

- Check for cracks in welds and loose or missing bolts. Fix, replace or tighten all hardware before attempting to tow.

- Be certain that your mirrors will provide a full view of all critical areas behind and along the side of your combined rig.

- Tire pressure is always important, but even more so with larger trailers such as a 5th wheel. Always check this before towing and periodically during your trip. Refer to Book 2.

- Consider the usage of an electronic tire pressure monitoring system for the trailer wheels. Such systems can greatly increase your safety by giving an early alert to a tire problem. Often the driver is very isolated from the trailer, preventing first-hand knowledge of what is occurring behind. Refer to Book 2.

SUMMARY

There is a lot of information and detail that is incumbent when an RVer decides to tow, yet most RVers have made the decision to tow something. After completing Book 7, you should have a much better feel for the primary issues involved. All we need do to assure safe travels is to apply that information to our daily RV lives. Be sure to share your knowledge on the subject with fellow RVers who may not have researched and studied the subject to the same degree prior to embarking on their RVing life.

BOOK 8: FIRE & LIFE SAFETY

CONTENTS

Author's Foreword 151
What's It All About? 151

FIRE BASICS — 152
A Lesson in Observation-the Witness Mark 152
The Four Elements of Fire 153
Putting the Pieces Together 154
Types of Fires 155

COMMON RV FIRE HAZARDS — 156
Identifying and Eliminating RV Fire Hazards 156
The RV Chassis 156
The RV Living Quarters 159
Lifestyle Issues 160
Summary of Common Fire Threats 161

YOUR PERSONAL PLAN OF ACTION — 162
Plan of Action Checklist 162
Escaping an RV Fire 163
An RV Fire Discussion 165

RV FIRE EXTINGUISHERS — 166
Types of Fire Extinguishers 167
Selecting the Best Portable Fire Extinguisher for Your RV 168
Know Your Fire Extinguisher Before You Need It! 169

FIGHTING AN RV FIRE — 170
PASS 170

FIRE EXTINGUISHER MAINTENANCE — 171

LIFE SAFETY MEASURES — 172
Summary 172

Book 8: Fire & Life Safety

AUTHOR'S FOREWORD

Fire and life safety is an integral part of *The RVer's Ultimate Survival Guide* because many, if not all, aspects of the RV lifestyle carry with them the potential of fire. Certainly nothing is more frightening to contemplate than a fire in our RV. Whether it's driving down the highway or barbecuing our dinner on the grill, we are dealing with components, materials and activities that, if not carefully monitored and controlled, could present a fire hazard. When you combine all of the aspects of RVing life and consider all of the potential ramifications of the equipment utilized in our RVs e.g. the propane system; 12 VDC, 120 VAC electrical systems; automotive fuel (gasoline or diesel); and heavily loaded vehicles working at their maximum at all times, we begin to recognize that the potential for fire exists. *The RVer's Ultimate Survival Guide* provides individual books on each of these subjects, covering the specifics in some depth. This book ties much of that information together with a focus on the fire hazards presented and how to handle such an occurrence in your RV.

WHAT'S IT ALL ABOUT?

Much of what you have learned thus far in *The RVer's Ultimate Survival Guide* has discussed mechanical systems, components, materials and operational issues that can lead to fire in your RV if misused or mishandled. Indeed, fire is a terrifying thought within the tight confines of an RV. Fire is one of those potentialities in life that few of us ever have the need to face "up close and personal." For continuing safe RVing, a study of the whole subject of fire safety and repetition of that material is essential for RVers and others onboard the RV.

If we are going to continue the RVing lifestyle in comfort and safety, it is essential that we immediately begin the process of fireproofing our lives and our vehicles.

The fireproofing process is not as intimidating as it would first appear. What is required is an understanding of the hazards around us and the creation of a plan designed to put into action what you will learn in this book. Combined with a constant diligence in maintaining our vehicle in a safe condition and operating it within its limitations, this knowledge could save your life. What better reason is there to get comfortable and get busy now?

> "...many, if not all, aspects of the RV lifestyle carry with them the potential of fire. Certainly nothing is more frightening to contemplate than a fire in our RV."

RVers' Ultimate Survival Guide

FIRE BASICS
A LESSON IN OBSERVATION--THE "WITNESS MARK"

As we travel the highways in our RVs, enjoying all the wonderful beauty that this country and lifestyle have to offer, we must constantly remind ourselves that the world is also filled with hazards. Occasionally, we come upon an accident or some other incident on the highway that serves to remind us (ever so briefly) that, indeed, we must keep up our guard lest such misfortune also befall us. Some of those lessons are obvious, while others are much more subtle. All should be taken fully to heart.

Sometimes an object is damaged by a direct physical action; e.g., the scratch left in the paint when we travel too close to the tree branches or when our clothes are torn or stretched when we walk too close to a nail in a wall. That scratch or tear is a "witness mark" to the action that caused it. As we look around, we are constantly reminded by "witness marks" of the hazards and conditions that can render damage to our body or property, and we are intuitively warned to take caution. When driving, much of what we routinely observe is a "witness mark" provoking similar caution. The roadway itself can often bear evidence of the serious consequences that are potentially lurking, waiting to victimize the unsuspecting motorist. No "witness marks" are more important than the vehicle burn marks found along the shoulders of roadways. Highways with as many as two or three fire "Witness Marks" per mile are not uncommon in the hotter western states while virtually all highways have a surprising quantity of such reminders. Get in the habit of noting the roadside burn marks, as they are vivid reminders of the hazards confronting motorists from fire. When observed, take just a moment to reflect that someone, perhaps a fellow RVer, saw his happiness to be "on the road" dashed at that very location. Recognize also that there are many more possible causes of vehicle fires in RVs than one would anticipate. With their tremendous complexity and extreme operating environment, RVs are seriously threatened by fire, which, once ignited, will leave the very same "witness mark" or burn patch alongside the roadway for others to observe and wonder as to its cause and consequences.

As you travel the highways, in particular, the Western highways with high mountains and difficult extremes of temperatures, you should make it a point to note and count the vehicle fire "witness marks." Those observations should then serve as a perfect reminder of the day-to-day hazards facing each of us. Take those somber moments to renew your personal conviction to avoid all possible fire hazards in your RVing life.

A tragic end to a wonderful vacation.

THE FOUR ELEMENTS OF FIRE

Fire Is a Necessity of Life
Without fire, life would not exist as we know it today. Many movies depict the importance of fire to primitive and modern mankind by illustrating the quest of early man to obtain and control fire. Today fire is ever more useful--even essential in our lives. In the furnace, it keeps our RVs warm in cooler weather. In our stoves, it cooks our food and heats our water, and in our refrigerators, it keeps our food cold. In campgrounds, it gives us heat, light and comfort. All of these positive uses of fire are possible because the fire in each case is carefully controlled. A controlled fire is one that starts, stops and burns at a rate that is appropriate for our usage. It is only when fire gets out of control that it is dangerous--very dangerous. Each year there are approximately 20,000 uncontrolled RV fires, destroying about 6,300 RVs and killing approximately 20 RVers. If you understand how fire works, you will be able to protect yourself better from its dangers.

In order for fire to occur, four elements must be present. If any one or more of these four basic components is missing, a fire will not burn.

Fuel
The first essential element of fire is fuel. Quite simply, fuel must be present for fire to exist. Combustible material (wood, paper, cloth, gas, oils, and fiberglass) constitutes fuel for a fire. Most everything on or in our RVs is class "A" combustible material. It is well-known that liquid or solid materials generally do not burn until they become a gas (vapor). The wax of a candle is an excellent illustration of this phenomenon. The wax does not burn while it is a solid, but, when it melts, and then vaporizes initially by the match, and then by the candle flame itself, it burns quite well, giving off heat, light and noxious fumes. Note that some familiar materials commonly thought to be nonflammable can become combustible if adequate heat is applied. You will read later in this text that even antifreeze, a liquid used to cool our engines, can be heated to the point that it can become the fuel for a fire. The amount of heat required to make materials combustible varies immensely. Consider for a moment that we all know that motor fuels (gasoline and diesel) are combustible. While that is generally true, what is not so readily apparent is that the diesel fuel (liquid) must be heated to approximately 150ºF before the fumes (vapor) can burn. In contrast, gasoline will vaporize at room temperatures creating a combustible vapor at normally encountered temperatures. Thus, gasoline poses a greater fire threat than does diesel fuel. Book 3 covers this subject in some depth.

Oxygen
The basic definition of burning is the oxidation of a material. The source of the oxygen to complete that process generally comes from air that has an oxygen content between 17% and 21%. Other sources of oxygen are possible; i.e., an oxyacetylene torch provides its own oxygen in a separate gas mixed at the tip; thus, it will burn in the absence of air, even underwater. Other materials can also provide their own source of oxygen when burned, so they are capable of sustaining the combustion process even without air. Magnesium (a solid metal) is an example of this material. Because of this quality, some fires cannot be extinguished by eliminating the source of air (smothering). In these cases, a different firefighting technique must be utilized.

Heat
Heat is also a basic component of a fire. It is the heat that raises the temperature of the fire's fuel to the degree that it produces a combustible gas. Some materials require very little heat while others require a great deal of external heat adequate to produce fire. The RV's brakes, the engine, the exhaust system and its gases, and the transmission are all common sources of heat in an RV. Obviously, any open flame such as exists in our refrigerator, water heater, furnaces, stoves, etc. can also provide adequate heat to initiate, promote or perpetuate a fire in our RVs.

Heat is not only a product of fire, it is also the mechanism that spreads the fire. There are three basic heat distribution methods that come into play in spreading a fire. The first and most obvious mechanism is "convection." The best illustration of this principle is the heat rising from a burn barrel in which the rapidly rising smoke and gases carry with it burning embers and ash, which can quickly ignite combustible material wherever it falls. At the same time, "conduction" is at work by heating the barrel itself. When it reaches an adequate temperature, you will observe that combustibles in contact with the barrel, but away from the actual flames (such as dried grass around the barrel base), will burst into flames. The final heat transfer mechanism is "radiation." In its simplest terms, we know that any material at an elevated temperature will "radiate" heat. This is how our radiant bathroom heaters operate: The element is superheated with electricity, gas or catalytic action to a very high temperature, and the heat contained in the element is then transferred to other items (people) in the area. Radiant heat can be directed or reflected by the use of a polished or reflective surface to focus the heat. All this is very useful in the bathroom, but in an RV fire the radiated heat in one area can heat another area to the degree that the remote area will spontaneously combust (burn).

Chemical Chain Reaction

A fire also requires a chemical chain reaction in order to continue burning. It is the chemical change in the material (fuel) that continues the process until the fuel is fully consumed or the source of oxygen is depleted. The process of manufacturing charcoal, such as used in our barbecues, illustrates this chemical reaction. In this process, a hardwood is heated to a very high temperature in the absence of air (oxygen) until the chemical reaction within the wood leaves only concentrated combustible materials, which can then be readily ignited in our barbecues and used for cooking. In RVs, batteries can also provide a chemical action to produce both heat and a source of combustible material (explosive vapors).

PUTTING THE PIECES TOGETHER

In order for fire to occur, four elements must be present. If any one or more of these four basic components is missing, a fire cannot burn.

FIRE TETRAHEDRON

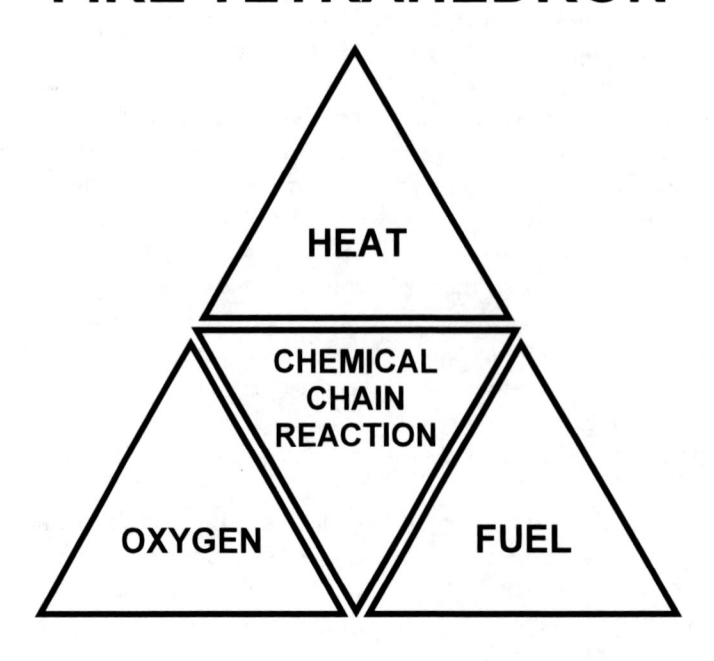

TYPES OF FIRES

There are various fire types (classes) that have been defined by fire prevention personnel, all of which might be encountered in an RV. Since the type of fire you confront dictates the type of fire extinguisher to use, this is a very important topic. To illustrate the importance of this, consider, for example, if you spray water onto a grease fire in the kitchen, the water will cause the grease to splatter, and the fire will likely spread. If you put water onto electrical equipment that is on fire, you will be in danger of severe electrical shock. Some types of fires may be successfully fought with differing types of fire extinguishers, and with varying levels of success. Depending on their intended use, a variety of fire extinguishing agents are often readily available for putting out a fire. Fire extinguishers are divided into classifications based on what types of materials they are suitable for. This makes an understanding of the common fire classification system very important. The most common classes are "A," "B" and "C." Following is a discussion of what each class includes in a typical RV.

RV Material Fire Classifications

- Class "A" combustibles consist of the ordinary products and materials around the RV that will leave ash when they burn. In an RV, the fiberglass used for insulation and skin construction, cloth utilized in the interior of RVs for curtains, upholstery and bedding, wood used in the construction of cabinets and furniture, the tires, and the RV's 12-volt electrical system components and insulation are all examples of class "A"-type combustibles. The vast majority of the material used to construct an RV is class "A" and will leave an ash when consumed by a fire.

- Class "B" combustibles are the liquids onboard your RV. Gasoline or diesel fuel, and propane while contained within its pressurized tank, are common examples of class "B" combustibles. Gases such as propane (after it has passed through the regulator) used for cooking, cooling, heating and barbecue grills are also a class "B" combustible. There are other materials commonly found onboard an RV that can also fall into this category. Common cleaning fluid, lighter fluid, cooking oils and even the liquid candle fuel that adorns our tables also falls into this category of combustible material.

- Class "C" combustibles are energized 120 VAC electrical equipment. This is probably the most misunderstood type of combustible material. The 120 VAC wiring, fuse boxes, circuit breakers, 120 VAC electrical machinery, TVs, appliances, shore power, generator power, inverters and battery chargers are all examples of class "C" combustible materials. Note that when you de-energize the source of a class "C" fire (unplug or disconnect), it then becomes a class "A" or "B" combustible material. Note also that an inverter and a generator are particularly important considerations because they can provide a 120 VAC source even with the RV fully disconnected and isolated from a shore-power 120 VAC source.

What You See and What You Don't

When the four elements of fire are available and come together in the proper proportions, they combine to make fire and produce heat, light, smoke and various gases. When sitting around a campfire, it is possible to feel the heat that fire produces. In addition, you can see the light and the smoke, and you may get a sense of the gases developing even though you may not actually see the hot gases that are rising above the fire. The gases produced in a fire are generally invisible but can be poisonous or toxic.

When a fire starts in an RV, the ceiling of the RV traps hot gases and the smoke. Because our RVs are generally much smaller than our traditional homes or apartments, it requires much less time for smoke and gases to accumulate to dangerous levels. Should a fire originate while you are sleeping, the poisonous gases may concentrate and potentially kill even before waking you. Smoke and hot gases make it hard to breathe and see, but perhaps even more insidious, they may cause you to become confused and incapable of clear thought, making your escape more difficult or impossible. Smoke and gases produced from a fire are so dangerous that it is essential that you flee from the fire immediately, even if you do not see flames. You may not get a second chance.

COMMON RV FIRE HAZARDS
IDENTIFYING AND ELIMINATING RV FIRE HAZARDS

The recognition of common causes of RV fires is the first vital step in preventing a fire in your RV. The recognition of fire hazards goes a long way towards assuring your escape should your RV suffer a fire. A monthly fire safety inspection may provide a timely warning permitting you to respond to potential fire hazards in your rig. Your understanding of potential fire hazards is also helpful in preventing fires in other RVs. Since RVs are generally parked in close proximity at rallies and RV parks, any fire affecting a neighboring RV can affect yours as well.

While it may seem that the whole world is filled with hazards, the truth is that there is actually a relatively limited quantity of issues that we must address. If we prioritize those issues, it is possible to get through the list quite expeditiously. The first step is the hardest: getting started. There is no time like the present.

THE RV CHASSIS

Overheated Engine/Transmission
A hard-working RV engine will operate at a temperature of over 200° F. This is normal and not a problem to an engine, but other parts of the engine get as hot as 350° F, and the exhaust manifolds may actually reach 1200-1500°F when used hard. A turbocharger (if present) or the catalytic converter will also operate at extreme temperatures--often over 1000°F. The tight confines of the engine compartment and the use of heavy insulation in that compartment reflect much of that heat back onto the engine, easily allowing a fire to break out if any combustible material is present. It is necessary to check this area for foreign material or debris that can blow in or be carried in by "critters." With the current design of many motor coaches, getting to the top of the engine is often very difficult. This will make keeping the area clean and free of debris much more difficult and may result in problems in putting out a fire that might result from these conditions. Never keep a rag "tucked" into the engine compartment to ease checking the engine/transmission oil. The oil-soaked rag in this area is a very serious potential fire threat.

Having the proper engine/transmission gauges can warn the driver of a potential problem that could result in abnormally high operating temperatures. With gas-powered vehicles (either a motorhome or pickup), a transmission temperature gauge, vacuum gauge, tachometer and oil temperature gauge can head off many problems with engine or transmission overheating. For a diesel pusher or puller motorhome or diesel-powered pickups, a pyrometer (exhaust temperature), transmission temperature gauge and a turbo boost gauge will keep you informed about how hard the engine and transmission are working. In many cases, added gauges such as these are necessities, not luxuries. It is also fairly well-known that any vehicle equipped with a catalytic exhaust converter must exercise extreme care when driving off-road. The presence of dry weeds and grass in contact with the exhaust system are very real fire risks. In a similar fashion, the exhaust system of an onboard generator may also present a similar hazard. It is highly recommended that all combustible material be removed from the proximity of the exhaust system.

Motor Fuels
Gasoline and propane motor fuels pose an obvious explosion and fire danger. Diesel fuel is the least volatile of the two fuels, but it also dissipates much more slowly, providing a longer-lasting fire hazard. Deal immediately with any leak or spill of any motor fuel and use them only for the purpose they are intended. As with so many fire hazards, the primary emphasis for motor fuel safety is diligence in the maintaining your RV. That maintenance, when combined with constant awareness on the part of the RVer, is what it takes to assure your safety. Recognize that your RV was designed and

built with great concern for its safety, and now it is up to you to maintain it properly. Once purchased and operated by an RVer, we assume that responsibility. Book 3 contains a full discussion of the very important topic of motor fuels.

Overheated Tires

Overheated tires are a common source of RV fires. A dragging brake can create enough friction to heat a tire or the brake fluid to a temperature adequate for self-ignition. Some of the most difficult fires to detect and fight are those caused when one tire of a dual pair goes flat, scuffs and ignites--often long before the driver becomes aware of the condition. The first warning of a problem may come when a passing automobile or truck gestures that something is wrong. To minimize this hazard, at each stop give tires a complete visual check and use the back of your hand to check for excessive temperature. Please consider that a tire pressure gauge reading on hot tires is not accurate. Pressure readings should be taken when tires are cold. For "hot" tires, it is possible to "tap" your tires with a club and listen for a difference in sound from one tire to the next, which can be interpreted as a significant difference in the pressure of the two tires. No matter how and when you identify that a tire is low, immediately take the time to find out what is causing the low pressure and correct the condition.

An effective proactive approach to prevent tire fires is to equip your RV with the latest generation of electronic tire pressure sensors (TPS). These devices reliably provide an ongoing real-time verification of the correct tire pressure--a fact that will greatly reduce the likelihood of a tire fire. Please consider also that to a tire under-inflation and overload are the same and carry the same dire consequences. Since there is only one correct pressure for any given load, a vehicle that is overloaded can create the conditions necessary for a tire to overheat, possibly to the point that a fire may occur. Consider also the ramification of the fact that many RV manufacturers route propane lines through the wheel wells of the RV. In this area, they are in harm's way should a tire problem exist. Whether it is a blown tire or one that is overheated, the existence of propane can make a bad situation much worse. Book 2 contains a full discussion of the very important topic of tires and their maintenance requirements.

Hot Brakes

Hot brakes represent yet another common RV fire hazard. Improper usage of brakes, particularly in mountainous terrain, can overheat brakes to the danger point. Similarly, brake malfunctions, that result in a "dragging" condition can also present a fire hazard due to the generation of excessive heat. Towing too large a trailer or towing an automobile not equipped with an auxiliary braking system means relying on the coach or tow vehicle's braking power to stop both vehicles. In many cases, this may not be adequate. Do not gamble with your safety. Make sure you have enough braking ability for the weight being towed. Stopping a combined vehicle with inadequate brakes will result in too much energy absorbed by the tow vehicle brakes resulting in excessive heat and rapid wear. Heat build-up in a drum brake can cause brake fade after only a few applications of the brakes. Disk brakes can dissipate the excessive heat much better, but are still subject to rapid wear, overheating, etc. When brakes fade, braking power is greatly diminished and stopping distance greatly increased. Trailer electromagnet drum brakes can retain heat often to the point of damage to the braking components. That damage combined with deterioration from rust, age, wear of the magnet, etc., may result in unequal braking and uneven wear within the brakes. When a trailer is two to three times as heavy as the puller, the result can be disastrous. For this and a multitude of other reasons, it is essential that RVers maintain their vehicles in excellent running condition. Recall at all times that an RV is essentially operated at 100% of its capability 100% of the time. No other segment of the automotive world even comes close to that reality. Your safety as an RVer is dependent upon an assurance that everything is operating correctly (as designed).

The braking system on your motorhome or truck/trailer type RV is probably the most critical safety system you have. It has the potential to fail to deliver adequate stopping ability and to cause or contribute to a fire onboard your coach. Your RV braking system demands proper usage and adequate preventive maintenance to assure your safety. Auxiliary braking equipment is readily available to upgrade RV braking systems. These devices come in a wide variety of components and are generally highly sought after by RVers. Upgrading braking systems must be done with great care and caution due to the nature of the equipment involved. When properly modified, auxiliary braking equipment can represent a major boost in safety and peace of mind. Book 6 (Driving) and Book 7 (Towing) present a full discussion of the very important topics of driving and towing along with the attendant driver requirements.

Engine Exhaust and Catalytic Converter
A hot engine or generator exhaust pipe or the vehicle's catalytic converter (if equipped) can ignite dry grass or debris under your RV. In particular, the catalytic converter can operate at temperatures in excess of 1500ºF under normal conditions. Under abnormal conditions e.g., excessive or prolonged engine idling, the temperatures can exceed those already dangerous levels. Partial plugging of the converter can also create the same excessive internal temperatures and thus represents a similar fire hazard. Do not leave your RV unattended while the engine or generator is running. If camping in dry grass, clear a three-foot circle down to bare ground around the exhaust tip, or use an up-pipe on the tip of your generator exhaust. You may also want to place a large container or jug of water near the exhaust outlet just in case of a small grass fire. Maintenance of these critical systems is urgent to assure your safe RVing.

Engine Accumulations
Grease, oil and road dust commonly build up on the engine and transmission. This is much more than just a housekeeping issue. Insulating those components makes them run much hotter than normal. While the grime itself may or may not readily burn, it can combine with a fuel leak, antifreeze, lubricant, power steering leak, or a short-circuited wire to provide fuel for a fire. Keeping your RV's undercarriage and engine clean will help it run cooler, more economically and longer.

Rubber Fuel Lines
Rubber fuel lines are commonly used to connect the various metal fuel lines and components used by the engine. Newer gasoline and diesel engines generally contain fuel return lines and added components to the fuel system, adding greatly to the complexity of the fuel system on those RVs. Each and every joint or connection in the fuel system is a potential leak. Regulations limit the total amount of rubber materials used in the fuel system because of the potential for leakage created by deterioration or damage to the rubber materials. During your monthly safety inspection, check all the lines and connections between the fuel tank and the engine. If there is any sign of a leak, have the lines replaced and the entire system inspected by a qualified RV mechanic as soon as possible.

Antifreeze
While most of us tend to think of engine antifreeze as a nonflammable material (after all, it is approximately 50% by volume of water), it is possible for it to catch fire and burn. Thus, it is a somewhat common source of RV fires. A pinhole leak in a radiator or heater hose can spray (atomize) antifreeze onto or near very hot engine parts. Antifreeze is comprised of concentrated ethylene glycol and water. When the water boils off, which it will do immediately, the remaining ethylene glycol is capable of self-ignition at 782º F. Many engine components (in particular, the exhaust manifolds during a long, hard pull) will easily exceed this temperature, providing the source of the heat required, to initiate the combustion process. During your monthly fire inspection, check all coolant hoses for firmness, clamp tightness and signs of leakage. Remember that the cooling system contains many rubber components that have a relatively short life even if used infrequently such as in an RV. Rubber coolant components should be changed as a precaution after approximately a 3-4-year life. Note also that silicone rubber components have a much greater heat tolerance and longer life making it a desirable material to use when replacing hoses, etc. Inspect your radiator frequently, and have it repaired by a qualified person as soon as possible if any discrepancy is noted. Caution is required when working with "hot" coolant lines because the entire system operates under pressure. Pressure is used to raise the boiling point of the coolant, keeping the cooling system working at temperatures well above the boiling point of water.

THE RV LIVING QUARTERS

Cooking Stoves
Galley stoves must not be left unattended. Should the flame go out for any reason, propane gas will continue to flow and accumulate until it could result in an explosion. Cooking stoves are not vented; thus it is necessary to open a window or vent while cooking to provide a source of fresh air. Also, for this reason, the cooking stove should never be used to heat your RV. Propane flames put out high levels of carbon monoxide and will quickly deplete your RV of oxygen. They are not designed for heating purposes and pose serious fire and asphyxiation hazards when they are used for a purpose for which they were not designed. Cooking stoves also operate with an open flame, making them vulnerable to igniting any combustible material in the area and even burning the RV's occupants.

Cooking Carelessness
When cooking in an RV, it is necessary to use greater caution than at home because in the compact RV galley combustible materials (paper towels, curtains and dish rags) are apt to be much closer to the stove than at home. Never cook with an open flame while traveling. Wear short or tight-fitting sleeves when you cook. Position the handles of pots and pans turned inward (away from the traffic) to prevent them from being knocked over or pulled down. If a grease fire should occur, the most effective action is to rapidly and carefully slide a metal lid over the pan to quickly smother the flames. It is recommended that a solid metal lid be kept close to the stove just for this eventuality. Similarly, a box of baking soda (the ingredient in dry-powder fire extinguishers) can be used in lieu of a fire extinguisher for minor galley flare-ups. Should a large stove fire occur, it should be treated as a major emergency by evacuating the area and then using an adequate fire extinguisher of the correct type to fight the fire.

Never use foil or other metals in a microwave oven. Also use caution when heating water and other liquids in a microwave. Even though they are extremely hot, they may not boil (bubble) in the microwave as they do on the stove. When removed from the microwave oven, the superheated liquid may explode (splatter) unexpectedly by placing a spoon or fork into the liquid. The result could be severe burns for the unwary cook.

Refrigerators
The refrigerator itself presents only minor fire risks; however, the propane that fuels it presents many potential fire hazards. See Book 4 for a full discussion of this very important RV safety topic. The primary fire safety concern is the result of using the refrigerator on propane while traveling. It is not essential to run your refrigerator or other propane appliances while you drive. Most units will keep food cold or frozen for many hours if they are left tightly closed. Driving with propane ON can add significantly to the potential fire danger if you are involved in an accident or experience a fire from any other source. Note: To fully protect yourself, it is necessary to shut off the propane at the tank (not at the appliance).

If you detect the smell of ammonia and have not recently used an ammonia cleaning product, it is likely that your refrigerator has a leak in its cooling unit. Concentrated ammonia gas can be very dangerous. Get out of the RV, leave the doors and windows open to ventilate the RV, and do not return until the problem has been repaired.

Batteries
RV and chassis batteries produce hydrogen gas as a by-product of converting their chemical energy into electrical energy and during its subsequent recharging operation. RVs, by virtue of their self-containment, often carry a large quantity of batteries and utilize high-powered battery-charging capability frequently. Hydrogen gas is flammable and, when concentrated in proper proportions, it is explosive. It is imperative to keep all flames, cigarettes and sparks (such as from jumper cable clamps or tools) away from batteries. Be sure your battery compartment is properly vented. Your RV should have been designed and built correctly by the manufacturer, recognizing the inherent hazards of these products; however, it is the responsibility of the RVer to assure that all safety features and vents are

retained and are fully functional. Always shield your eyes with quality safety glasses when working on or near batteries. Keep vent caps tight and the batteries level. This is especially important for lead-acid-type batteries, which contain liquid sulfuric acid. If, during your monthly safety check, you find the battery is leaking or swollen, replace it immediately. Use extreme care when handling batteries. They can explode. Keep batteries out of reach of children and vice versa. The stored electrical energy in batteries is significant. If a metal object is allowed to short across the battery terminals, a very hazardous condition immediately occurs. Initially, there may be heavy arcing and sparking as the contact is made, then the electrical energy will quickly heat the shorting object, possibly to red hot (depending upon the size of the item), all while the battery generates explosive hydrogen gas. This process provides all the ingredients for an explosion and fire accompanied with potential personal injury.

Electrical Problems
Electrical malfunctions, in particular 12 VDC problems, are probably the greatest potential source of fire in your RV. As a responsible RVer, consider, as a minimum, the purchase of an RV that has the RVIA seal (establishing stringent electrical standards), have any add-on wiring performed by (or checked by) a qualified electrician, and always use correct procedures and common sense when operating any electrical device. Check all accessible 12-volt connections before and after every trip. Recognize that low-voltage shorts (12 VDC) account for about 35 percent of reported RV fires. If an appliance smokes or has an unusual smell, unplug it immediately and replace it or have it repaired. Replace cracked or frayed electrical cords. Do not overload extension cords or run them under rugs. Do not tamper with the circuit breaker box or use improperly sized circuit breakers or fuses. Be sure that any appliance used in the RV is approved for RV use. Look for a tag saying the appliance is UL approved for RV and mobile home use, or check with the manufacturer or dealer. The use of a quality electrical monitoring system allows you to monitor the quality of the 120 VAC electrical power coming into your RV as well as that being produced onboard your RV with the inverter or generator. The good quality 120 VAC power is very important for the well-being of your electrical system and components. Book 5 provides a complete discussion of the various electrical systems utilized in your RV.

LIFESTYLE ISSUES

Damp Charcoal
Some of the fire hazards facing us as RVers occur outside the actual RV. For instance, many RVers carry a supply of charcoal for their BBQ grills. It is important to recognize that spontaneous combustion can occur in damp charcoal. To avoid this hazard, buy charcoal fresh, keep it dry and store it in a covered metal container. Do not forget that the rag we used to clean up the BBQ is also soaked with highly combustible food fat. Dispose of this waste to avoid any fire hazard. In a similar fashion, rags soiled with auto wax or cleaners that contain oil products or other petroleum-based cleaning materials can also spontaneously combust at a surprisingly low temperature, particularly if kept in a combustible container such as paper or a cardboard box. Store dirty cleaning rags in a metal container with a tight-fitting lid for safety. Probably the most obvious example of this is a rag that RVers use to wipe the engine or generator dipstick when the engine oil is checked. It is common to tuck that rag into a location close to the dipstick because it will be conveniently there the next time that we check our oil. That oil-contaminated rag in close proximity to the very hot engine components is an effective recipe for an engine fire.

Portable Heaters
Portable electric and liquid-fueled (Propane) heaters are very convenient and widely used in RVs; however, they need to be kept at least three feet from combustible material. In the tight confines of an RV, that requirement is not always fully satisfied, resulting in many RV fires. The tight confines of the RV often result in electrical heaters being knocked over or displaced allowing them to contact a combustible material--a fire is a likely result. Never leave portable heaters on when you leave your RV or go to bed. Keep all children and pets well away from portable heaters.

Remember that not all portable heaters are electrical. Some burn propane or kerosene or may be either a combustion or catalytic type. This type of heater requires an open window at all times. All of these heater types consume the oxygen in the air and are a source of carbon monoxide. While these are an excellent source of heat, they are safe only if operated correctly and kept clean and in good working condition. A portable heater of any type should also be equipped with an automatic shutoff device which will safely shut off the fuel supply should the heater be turned over.

Vehicle Storage

If you store your RV or park for extended periods of time, be certain to check the various flues and vents (actually, all openings) on your propane appliances before switching to operate on propane. Birds and insects commonly build nests and clog these openings. This can cause a fire hazard when used and the hot combustion gases come in contact with the debris. An additional hazard associated with the blocking of vents is that it may allow an excess of carbon monoxide (CO) to enter your RV creating a life-threatening hazard.

SUMMARY OF COMMON FIRE THREATS

What has been presented in the above listing of RV fire safety issues must be considered to be only a partial listing. This list has been compiled by experts based on a review of the most common causes of RV fires. It is entirely possible that there are many--perhaps hundreds--of additional potential fire hazards that we should be equally concerned with for our own safety.

There are common threads in the above discussion of potential causes of RV fires.

- The first is that your RV has been designed and fabricated using the best-proven technology currently available to provide a safe environment for our usage. As an RVer we can take some solace in that knowledge, but must also recognize that industry standards are not static. There are thousands of individuals working daily to improve the materials or processes that will further enhance our safety. Thus, it may be necessary to continue to upgrade our own RVs to maintain our vehicle in the "state of the art" safety condition.

- As an RV owner/operator, it is imperative to be always diligent as we use our vehicles. It is our personal awareness of our surrounding, our knowledge of the correct functioning of our vehicles and the environment around us that will give us early warning of an eminent safety issue.

- The best offsetting action for many of the discussed safety issues is the timely and proper maintenance of your RV. RV maintenance is not an easy matter. RVs are terribly complex vehicles. RVs travel extensively, routinely encountering ongoing vibration and shock, and quality RV maintenance is not as readily available as we might hope. Yet we must find the means to have our RVs inspected and repaired as required to assure our safe travels.

YOUR PERSONAL PLAN OF ACTION
PLAN OF ACTION CHECKLIST

Now that you recognize common fire hazards and, hopefully, have eliminated them, proceed to the next step--that of developing a safety plan of action specific to your needs. A personal plan of action is a proactive plan intended to help prevent serious injury should a fire occur and is essential to enhance your survival. Practicing your plan of action will further assure that it is appropriate and can be implemented quickly, fully and with maximum efficiency. For an effective plan, be sure to consider and include the following:

- Make certain that all occupants of your RV (including guests and especially children) know what the smoke, carbon monoxide and propane gas alarms sound like. They should also be thoroughly briefed as to what to do when they hear any of these critical alarms sound.

- Upon arrival at any new destination, verify what the local emergency phone number is (911 or 0) along with the address required for emergency vehicles to assist you. Adults and young travelers should be shown how to dial 911 or 0, and how to summon emergency help on the CB, VHF or ham radio (if available). It is crucial to know where your RV is located so firefighters can find you. Remember that 911 automatic locator systems currently do not work with most cell phone systems.

- Preplan to have at least two escape routes from your RV. One should be in the front of the RV and the other in the rear. As soon as RVing children are old enough, teach them to open doors, escape hatches and emergency window exits. If tools are needed, mount the tools on walls in the immediate vicinity of the escape hatch.

- Predetermine a rallying point safely away from the endangered RV where everyone will meet immediately after escaping. The immediate gathering at a predetermined location will allow a quick count of all persons present to verify a complete evacuation.

- Review with everyone the "Stop, Drop and Roll" rule so they know what to do should their clothing catch fire.

- Make sure visitors are briefed on opening the front door. Not all manufacturers use the same style lock and latch assembly, with the result that the opening procedures may differ significantly.

- Show family members and traveling guests how to unhook shoreline electricity (screw-on cords can be tricky and time consuming) and how to close the propane shut-off valve in case either of these measures is called for. Reiterate that personal safety takes precedence over those acts that are intended primarily to make it safer for others (including fire fighters) responding to the fire.

- Make sure family members and traveling companions know how to use the fire extinguishers and understand which extinguishers are effective on various types of fires. The P A S S method of using a portable fire extinguisher to fight a fire is discussed in depth later.

- Re-emphasize to everyone aboard that objects can be replaced, people cannot. Never stay behind or re-enter a burning RV to retrieve anything.

- Practice unhooking your tow vehicle as quickly as possible to avoid having the fire spread to a second vehicle. As a goal, you should strive to be able to unhook the vehicle in less than 15 seconds. To meet this very demanding performance standard will require considerable practice, and, in some cases, it will involve the use of special attachment hardware. Note also that in most cases the use of anti-theft locks of any type will preclude you from safely disconnecting in the available 15 seconds. Of course, as has been often repeated, saving property should not be attempted except where it can be accomplished with safety. No amount of property is worth personal injury or death.

Book 8: Fire & Life Safety **163**

ESCAPING AN RV FIRE

By "Mac the Fire Guy" McCoy

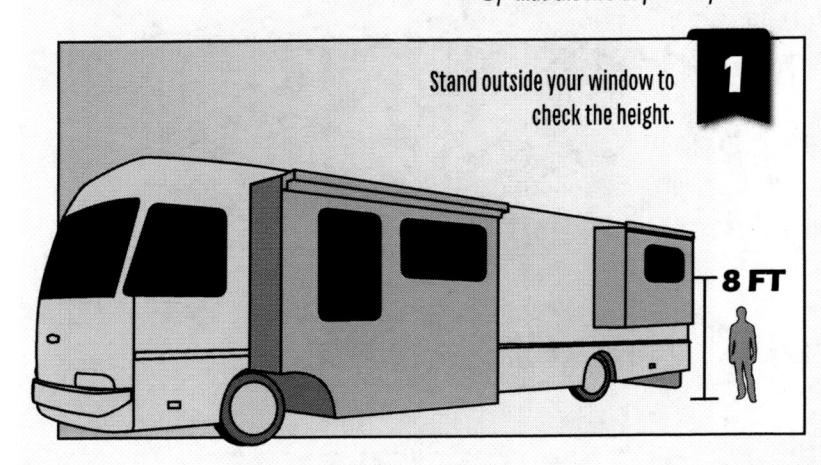

1 Stand outside your window to check the height.

8 FT

The first thing you need to do is stand outside your window to check the height. How far can you expect to drop? For the purpose of practicing, you might push the RV park's picnic table under the window.

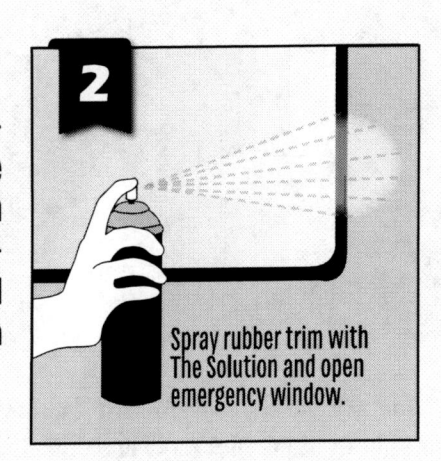

2 Spray rubber trim with The Solution and open emergency window.

Next, open your emergency window. If your window sticks or is difficult to open, try spraying the rubber trim with The Solution, a simple dry wash containing polymer wax, detergent and UV protectant. You can also use 303 Lubricant. This will make it open easily, and you will want to do this a couple times every year.

3 ← Use dowel stashed nearby to hold the window open.

The emergency window may be large and heavy. You will want to have a dowel stashed nearby to hold the window open. It would be quite difficult to slide through the window space with the weight of a heavy window hanging on top of you.

RVers' Ultimate Survival Guide

The window sills are metal, so throw a blanket over the edge, corner to corner, and use it for padding on the way out. The stronger person can hold one end of the blanket, letting the other use it to slide down. This blanket will also come in handy to cover up in inclement weather or if you are under-dressed.

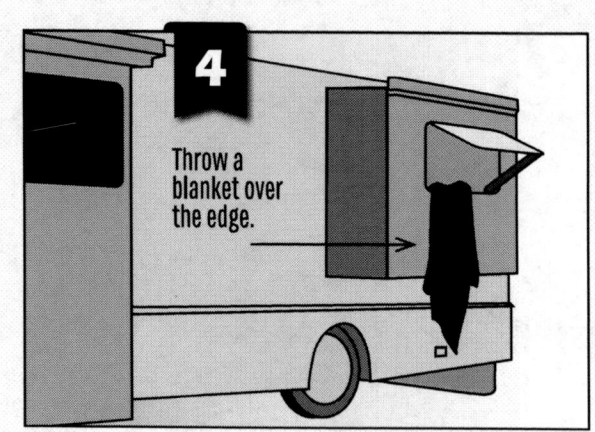

Throw a blanket over the edge.

Exiting through the RV window.

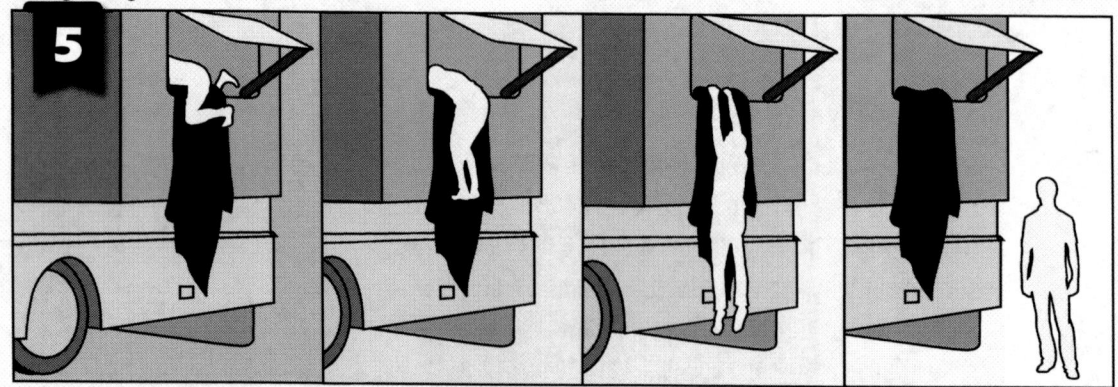

Getting out through the window can be difficult for some of us because we tend to lose upper body strength as we age.

It might be a good idea, if you are parked along the highway, to throw a flare out the window and a few feet away from the coach so cars and trucks will drive around you and you won't get run over while escaping. These flares are small and won't take up much room next to the bed.

How much preparation you can do will depend on your emergency situation. You may not have time to throw out a flare or even a blanket, but having a solid fire escape plan may help you replace panic with logical, life-saving actions if a fire occurs.

Mac McCoy has 35 years of fire safety experience, a BS degree in fire science, and a master's degree in fire administration. Mac has taught firefighting skills and techniques to RVers, military personnel, firefighters, and law enforcement, both in the United States and abroad.

AN RV FIRE DISCUSSION

A fire can hit your RV at any time and may come in a wide variety of ways. You may or may not be aware of smoke and gases before you see flames, while in other cases the smell or sight of flames may be your first indication of a problem. In other possible scenarios, your attention to a fire may come from a passing motorist, from a smoke alarm, a fire detector, or from an indirect indication such as from an amp meter or temperature gauge reading indicating that there might be a problem onboard the RV, and quite possibly, that problem is a fire.

A constant vigilance to anything awry is generally an RVer's best defense.

Once your smoke detector goes off or your awareness of fire galvanizes you into action, you may not have much time. Your best course of action is to get out of the RV immediately! Do not stop to take anything with you. Exit the RV at the nearest exit, which may be the main door or the escape hatch in the bedroom area. If the only way out is through accumulated smoke, crawl under the smoke on your hands and knees. Note that hot smoke and gases rise and will generally fill the RV from the top down, so by crawling on your hands and knees, you breathe the cleanest air available. That clean air may be only a few inches above the floor. It is essential that you breathe relatively clean air to prevent damage to your lungs and to assure clear thinking permitting you to focus on your escape from the burning RV.

After everyone has safely exited the RV and is a safe distance away (verified by head count), make sure the fire department has been called. If time permits, you have the opportunity and the equipment is available, there are some steps that you can take to minimize fire damage. Such actions should not be heroic or macho but may save invaluable personal effects and speed your personal recovery from what is certain to be a traumatic, if not cataclysmic, event.

Remember that the first rule of RV firefighting is to save lives first and property second.

Only if you can do so without endangering yourself or others should you use any firefighting aids on hand. Use your water supply hose and those available in the area to fight the fire and to protect anything in the immediate area that is threatened by the fire. If you equip your hose with a quick-disconnect fitting, they can be unhooked quickly and used to fight a fire. While you are in the area, disconnect the electric shore power cord or shut off the power to keep the fire from becoming a class III fire. If a nearby RV is burning and cannot be moved, it may be possible to safely stay close enough to keep your RV hosed down, saving it from major damage. Regretfully, in most cases, the best advice for your own safety is to wait for emergency assistance at least 1,000 feet upwind and uphill. Do not stand in the smoke as it is often toxic and is full of very deadly gases and fiberglass particles that can be harmful to your health.

It has become quite commonplace (and is required at some RV campgrounds and resorts) for the RVer to place an extra 50-foot hose alongside his/her RV for emergency usage. This firefighting hose is connected to the water faucet with a "splitter" device permitting it to be used even while the RV water hose is connected to a single water faucet hookup. This hose and those of others in the area are intended to provide immediate fire-fighting capability in the event of fire.

RVers' Ultimate Survival Guide

RV FIRE EXTINGUISHERS

The handheld portable fire extinguisher is the most common fire-protection device in use today. The National Fire Protection Association (NFPA 1192) requires a dry-powder extinguisher capable of putting out a 10-square-foot class "B-C" (10 "B-C") fire in all motorhomes and one that can extinguish a 5-square-foot class "B-C" (5 "B-C") fire in all other recreational vehicles. This is the minimum that is required by law, and virtually all manufacturers comply with this requirement. The placement of this fire-fighting equipment is also specified in that it is to be placed near the vehicle entrance. You will remember from earlier discussion that a class "B" fire involves liquids or gases and a class "C" fire involves energized 120-volt electrical equipment. The NFPA guidelines do not require that your extinguisher have a class "A" rating, which would make it effective in extinguishing fires involving materials, like wood and cloth that make up the bulk of the interior of your RV.

The NFPA-required minimum fire protection device in your RV might not be adequate for your protection and peace of mind!

Fire experts agree that it is possible and quite common that manufacturer-furnished NFPA-approved fire extinguishers will not be effective to fight fires in your RV. A check of your RV's extinguisher's markings will identify what materials it is designed to work on effectively. Ideally, you should have extinguishers with symbols for all three fire classes ("A," "B" or "C") on them; however, in order to get a multi-use ("A-B-C") dry-chemical extinguisher effective for even a small fire, you would have to purchase a large, heavy extinguisher, which may not be suitable for RVers. The primary reason for this limitation is that dry-powder extinguishers use baking soda that is dispersed by air pressure to smother a fire (preclude the presence of oxygen). It takes a large amount of dry powder to accomplish this even for a modest-size class "A" fire. The typical dry-chemical fire extinguisher also has the very serious consideration (potential limitation) of widely dispersing throughout the RV when used. What this means is that, when dry powder is used to successfully fight even a small fire, the cleanup is extensive and can be quite expensive due to this dispersal quality.

A dry-chemical fire extinguisher also has a monthly maintenance requirement that is commonly neglected in RV usage. The purpose of this maintenance is to assure that the powder is not tightly packed and that the pressure source is adequate to propel the powder when required.

Many RV dry powder fire extinguishers fail when called upon due to lack of maintenance.

What might be a better solution for many RVs is to supplement the factory-installed fire extinguisher with a non-corrosive "designer foam" extinguisher. This type extinguisher is effective on class "A" and class "B" fires, which combined include over 90% of all RV fires. "Designer foam" extinguishers are user-friendly, environmentally safe, compact, lightweight and convenient for RV travel. As a responsible RVer who is concerned about the safety of those onboard the RV and those around it, it is a wise precaution to supplement the minimal fire protection equipment provided with your RV.

One fire extinguisher is simply not enough for your RVing safety!

While the NFPA does not require that the manufacturer provide (or for you to carry) more than one fire extinguisher, the best advice available is "don't take chances." One fire extinguisher is simply not enough. Fire and life safety instructor Mac McCoy recommends having three extinguishers inside your coach. This also gives you the opportunity to equip your RV with extinguishers capable of fighting all classes ("A-B-C") of fires. Remember that class "B-C" extinguishers are non-conducting and can, therefore, be used for class "C" electrical fires. The best locations for these additional fire extinguishers are near the entrance, in the kitchen and in the bedroom. These recommended locations provide for the maximum interior protection and personal safety of the occupants. Two additional extinguishers should be located outside the RV--one in an unlocked outside compartment and the last in your towed or towing vehicle. This will provide the maximum protection for your RV (and those around you) along with peace of mind that you have done all that is possible to assure your own safety. Be sure to mark the location of extinguishers. A standardized marking system is with a large red arrow located at eye level and pointing to the extinguisher. This will save you valuable seconds in case of an emergency.

TYPES OF FIRE EXTINGUISHERS

It is vitally important that RV owners become knowledgeable about the different types of portable fire extinguishers available and equally knowledgeable of their correct use. There are many differing types of portable fire extinguishers suitable for use in an RV. Following are some common extinguisher types RV owners may encounter:

Dry Powder Extinguishers
Dry powder extinguishers are probably the most common portable fire extinguishers in RV usage today because they meet the NFPA-prescribed minimum requirements. These extinguishers are used on class "B-C" fires. Dry-powder fire extinguishers use baking soda as their extinguishing agent. The dry powder is dispersed by compressed air or CO_2 gas. This is the most effective type extinguisher for propane valve or propane regulator fires where the leak is low pressure (only) resulting in minor propane leakage. A dry-powder extinguisher can create a very large mess: for this reason, it is best used outside the RV. This type of extinguisher is much less useful for the RV interior, and it is not suitable for class "A"-type fires. Once discharged, a portable dry-powder extinguisher must be recharged or replaced before it can be used again. This is necessary even if the entire contents were not expelled. Portable dry-powder extinguishers stored in an RV must be inspected and inverted (shaken) monthly (at minimum) to prevent the powder from packing, rendering the extinguisher inoperative without warning. Check your RV's extinguisher(s) before each trip in the RV, particularly if it has been in storage. See the fire extinguisher maintenance section for specific instructions on how to check it. The life limit for a domestic dry powder extinguisher with a plastic top is six years, while the metal top versions have a life limit of 12 years. The date of manufacture should be contained on the extinguisher label.

Dry Chemical
The terms "dry chemical" and "dry powder" are often used interchangeably. Although this usage may be correct, there is more to it. A dry-chemical extinguisher is a dry-powder extinguisher with an additional chemical agent added. Dry-chemical extinguishers are suitable for use on class "A-B-C" fires. As a general rule, the suitability for usage on class "A" fires dictates a considerable higher volume of dry chemical, making the fire extinguisher larger for a similar fire size rating. Like other dry-powder extinguishers, they must be recharged or replaced when used, and they must be inverted and shaken monthly to avoid powder packing. The regulated life for a domestic dry chemical extinguisher with a plastic top is six years, while the metal top versions have a life limit of 12 years.

Stored-Pressure Water/Foam Extinguishers
Stored-pressure water extinguishers, also referred to as "P" (pressure) cans, are useful for small class "A" fires and are often used for extinguishing confined (limited) hot spots. Stored-pressure water extinguishers can be refilled and recharged easily after usage and require no routine maintenance except for verifying correct air pressure on the gauge.

Class "A-B" "designer foam" concentrates can be added to a stored-pressure water extinguisher to enhance its effectiveness. The addition of designer foam provides a wetting agent that aids in extinguishing deep-seated fires and vehicle fires. When class "A-B" designer foam and water are mixed, the resulting foam-extinguishing agent floats on the surface of fuels that are lighter than water. The film of foam that extinguishes the flame also serves to prevent reignition of any remaining fuel by creating a vapor seal. Some designer foams also have a detergent base that helps to break down hydrocarbon fuel.

Designer foam fire extinguishers are the most useful and user-friendly extinguishers for use in an RV.

The useful life of a designer foam agent is 5-30 years (depending on manufacturer) and, in general, requires no maintenance beyond verifying that the unit contains proper pressure. Designer foams are nontoxic, noncorrosive and require less cleanup than traditional dry-powder extinguishers, making them the most logical choice for an RVer seeking greater protection than that required by law and provided by the RV manufacturer.

Halon Extinguisher

Halon or any other halogenated firefighting agent extinguishes fire by a process that is not definitively understood. Research suggests that those agents interrupt the chain reaction of the combustion process. Because of their ozone-depletion potential, halogenated extinguisher agents are included in the Montreal Protocol which bans substances that deplete the ozone layer. International agreement required a complete phase-out of the production of permitted halogens by the year 1995. As of 2002, Halon is no longer available to the public. The only exceptions under the agreement are essential uses where no suitable alternatives are available. Since 2010, Halon has been unavailable for use. There is no requirement for RVers who currently possess a Halon extinguisher to dispose of it. It may be retained and used for the purpose for which it was designed and manufactured. Responsible RVers may wish to consider properly disposing of the Halon extinguisher and replacing it with a suitable alternative. Proper disposal of all types of fire extinguishers is best left to firefighting professionals, so take them to your local fire department for proper disposal.

The most common type of Halon extinguisher contains Halon 1211. These extinguishers are intended primarily for use on class B-C fires; however, Halon 1211 extinguishers of less than nine pounds in capacity are not powerful enough to extinguish large fires (typical ratings are between one and four square feet depending on size). When used on a fire, the Halon and the products of combustion combine to give off very deadly gases. In the confined space of an RV, these gases could prove fatal to occupants. The user of a Halon extinguisher must stay in fresh air while using the extinguisher. Halon 1211 extinguishers are no longer manufactured for personal use and are highly regulated by the EPA.

Selecting The Best Portable Fire Extinguisher For Your RV

When used properly and under the proper circumstances, a portable fire extinguisher can save lives and reduce property loss by putting out the fire or at least keeping it confined to a limited area until the fire department arrives. Choosing the right portable fire extinguisher depends on a number of factors, including:

- Classification of the burning fuel
- Rating of the extinguisher
- Hazards to be protected against
- Severity of fire
- Atmospheric conditions
- Availability of trained personnel
- Ease of handling extinguisher
- Life hazards or operational concerns

The extinguisher must be large enough to put out the fire. Be aware that portable fire extinguishers are not designed to put out large or rapidly spreading fires.

An extinguisher is not an alternative to calling the fire department. Many portable fire extinguishers discharge completely in as few as 15-20 seconds.

KNOW YOUR FIRE EXTINGUISHER BEFORE YOU NEED IT!

Cylinder
This is the body of the extinguisher. It is pressurized and holds some combination of extinguishing agent and a gas to expel it.

Handle
This is nothing more than a grip for carrying or holding the extinguisher. The handle design may vary according to the manufacturer. By design, lifting an extinguisher by the handle will not cause the unit to discharge.

Trigger
This is normally a short lever or button mounted above the handle at the top of the extinguisher, although some units differ. The unit will discharge when you squeeze the trigger or depress the button.

Nozzle
This is at the top of the extinguisher where the extinguishing agent is expelled and may have a hose attached, which can be directed by the operator's free hand.

Pressure Gauge/Pressure Pin
The effective range of an extinguisher and its ability to expel the agent decreases as pressure drops. Most gauges or pressure-indicating pins are calibrated to reflect the minimum pressure required to fully expel the fire-fighting agent. Any extinguisher not up to the minimum pressure must be serviced or replaced.

Locking Mechanism
All portable fire extinguishers come with some type of locking mechanism to prevent accidental discharge. The mechanism may be a simple pin or clip that must be removed or released for the extinguisher to work. In many fire extinguisher types, the locking mechanism is retained with an easily breakable seal to prevent the lock from falling out, allowing the "armed" extinguisher to go off unexpectedly.

Always leave large fires to the fire department!

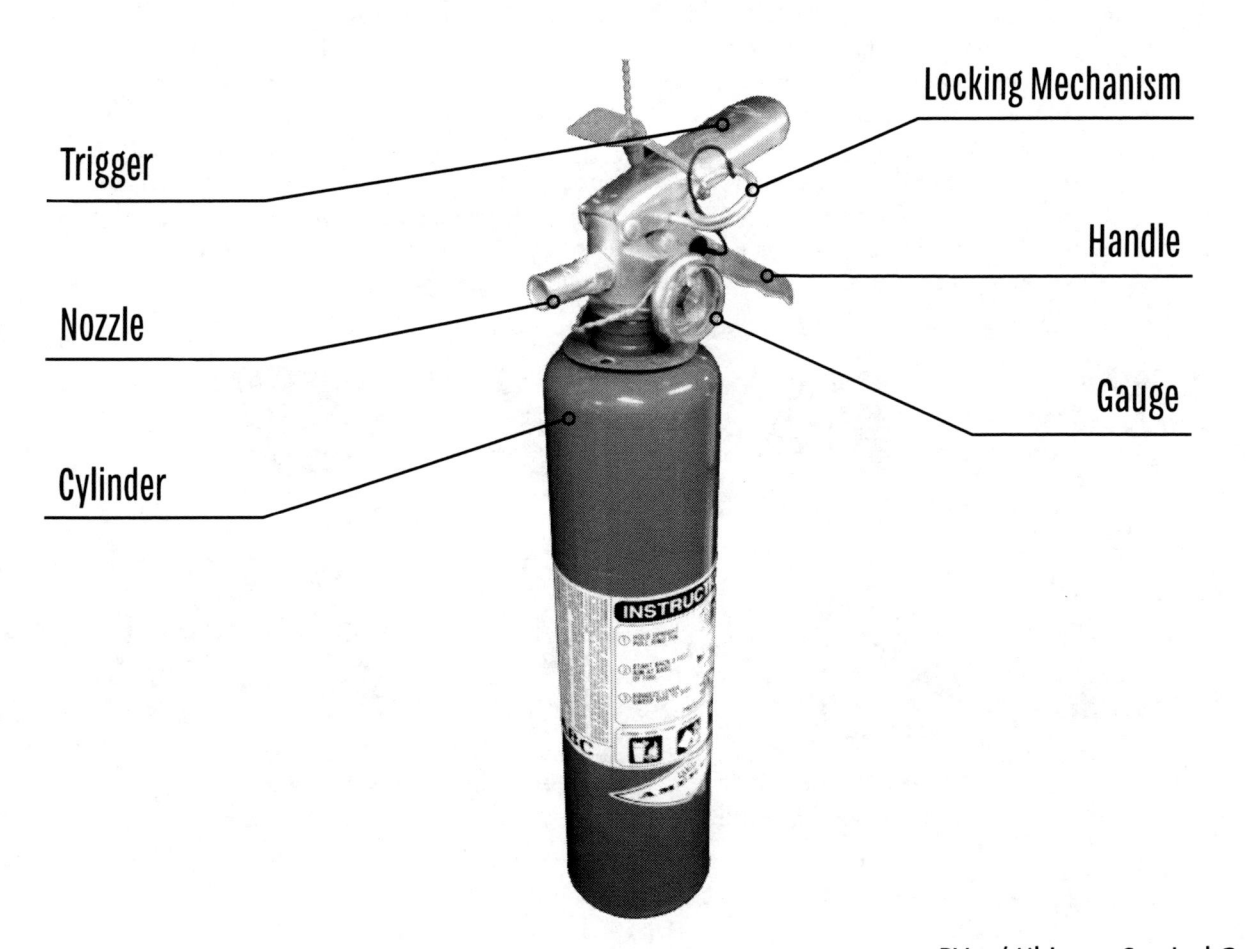

FIGHTING AN RV FIRE

Always leave large fires to the fire department. Fight only small fires that are limited, within easy reach and that you can fight with your back toward a safe escape. If you have the slightest doubt that you should fight the fire, do not attempt it! Instead, get out and move far away fast.

P.A.S.S.

Pull the Pin
This unlocks the operating lever and allows you to discharge the contents of the extinguisher.

Aim Low
Point the nozzle or hose at the base of the fire.

Squeeze the Lever Above the Handle
If equipped with a button, press the button. This discharges the extinguishing agent. Releasing the lever or button stops the discharge.

Sweep from Side to Side
Moving carefully toward the fire, keep the extinguisher aimed at the base of the fire and sweep back and forth until flames appear to be out. Watch the fire area. Should the fire restart, repeat the process.

Always leave large fires to the fire department.

One necessary addition to this procedure is to "cool the fire." This is particularly important for RV fires where motor fuels and overheated components and lubricants are often the source of the flames. When using an extinguisher to put out surface flames, make sure to totally penetrate the fuel so that it is cooled; otherwise, the fire may flare up again. This is when having additional fire extinguishers is doubly important. If you use your only extinguisher to stop the fire and do not have another to cool the area down, the fire is likely to restart. This time you will not have anything with which to fight it. This is also where a designer-foam extinguisher has a great advantage because it cools the fuel effectively, preventing a rekindling of the flames. Always be sure the fire department inspects the area, even if you believe that the fire is fully out. In addition to using portable fire extinguishers, your water supply hose (and those of neighbors) can be unhooked and used as a tool to fight the fire. If a nearby vehicle is burning and you are unable to safely move your RV but can safely remain close enough to keep it hosed down, it may be possible to save it or minimize the damage to your RV and surrounding property.

Pull the pin in the handle.

Aim the nozzle at the base of the fire.

Squeeze the lever slowly.

Sweep from side to side.

FIRE EXTINGUISHER MAINTENANCE

Once you have determined that you have the correct type of extinguishers, your next priority is to keep them properly maintained by checking them periodically. This is the RVer's personal responsibility!

The first thing to verify is the date of manufacture of your fire extinguisher because of the NFPA 10 life limit on domestic fire extinguishers. Somewhere on the label, generally near the notation regarding extinguisher classification, there should be a box with a date code, e.g., 2005. That would be the date of manufacture. Plastic top domestic extinguishers have a six-year life limit while metal top extinguishers have a 12-year life limit. During your monthly inspection, you should check the fire extinguisher gauge or depress the pressure pin to determine if there is adequate pressure in the extinguisher. If the gauge or pressure pin indicates empty or inadequate pressure, replace or recharge the extinguisher immediately. To test non-gauge extinguishers, push the plunger indicator (usually green or black) in. If it does not come back (rebound), the extinguisher has inadequate pressure to expel its contents. If you need help testing your fire extinguishers, visit your local fire department.

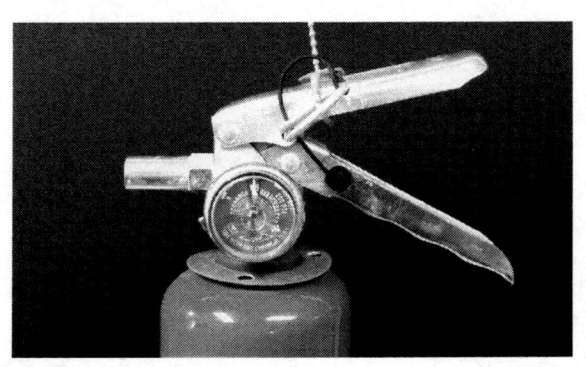

If you use any portion of a powder extinguisher, have it refilled or replaced immediately. When an extinguisher has been partially used (even a small amount), a particle of the dry powder or dry chemical may become trapped in the valve causing the valve to leak pressure. Never put the dry powder or chemical fire extinguisher back into the bracket thinking that you "only used a little." Once the extinguisher has been discharged (even a little), it must be replaced or serviced. Should you desire to have a fire extinguisher refilled, request that they first shoot off the old charge (most refill stations have a special place where this can be done safely). If you can observe the procedure, it may let you witness how far it shoots and how long the charge lasts.

Do not pull the pin and expel the contents to test your powder extinguisher.

Invert and shake your dry-powder or dry-chemical extinguisher to loosen the powder. Smacking the inverted extinguisher with your palm or a rubber mallet can help. The vibration of your RV while you travel down the road packs the powder tight. This may make your extinguisher ineffective in fighting a fire. If you cannot detect movement of the powder within your extinguisher, replace it immediately or have it checked by an expert.

For stored-pressure water/designer foam and Halon extinguisher, the maintenance process is considerably easier. They need only to be inspected to verify that the pressure gauge has adequate pressure as evidenced by the normally green band on the gauge.

LIFE SAFETY MEASURES

There are several fire and life safety tools that can be used to save lives in your RV. Keeping them well maintained and in good working condition is equally important as knowing how to use them properly.

Smoke Detectors

Smoke detectors are intended to alert you or to wake you when there is a dangerous concentration of smoke in your RV. The National Fire Protection Association requires the RV manufacturer to put one detector in your RV. Depending upon the size and configuration of your RV, you may want to place a second one in the sleeping area. Choose only a UL (Underwriters Laboratory) RV-approved smoke detector. Test your detector(s) weekly to make sure they are working. Most RV smoke detectors are battery powered, meaning that batteries must be changed routinely. The National Fire Prevention Campaign suggests that you change home smoke detector batteries twice a year when you change your clocks to and from daylight saving time.

RVs are generally relatively small vehicles (compared to your conventional house) resulting in a common complaint that the smoke detector goes off with the slightest provocation. This can be easily solved by changing to a smoke detector that includes a button which, when depressed prior to cooking, will shut off the detector for 15 minutes. It will automatically reset itself and sound a brief chirp when it does to let you know that all is well. In addition, this type of detector will still operate normally during the 15-minute period if heavy smoke is detected.

Carbon Monoxide (CO) Detector

Deadly, invisible, odorless CO (carbon monoxide) gas usually results from engine or generator exhaust leaks or misuse of portable gas-powered heating devices. CO can also come from someone else's vehicle or from their generator used while camped tightly at RV rallies or shows. Be sure to position your CO detector in the bedroom. The proper location of this very important device is on the ceiling or on an inside wall where it should be located at least eight inches from the ceiling and at least five feet from the floor.

Propane (LPG) Leak Detector

LPG is heavier that air; thus, like gasoline fumes, LPG will tend to collect in low spots in the RV. Once pooled in this fashion, it remains there until air movement dissipates it or until a spark sets it off explosively. Your propane detector should be placed in the kitchen area at floor level. If your detector sounds a warning that you have a leak, or if you smell the garlic warning odor of propane gas, shut off the propane at the tank. When any propane leakage has been noted, quickly proceed as follows:

- *Get everyone out of the RV immediately.*
- *Don't smoke, light matches, operate electrical switches, use either cell or telephones, or create any other source of ignition.*
- *Call the area fire department emergency number or 911 from the nearest phone.*

SUMMARY

At best, a fire is always a scary experience. In the tight confines of a recreation vehicle, the thought of fire is doubly terrifying with the potential of total loss of one's home, the destruction of one's personal possessions and the threat of loss of life itself. However, that need not be the case. It is entirely within the capability of RVers to protect themselves and their property to a large degree. What is required is a plan that is fully thought out well in advance of that eventuality. With a plan and the judicious addition of fire-fighting equipment carried onboard the RV, there should not be excessive fear of fire.

BOOK 9: PERSONAL SAFETY

CONTENTS

Author's Foreword 175
What's It All About? 175

PERSONAL SAFETY FOR RVERS   176
Boondocking Security Concerns 176
Tips for Discouraging Thieves 176
Enhancing Your Security 177
Tips to Avoid Being a Crime Victim 178
Personal Safety Philosophy to Live By 179
Weapons as Defensive Tools 181
Non-Lethal Weapons 181
Lethal Weapons 182
Choice of Firearms 184
Communications 186

WEATHER AND MEDICAL HAZARDS   188
Surviving Nature's Hazards 188
A Winter Travel Emergency Kit for RVers 192
Desert Travel Issues 193
Surviving On-the-Road Health Problems 194
Locating a Doctor While Traveling 196
Have Pills—Can Travel 198
Summary 199

AUTHOR'S FOREWORD

With the completion of this book you will have completed the entire curriculum of *The RVer's Ultimate Survival Guide*. We hope that at this point you are feeling pretty good about your accomplishment. Personal safety issues are numerous. Indeed, it would be easy to add additional chapters. Without doubt, we have addressed many of the most obvious personal safety issues confronting each of us. We hope your study has prompted you to consider your whole RV lifestyle and the safety issues in it.

> "...millions of RVers travel with the full expectation that RVing is a safe lifestyle without needless risks involved."

WHAT'S IT ALL ABOUT?

The recreation vehicle (RV) is a wonderful invention. No one actually knows when and where the first RV was developed and put into use. No doubt it was home-built and met the owner's need to travel comfortably early in the 20th century. There are many pictures dating to that era showing various "camp-mobiles," which were generally constructed from a Ford Model "T" or some other truck chassis of the time.

In its current state of development, the RV provides the opportunity for a tremendous number of individuals (some 6+ million RVs are registered) to travel extensively for reasons as diverse as the RV itself. Some who follow the RV lifestyle do so of necessity traveling to new destinations as their jobs dictate. Others use the RV exclusively as a vacation travel vehicle, and some only use it as a platform for tailgate parties at games and sporting events. The snowbird uses his or her RV extensively to follow the sun into the southern parts of the country during winter, and the full-timer forsakes all other residences to live and travel full-time in pursuit of a nonstop life experience. For every RVer, there is a unique story-- some of which are most fascinating and wonderful. Each of the millions of RVers travel with the full expectation that RVing is a safe lifestyle without needless risks involved. On the whole, it is. Yet there have been rare security incidents resulting in countless discussions around the campfire where RVers gather. This has prompted a compilation of personal safety issues and concerns to be included in this book. Recognizing the widely varying makeup of RVers, the diversity of activities they pursue and the geographic extents to which they travel, this book contains an equally diverse collection of topics.

PERSONAL SAFETY FOR RVERS
BOONDOCKING SECURITY CONCERNS

What Is Boondocking?

Dry-camping is often called "boondocking." Essentially, this entails camping without hookups for some period of time. Boondocking may be your personal preference, an occasional option or a necessity when a campground vacancy cannot be found. Note: Some RVers actually take boondocking to great extents preparing their RVs and themselves to maximize the length of time that they can remain in the "boondocks" without support services. No doubt there are some RVers out there who can and do boondock full time. The annual RV gathering of tens of thousands of RVs in the Arizona desert at Quartzsite is an excellent example of the whole boondocking experience.

Boondocking takes place on federal lands, such as Bureau of Land Management (BLM) areas, in national forests and even in state parks where hookups are not commonly available. Boondocking in such places is generally permitted by law and accepted by everyone. Only when it is done in metropolitan areas does it become controversial. Since boondocking generally involves being somewhat isolated, safety should be your primary concern.

All people, including RVers, expose themselves to risks at various times. We neglect to lock the door; we open the door to a stranger's knock; we pick up a hitchhiker or we use isolated public rest rooms. Each of these commonplace daily occurrences can be an opportunity for a criminal.

Criminals are opportunists who look for the easy way through life and in their criminal activities. Since that is true, why would a criminal attempt to break into a locked RV at a roadside rest area, when there are nearby automobiles that are easier targets? The window of an automobile permits observation of both the contents of the vehicle and any potential victim(s). In stark contrast, the thief has no way of knowing how many people are inside the RV or if they are armed and waiting for him. Yet many RVers are afraid to spend a night in their RV unless it is parked in a secured campground. Fear is a psychological barrier because it does not need to be completely logical to become a personal issue. Fear is a thief of our freedom to fully enjoy life.

Whether you boondock frequently or only occasionally, it is sensible to have some additional safety measures in place.

TIPS FOR DISCOURAGING THIEVES

- Do not leave valuables lying either outside the RV or in plain sight in the tow vehicle.

- Do not keep unnecessary cash around. With ATMs (automatic teller machines) across the country, cashing checks is not a problem. Whenever possible, use credit cards instead of cash. Find a safe place to hide your extra cash. Most RVers agree that it is better to put the money in two or three separate hiding places.

- When you leave your RV, close the drapes and leave a light and a radio on, so prowlers will think that the vehicle is occupied.

- Do not open the door to anyone unless you know who it is. If you have your name anywhere on the outside of your rig, as many RVers do, be aware that if someone calls out your name, it could be a criminal trying to lure you into opening the door. You may wish to rethink posting your name outside for security reasons.

Remember, your RV is a fortress only as long as you remain on the inside and your adversary is on the outside.

ENHANCING YOUR SECURITY

Alarm Systems

Most alarm systems operate on 12 VDC and require a professional to install, but, there are some you can easily install yourself. Alarm systems vary depending upon the technology they use to operate, the complexity of the system and the cost of the system. Some common RV security systems are motion-sensor type alarm systems that activate a loud alarm if the RV is jarred excessively. Because of this limitation, it is not a practical system to use on an occupied RV, yet it might be suitable as a theft preventive device for a parked RV.

The intrusion-type alarm is set off if the door, window or hood of your vehicle is opened without first turning off the activating switch. The switch is key-operated and usually installed on the outside of the vehicle. If it is mounted on the inside, it must be equipped with a time delay that allows the owner time to unlock and open the door and turn off the switch.

The ultrasonic-type detection system might be useful for an RV that does not contain pets. The ultrasonic system is a motion detector, which senses movement within a certain area of the vehicle, setting off an alarm to scare away any intruder. A wandering pet or occupant could also unwittingly trip such a system.

Another common security (theft) system type is not actually an alarm but serves as a deterrent because the motor cannot be started until a hidden switch is activated. In this system, a switch is spliced into the "hot" wire that feeds the ignition coil. The switch should be installed anywhere it can be hidden and not easily found. If your vehicle has an electric fuel pump, an alternative is to use the switch to open the circuit to the fuel pump preventing it from operating until the switch is activated.

Alarm systems may not discourage the professional thief, but they can be valuable when you occupy the RV, because the alarm will alert you, giving you an opportunity to prepare yourself.

Many RVers believe the best alarm system is a dog. A dog's keen senses and its barking will alert you to the prowler as well as warn you of other dangers such as smoke from a fire. Often a barking dog is enough deterrent to make the thief look for an easier target.

Outdoor Security Lights

If you do not already have a light outside your RV door, it is a good idea to install one that will operate on your 12-volt system. Then, by flipping a switch, you can light up the area outside your RV door even if you are without electrical hookups.

If you have a trailer, you may also want to install a switch that will allow you to turn on your entire trailer and tow vehicle clearance lights, along with the taillights on both vehicles, without leaving the security of your trailer. Turning on outside lights tells a potential thief that you know he is there. Knowing that he will face an alert RVer may be enough incentive to scare him away. With the outside lit and the lights off inside, you will be able to see him without his knowing where you are in the RV. The addition of such a system and possibly encompassing a siren as well is quite easy and can be accomplished by most RV owners.

Deadbolts

Many RV doors have similar locks and keys, so the first step toward better security is to add a dead-bolt lock. The simple slide-bolt type of dead-bolt lock may not be adequate if your RV has a window within 36 inches of the lock. A thief could easily break the window, reach inside and unlock your door. In this case, you need the double-keyed type because it can be locked from either side of the door and requires a key to unlock it. The drawback to the double-keyed type is that, if there is a fire or similar emergency, you lose valuable time getting the key from its storage place before you can unlock the door. Yet, if you leave the key in the lock, it defeats the purpose of a double-keyed deadbolt. The best bet is to obtain an extra dead-bolt key and hang it near the deadbolt but not within reach of the window. It is not expensive to have the deadbolt lock installed by a locksmith, but since detailed instructions come with the lock, you can probably install it yourself.

Peephole Viewer

In addition to a dead-bolt lock and scare lights, you may want to install a peep viewer on or near your door. This wide-angle viewer can be obtained from a hardware store for only a few dollars. Once installed, a wide-angle lens allows a good view of the entire area outside your door without opening the door.

Steering Wheel Lock

A steering wheel lock requires no installation, yet is an effective theft deterrent. This device, preferred by many RVers, has the advantage of being visible to the thief before he breaks in and, because it is made of hardened steel, it cannot be easily defeated. Some steering wheel locks extend down around the brake foot pedal; thus, when locked in place, the brake pedal is secured to the steering wheel so that the thief cannot steer or stop the vehicle.

Accessory Padlocks

You may want to add quality padlocks to secure the spare tire, propane tanks and the battery case if equipped. With the price of gasoline, it is also a good idea to have locked caps for your motor fuel tanks. During previous fuel shortages the theft of fuel was a common occurrence. What better target than an RV with a large fuel tank?

If you have a trailer or "toad" behind your motorhome, you may worry about someone stealing it. You can install one of the special hitch locks available for this purpose. One type requires a special key as well as a particular type of Allen wrench to remove the jam screw, while others simply utilize a padlock. Locks of this type make it nearly impossible for anyone to move your trailer or to steal your "toad" when the lock is in place.

A professional thief can steal your RV, no matter how many quality devices you use, but, the more deterrents you have, the more likely it is that a thief will decide to steal someone else's vehicle instead of yours, so everything you do to discourage a thief from targeting your vehicle is worthwhile.

TIPS TO AVOID BEING A CRIME VICTIM

Tip #1: Never fight over property!
You must not use deadly physical force to prevent a property crime. It is just "stuff" and can be replaced. Many good people, including RVers, have been killed or severely injured contesting the loss of a wallet or purse with less than $20 in it. You might resist a property loss such as a carjacking if the attacker is obviously unarmed, but if he has a knife or gun, assume that he will use it. Leave the car.

Tip #2: If you need a cane, consider an alternative.
The use of a hiking/walking stick in place of the cane will not convey the same message to a criminal. A $50-$100 collapsible (foldable) stool can also serve as a defensive measure. The hardened steel tip makes a decent defensive fighting tool, but it does not look like a cane or indicate that you have a disability. Remember that criminals will not feel sorry for you just because you are disabled. In actuality, they are more likely to choose you to attack because you cannot chase them.

It is good practice to try to think like a criminal. How would you attack? Who would you go after? Where would you make your move? What might scare you off? Make it a game and, when you start selecting your "potential victims," you will begin to understand what the criminals see. Practice your people-watching skills with this new slant, and you will be amazed at the insight that you gain.

Tip #3: Lock your doors!
LOCK YOUR DOORS on your tow vehicle, towed car and your RV every the time you enter or leave the vehicle. Make this just as important and automatic as putting on your seatbelts. It is not 1950 anymore (the good old days) and every day folks are attacked on busy city streets and in mall parking lots. Simply locking vehicles could have prevented many of these unfortunate occurrences or would have allowed the unwitting RVer to escape unharmed.

Do not open the door of your RV unless you can see who is there and then only if you are certain that you know the person. More than a few unfortunate individuals have fallen prey to the "sick baby" or "I've been in a car accident" ruse, only to find the poor woman has her ex-felon boyfriend hiding nearby. Extreme examples? Maybe, maybe not. Why take a chance?

PERSONAL SAFETY PHILOSOPHY TO LIVE BY

Personal safety and survival is 95% attitude and knowledge, not reliance on hardware (weapons) or brute strength. While the law does not require you to retreat from your property, standing your ground in defense of it can be a bad decision, tactically as well as strategically. Security experts advocate a three-step mindset to make your life safer from crime. Do everything that you are capable of to:

- Avoid being selected as a criminal's victim.

- Escape it if you are not able to avoid the attack.

- Win if you cannot escape. If he breaks off his attack and flees, you have won!

This self-defense philosophy is also recommended in the event of attacks from large animals.

Avoid

Crime is real and very personal when it happens to you, regardless of statistics and the reported crime rates. The crime rate is 100% when you are picked to be a victim. Until you accept that you are at risk, you are not truly aware and are, therefore, at increased risk. Consider that we walk around and drive often talking on our cell phone instead of paying attention to our surroundings. When we do so, we are not watching for the "wolves." To best protect yourself, you must understand crime trends and criminal characteristics and believe that you can and will prevail in the end.

It is important not to be picked out of the group as the prime victim. You want to either look like the biggest, meanest member of the group or not stand out at all. Standing out as a weakest or most vulnerable of the group increases the chance that you'll be picked.

- Dress modestly. Dressing provocatively is more dangerous.

- Limit your jewelry to that which you are willing to lose. Heavy necklaces, especially gold chains, are not only attractive to snatch-and-run thieves, but can be used to choke and pull you to the ground.

- Carry a concealed purse or wallet. An inside the waistband or bra travel wallet offers some degree of security. Consider carrying an old purse with some makeup or old papers and some "mugger money" in it as a deterrent. Your real credit cards and other valuables are then concealed and protected.

- Walk confidently. An erect posture and vigorous gait are more defensive than walking slumped over, oblivious or with your hands in your pockets. Do not walk in a fearful manner. Look at the crowd and behind you occasionally. This is critical. Walk and carry yourself as if the sidewalk is yours. You should strive to look confident, aware, capable and ready to resist and fight back if need be--no matter your size or age.

- Avoid walking alone. Call a cab from inside the restaurant or ask a friend to accompany you or bring your car around. You do not want to look like easy "pickings" for a predator's next victim. Should you find yourself alone and approaching a group (generally males hanging out), you should avoid the confrontation by crossing to the other side or by turning around. Do not make it easy for a criminal to take you on or take you to a secluded place which could become crime scene #2.

Escape

Sanford Strong, retired police officer and personal safety instructor, gave us "The Four Survival Rules to Live By" in his book, *Strong on Defense: Survival Rules to Protect You and Your Family*.

- React immediately: Your best chance to escape violence and minimize injury is in the first seconds.

- Resist: Your only alternative is to submit. Both choices are lousy, but resisting gives you the best chance.

- Crime scene #2: Always more isolated than the initial point of contact and always worse for you.

- Never, ever give up: Your attitude can keep you alive even when you are badly injured.

Escape is effective only if you recognize the pending attack, react quickly and resist. A woman who is approached when she is getting into her car at the grocery store must stop fiddling with the bag of groceries and her keys, even if it means dropping them. It is time to flee or fight, not get pinned in and hit, or shoved into the opened car. The simple act of moving to the other side of the car, putting a barrier between you and the advancing person, may be effective. Do not hesitate to yell (do not scream) "HELP" or "FIRE!" to draw attention and assistance. Unfortunately, yelling "Police" may cause some bystanders to avoid getting involved. The earlier you recognize an attack is coming, the more time you have to react and follow your plan. This assumes that you have pre-visualized the "what if" before it really happens. This is the awareness that we suggest that you strive for. If your fast, aggressive and forceful actions change the attacker's mind and he flees, you have escaped.

Win
When both Avoid and Escape fail, you may be trapped, but you still have two choices: submit or fight. Submission may not save you from injury, death or worse. Experts recommend that you should resist fast and with conviction. Resist as if your life is valuable to you and your family (because it is) and it may be in jeopardy. This notwithstanding, recall that if this is a property crime with an armed felon and you are convinced that he will leave if you give up your possessions, you may simply surrender whatever he is after. That is where your stash of "mugger money" comes in.

Winning means employing both verbal and physical resistance in a manner that enables you to effectively escape or repulse the attacker. Causing the attacker to break off the attack and flee is winning! You must WIN! Remember that sometimes you must win both on the street and then in court.

Verbal Self-Defense Tactics Include:
- Yell (not scream) "FIRE" or "HELP". Screaming conveys a sense of fear.

- The words used must be direct, short and firm, such as "Stop right there!" "Back off now!" "Do not come any closer!" "You are bothering me!" Vulgarities are appropriate if used assertively and without challenging your attacker's manhood.

- Soft terms, "please," "would you," "excuse me," and "sorry" convey weakness.

- Do not start try to justify your right to be left alone.

- Do not be swayed by the attacker's admonitions that you are overreacting.

- Never back away! Taking a solidly placed step forward will affirm your verbally stated resolve.

- Never lose eye contact.

- Do not miss your chance to run (escape) when the time is right.

Physical Self-Defense Tactics To Consider:
You may wish to take self-defense classes. They are offered by several organizations. Note that we are not talking about martial arts, although they are a great hobby and appeal to many RVers. Much of the psychology of self-defense is mental, which can empower the mind with the result that vocalization unlocks literally explosive power and determination. Training is focused on self-defense skills that can enable you to avoid, resist and survive situations ranging from low levels of aggression to an extremely violent assault.

WEAPONS AS DEFENSIVE TOOLS

The topic of carrying a gun for personal protection is one that comes up frequently whenever RVers gather. This is despite the fact that many RVers conceal the fact that they are armed, causing us to wonder the true extent of armed RVers. No doubt there are many. We have already discussed to a considerable degree just why an RV is probably not a likely target of criminals and how with a few precautions, it is possible to further protect ourselves from being selected as crime victims. We have also looked at what to personally do if such a misfortune does befall us. Now we will turn our focus to defensive tactics including the use of firearms to protect ourselves. While this topic is immediately a reason for many RVers to simply skip over this section entirely, it is suggested that we all take the time to review the issue completely. This book strives to present the facts on both sides of the gun controversy completely and clearly. Recognize that since many RVers do carry arms for various reasons and we all travel together to some degree, we must understand the whole topic in order to respond appropriately if and when the occasion presents itself.

Proper weapons and training in their use can even the disparities of age, size, frailty, slower reflexes and, to some extent, surprise when the RVer is approached by a criminal. Weapons aren't for everyone but, for those inclined to utilize them or for RVers who find themselves in particular danger, they should be considered. There are essentially two classes of weapons: those that are lethal and those that are not.

NONLETHAL WEAPONS

Pepper Spray
Legal in nearly all jurisdictions for adults and law-abiding citizens, this is a relatively new version of an aerosol restraint spray made from red chili peppers. Oleoresin Capsicum (OC) is the product created when dried chili peppers are ground.

- Use only pepper sprays that are made from a law enforcement grade and brand. They are very effective on both humans and unleashed dogs.

- Pepper sprays were first used by the U. S. Postal Service letter carriers to control animals. Certain versions and designs are the best defense against bear attacks, including the fearsome grizzly. Since Canada only allows pepper repellent sprays for use against bears, the "bear only" versions are best.

- Choose a pepper spray that has a decent volume and range. The tiny key chain versions put out too little OC and have too short a range to be a serious deterrent. The burst spray type puts out a large cone of OC in a strong (effective) blast. A hand-sized burst canister may be emptied in one real defensive action, but you will consider its cost ($10) well spent. Some states have restricted pepper sprays to police only so you will have to check your local jurisdiction before purchasing this product as a defensive weapon.

Stun Guns
Electronic incapacitation devices (EIDs) are another purely defensive weapon. They have a deterrent effect for people who are afraid of electricity and require that you actually contact the criminal in order to use them for self-protection. Stun guns are not incapacitating, although they will make all but the most determined attacker release you permitting an escape. Stun guns can be taken away from you by an equally aggressive attacker and even turned against you.

Traditional stun gun technology weapons operate in a 7-14 watt range and interfere with the communication signals within the nervous system of the target, affecting the sensory nervous system. Be aware that a small percentage of people with a high tolerance for electrical stimulation can resist the effect and, therefore, continue the attack. The notable exception to this is the Advanced Taser, which became available for citizens in late 1999.

This personal safety device approaches a handgun in size, weight and effectiveness. Electro-muscular disruption (EMD) weapons use a more powerful 18 (civilian) to 26 (police only) watt electrical signal to completely override the central nervous system and directly control the skeletal muscles. This EMD effect causes an uncontrollable contraction of the muscle tissue, allowing the M-series to physically debilitate a target regardless of pain tolerance or mental focus. The Advanced Taser and EMD are weapons specifically designed to stop even the most aggressive combatant. Rather than simply interfering with communication between the brain and muscles, the Advanced Taser and EMD systems directly force the muscles to contract until the target is in the fetal position on the ground. The M-18L (with laser aiming) has a likeness to the Star Trek phaser, offering a 15' range and truly disabling, yet completely with a nonlethal effect. We recommend the laser-aimed version for both its deterrent effect and accuracy. The M-18L is not inexpensive, but it is comparable in price to a quality handgun. Some handgun-free states and cities treat these devices like handguns and will not allow you to possess one, even inside your dwelling (RV), despite the fact that they are completely nonlethal.

LETHAL WEAPONS

Firearms

The reality is, when the situation calls for deadly physical force for self-defense, there is nothing that is as versatile and as effective as a gun. It is believed that 50% or more of the RVing community already travel with a firearm, although no one knows for sure. While the law does not generally require you to retreat from your property, standing your ground can be a bad decision. Remember the three-step plan already discussed to make your life safer from crime and large-animal attacks. Avoid, escape and win!

As human beings, we must do everything possible to avoid the use of deadly force. The aftermath of any such incident is ugly, no matter how justified. Note that lethal force is not applied exclusively by use of guns. A knife, wrench or even your car can be used to defend yourself or your family. For this reason, you need to know and understand this area of the law, even if you choose not to carry firearms of any type.

Justification

You could lose your life, your estate and maybe even go to jail (if you act improperly), even if you feel you were justified in using lethal force. A universal rule of law is that "ignorance of the law is not a defense" (nor is intoxication).

Never use deadly physical force to prevent a property crime. To put to rest an old wives tale, you cannot shoot the criminal stealing your tow vehicle (or other property), then drag him/her inside your RV and claim self-defense. Deadly force is only justified for certain felony crimes (not including theft). Leaving the security of your RV home to stop a thief can get you killed or lead you to kill someone over a property crime.

Rule #1:

Before you shoot, you or a person you are protecting must be in imminent fear of serious physical injury or death.

- If an attacker is coming at you with a gun, knife or bludgeon (such as a tire iron), and you are in fear of serious physical injury or death, you can justifiably defend yourself with deadly physical force. If the attacker is armed with a dangerous weapon, but not a deadly weapon, you can still be justified in using a firearm to defend yourself. The key is "being in fear of your life."

- Being stabbed with a knife (even a small one) or smashed in the face with a baseball bat is often fatal or could leave you with a brain injury. A good knife fighter can cut both your carotid arteries in seconds, leaving you to bleed to death in less than a minute. When presented with a lethal attacker, police officers are trained not to take a baton to a knife or gunfight, nor should you.

- A police officer does not normally use pepper spray or a Taser to defend himself from an imminent gun attack. He/she shoots when there is no time to verbally command the advancing attacker to stop, from behind cover, and with significant distance. An attacker can advance over 21 feet before you react due to the lag time of your seeing the threat, identifying it as a threat and your brain commanding your body and hands what to do.

- A common question is, "Can you use deadly force against an attacker who is not armed?" The answer is yes if you are in imminent fear of serious physical injury or death. A large, mean male attacking an elderly or frail man or woman or someone with a disability can be shot in self-defense. This principle is called "disparity of force." Since women and elderly are easier "marks" for street criminals, only a fool would continue his attack against a firearm, unless he or she is also armed or very determined.

Rule #2:

Buying a firearm without knowing and fully understanding the laws, the realities of gun usage, and knowing how to operate, shoot, clean and store it can have fatal consequences. Many police officers and citizens die of excessive confidence in their "hardware." It is the mental attitude that counts. Some people feel just having a gun is adequate. Nothing could be farther from the truth. Some RVers think that all they need to do is point an empty gun at an intruder (because they could not bear to kill someone), and that would be sufficient. That threat might work in some specific circumstances, but, equally likely, that bluff might get you killed. If you own, carry and present a firearm under threat, you must be mentally and physically able to use it, as its presence will commonly prompt an equally strong reaction from the criminal.

Rule #3:

If you are justified to shoot, do not shoot to wound. Aim and shoot at the center of mass (largest target area) to stop a lethal attacker. Note that even trained police only hit with about one out of five rounds they fire in a gunfight. Since they are generally better armed, trained and practice more frequently than most citizens, the success of a citizen in knocking down a criminal is relatively low. It is generally recommended that you do not fire a warning shot. Continue firing until the lethal attack is stopped. A firearm for self-defense is solely for delivering deadly physical force.

CHOICE OF FIREARMS

Just as a small, conveniently located fire extinguisher is the best tool to immediately put out a grease fire on your RV stove, the firearm is often the most effective tool to stop a lethal attacker. Lethal attacks often come with little or no warning and generally from close distances. Just as you do not stand there watching the fire spread from the frying pan while you call 9-1-1 for assistance, you cannot expect the attacker to wait while you call for the police on a cellular phone. After you stop the attack, call 9-1-1 for medical, police and a lawyer who specializes in self-defense law.

Long Rifle Or Shotgun
A long gun, either a rifle or a shotgun, is often preferable to a handgun. Why? For the same reason that when you need to drive 16-penny nails, you do not choose a small tack hammer. Long guns offer superior "rapid incapacitation capability" (stopping power). They also have a greater sight radius, which means you can hit the lethal attacker sooner, from greater range (before he is on top of you) and with less chance of missing, thereby not endangering bystanders.

While long guns may be more effective in stopping power, their length and bulk also present problems as a defensive weapon. Should you miss with a rifle, the bullet will travel great distances with lethal results. Conventional rifle bullets will penetrate many layers of sheet rock (walls) or the walls of a whole row of RVs in a campground. There are special highly frangible ammunition and techniques intended to reduce this problem. The intruder, especially in an RV, will be in a confined area. Moving and presenting a hunting rifle with scope in the typical bedroom of an RV is not easily or effectively accomplished. Again, because of the size and bulk of a long gun, the glove box is out as a place to carry it close to the driver when on the road. A shotgun loaded with no larger than #6 birdshot is much more suitable for many of these same reasons. Do not use slugs or #00 buck. Small shot at close range is extremely effective and does not carry the same risk of traveling and doing damage at great distances. Consider that a shotgun at close range is not a "scatter" gun. The shotgun still must be properly aimed to be effective. To be specific, the pattern spread of a short-barreled shotgun is less than one inch per yard. Compare that to your typical RV (less than 40 feet) and you will see that the pattern remains less than 10 inches. Some RV security experts consider the shotgun to be the perfect self-defense weapon--in particular, the slide-action versions. Their rationale is that the sound of cocking the weapon is so unmistakable and fearful that all but the most determined intruder will be intimidated or run off.

Handguns/Sidearms
A handgun, also known as a sidearm, is the weapon carried by police officers and many civilians because of its small size and light weight. Its small stature means that it can be carried in a fast draw holster or it can be concealed if you are legally entitled to carry a concealed gun.

As a direct result of being small and light the handgun also lacks much of the rapid incapacitation capability needed to stop a lethal attacker. Remember, the goal is to stop the lethal attacker in his tracks, generally at close range. Many persons who are fatally shot take as much as 12 to 15 seconds before they are incapacitated, rendering them incapable of further attacks on you. It is only in Hollywood movies that folks are explosively thrown backwards from the force of a handgun. Once the decision to carry a sidearm is made, select only medium-caliber or large-caliber well-made handguns for self-defense. Misfires and misses may not matter on the target range, but in a deadly confrontation there are few second chances.

....

Only use handguns as an absolute last-ditch tool for very close lethal defense when avoiding and escaping have not worked.

....

Concealed Carry Weapons (CCW)
There are over 28,000 gun laws in the U. S. There are federal laws, state laws and sometimes even county and city laws, all unique and often contradictory. The legal issues of gun ownership can get really complicated for RVers, who by definition travel into numerous jurisdictions. Your fully self-contained RV may

be your second home, per IRS law, and might be treated as such in some jurisdictions if an intruder broke in while you were "home." You may always consider yourself "at home," but the law may not. For instance, you are at home when you are in a campground hooked up to utilities. However, when you are mobile, the law may define you as being in a vehicle. How many non-RVers understand dry-camping and boondocking? No hookups, but yet you are home and asleep at night. Just how local authorities will treat you remains an unanswered question until an incident arises prompting an official determination.

Once you step outside your home, you and your sidearm are either in an "open view" or "concealed carry" mode. Then, with a few exceptions, you need a CCW permit if your gun is concealed from sight. What are the exceptions? Some states allow you to carry a firearm temporarily concealed when going to and from the shooting range or hunting.

While driving, if the gun is on or about your person, such as in a glove compartment, you are generally considered to be carrying a concealed weapon. Traveling in a motorhome can be questionable for similar reasons--it is not clearly defined. However, having your defensive handgun back in your 5th wheel is of little use if you need it to defend yourself while driving.

Always consider that there are some prosecutors who do not like armed citizens defending themselves and act to discourage such practices at every opportunity. And there are also states in which the mere possession of a handgun by a resident, even inside their own home, requires a state license. If you need or want to carry a concealed firearm, even briefly, on your person or in your car, it is recommended that you get a CCW permit from your home state.

Most states will require that you complete a certified training course before they will issue a CCW permit, while others have no such requirement. Some have hefty fees, while others are quite economical. One advantage for an RVer is that some states offer reciprocity to other states, so your CCW permit may be good in more than just your home state as you RV around the country.

McClure-Volkmer Act

To a limited degree the McClure-Volkmer Act attempts to fix the interstate travel problem of the 1968 Gun Control Act. This 1986 law allows for travel through a state without hassle. In essence, you must be bound for another state where your weapons are legal, and any extended stops (other than gas or emergency services) obviate your rights of lawful passage. Stopping for a day of sightseeing, for instance, makes you now subject to the gun laws of the state you are in. In all cases, your weapons must be unloaded, cased and stored in a trunk or storage compartment not readily accessible. The McClure-Volkmer Act offers very limited protection, and many non-federal police officers do not know all of the details or even that it exists.

Canada and Mexico

Canada does not allow its citizens to own pepper spray, even for personal defense. However, "bear repellant" is okay. Handguns in private ownership and possession may not be transported into Canada under any circumstances. Canadian visitors must have a firearm declaration permit to bring in ordinary hunting rifles and shotguns. Contact the Canadian customs service for the latest Canadian gun information. Note that there is no provision to allow US travelers heading to Alaska to pass through with such weapons.

Mexico is similar. It is generally best to leave your guns at home. Special permits are required to bring hunting rifles into Mexico. Contact the Mexican Consulate for current updates.

After the Shooting

If you are forced to use deadly force to prevent being a victim of a lethal attack, your next battle begins immediately. Now you will be required to win in the legal arena also. While many a uniformed police officer may see your justification, the use of deadly force (homicide) will often go before a grand jury as a matter of policy in many jurisdictions. If the DA's position is to discourage private citizens from arming or defending themselves, you may find yourself having to prove your justification in court.

You will now find yourself as a defendant and will be required to justify the homicide. The prosecution must then show that your use of deadly force was not justified beyond a reasonable doubt in order to find you guilty. It might take a jury trial to prove whether the homicide you committed was justified or a crime. It may cost you thousands of dollars, months of time and untold stress to prove you were actually the victim.

During and after your use of deadly force, you will likely be in a mental state few have ever known. While you know fully of your innocence, your first task is to not incriminate yourself by misspeaking to investigating officers. Do not give a detailed statement to responding officers until you have an attorney of your choice present. Tell them only that you were in fear of your life and show them the weapon you used. Beyond that, tell them you have been trained to talk to your attorney first. Above all, do not lie to investigators; lie and the burden of proof of your justification will become a fight to prove your innocence.

Post-traumatic stress is very real. Police officers who are involved in shootings are afforded counseling, no matter how justified the shot was. There are tremendous psychological effects, even where there was no wrongdoing whatsoever. This is a very stressful period of time and it may be far worse for you. This is not a time to be macho. It is time for healing.

If you are going to carry a weapon, you need to learn how to shoot quickly and effectively in a realistic self-defense environment. The handgun is the most difficult of all firearms to shoot accurately, but it is the easiest to carry and fastest to deploy.

COMMUNICATIONS

For serious RVers, easy and effective communications are a necessity for our very existence. No matter how solitary an RVer might be, even he or she must keep in touch with family, friends, business contacts or some other entity--after all, you never know for sure when Ed McMahon might be calling with your million dollars. Recent years have made keeping in touch much easier with a variety of high-tech solutions that are perfect for the RV traveler; however, you still have to work at it, and there are expenses associated with communicating effectively. Without today's communication systems, there would be far fewer RVers traveling to the degree we do, because keeping in touch is just that important. That is the convenience factor regarding communications. We also must recognize the safety aspects of "being in touch." One never knows just when an accident or serious illness might befall us. When it does, it is our communications tools that we first turn to for assistance.

CB and Ham Radio

A CB radio is the least expensive communication tool readily available to the RVer; however, its range is limited to approximately three-five miles. CBs are very convenient to use because they require no license and can easily be installed by most RVers, and there are even handheld devices that can be packed away until needed. For those in trailers, there are special mounting brackets that allow you to transfer the CB unit from your tow vehicle to your trailer in a matter of seconds. Or, you can simply purchase two CB units--one that is permanently mounted in the trailer and the other in the tow vehicle. CBs remain a desirable communication tool for truckers as they travel the highways day after day, and they make almost constant usage of channel 19 to keep in touch. Be forewarned that the language used can be quite offensive to many RVers, yet this is the first place to turn for HELP on the highway.

When CB radios are used for an emergency, first use channel nine and call for assistance. In some areas the highway patrol monitors channel nine for this purpose. If no answer comes back, switch to channel 19 (or any channel that is being used) and break into the conversation, stating that it is an emergency. Request their assistance in contacting the local 911 or the appropriate services.

There are many devoted RVers who are also amateur (ham) radio operators. Ham radio is an attractive hobby for the RVer. As a result, it is quite common.

Ham radio allows for far better communications with less interference and great range making this a true communications tool. If the people that you desire to communicate with are also ham radio operators, it is possible to remain in almost constant touch no matter where you travel. If not, there remains the possibility of a local operator patching through a call from another ham on the road. It is all a very loose arrangement, but it works and is commonly called upon during times of emergencies for essential emergency communications. Ham radio requires passing a comprehensive test before you can get the required operator's license ,and the equipment can be quite expensive.

Although CB and ham radios are communication tools that may work well for boondocking RVers, they are not the preferred means of communication for most RVers who are interested in safety, protection and staying in touch.

Cellular (Mobile) Phone
Most full-time or serious RVers consider a cellular telephone to be essential for safety, as well as for staying in contact with family. It is usually the quickest and most effective means for routine communications. Cell phones are inexpensive to purchase, but the service can be costly. There are many competitive services with all sorts of program variations. Some have cheap rates for local calls but high "roaming" fees for calls made outside the "home" cell phone area. This type service is expensive for travelers, so keep looking until you find the one that suits your lifestyle.

Many travelers, especially full-time RVers, look for a service package that has a higher monthly fee but no roaming or long-distance fees. Since there are so many competitive services available, it is wise to investigate as many as possible before you make your purchase.

Cellular telephone service is especially important for single RVers. It is comforting to know you only have to dial 911 to get help and, if you have a breakdown, you can call your emergency road service from your vehicle, and they can tell you exactly when to expect help to arrive. Cellular phones are also obviously even more essential for travelers who have serious health problems. Equally important is when family members who have been left behind have health problems

or business issues that make it necessary for them to be able to contact the travelers.

The biggest disadvantage of cell phones is that there are some areas where the call signal is too weak or there are too many phones in operation to permit your communication to get through. There are a multitude of external antennas and other accessories such as "signal boosters" intended to minimize this problem, but there are still areas where you will be out of contact. Check the coverage area of your service provider. They are not all the same, so try to find the one that services the areas in which you plan to travel.

Recent changes in the laws covering cellular providers requires them to put through emergency calls (911) regardless of subscription to their service. What this means to RVers is that it is possible to carry a low-cost (or no cost) phone with them for possible use in an emergency should it ever occur. Used phones can still serve a valuable service for RVers who do not wish or need to subscribe to a cellular service. This type of program could be quite helpful in the case of a "snow bird" that only travels cross-country twice a year to a fixed location at either end where a conventional phone service is used. The desire for cellular security while en route could be accomplished merely by carrying a used or low-cost phone. Remember to keep the batteries charged at all times.

When using a cellular phone to report an emergency (911), you must know and report your location to the emergency operator; contrary to conventional phones where 911 calls are automatically identified and located, cellular calls are not.

While discussing cell phone and the related technology, it is important to note that this is probably the most common means by which many RVers have access to the internet. The proliferation of smartphones has put the internet into our RVs by the simple expedient of purchasing a smartphone and a related "data" plan. The phone then becomes our link to the internet or, in some cases, will become a "hot spot" to which we can link all of our internet devices directly to the internet. This type of unified service is very desirable and well within the range of affordability for many RVers.

WEATHER AND MEDICAL HAZARDS
SURVIVING NATURE'S HAZARDS

Our RVs are our home away from home, and we spend a considerable amount of time in them as we travel. It also is true that RVers generally avoid severe weather and inclement conditions like the plague. Yet we do occasionally get trapped in a situation where we must take defensive action or "ride out the storm" to prevent injury or death. Of necessity, our RV becomes our refuge when Mother Nature distributes her severe weather around the country. For this reason, we need to consider this issue thoroughly and make the proper preparation for the eventuality that we all hope will never come.

Nature's Booby Traps

Nature has a way of setting booby traps that come in all shapes and sizes from disagreeable dust storms to terrifying tornadoes and from summer thunder storms to winter blizzards. All these and more are situations to avoid whenever possible. However, if you have planned ahead about how you will handle these unlikely occurrences, you will not be one of those who panic, turning a bad situation into a disaster.

Government agencies, from Washington to state capitals to town centers, all set up contingency plans for almost everything from a nuclear attack to a storm-warning system. RVers should do the same. When you understand the hazard and are prepared, you will be calm in determining the correct plan of action. This could be the difference between life and death. Many people, including RVers, are killed needlessly because of the lack of planning for such eventualities. Hurricanes and other severe storms commonly shut down whole communities, including its water, electrical, sanitation and food services. In your self-contained RV, you are better prepared to wait out shortages that are crippling to others; however, it does little good to have the capability for self-containment if your RV is not ready for use when disaster strikes. What is the value of having a water storage tank if it is empty when the water supply is shut off? Even when your RV is parked in the driveway between trips, the batteries should be fully charged, the holding tanks empty, the fresh water tank full and the pantry stocked with at least a modest amount of storable food. These recommendations assume that your RV can be operated safely (within all load ratings) in this configuration. See Book 1.

Keep your gasoline tank full between trips, as you may need the gasoline to operate your generator in case of a prolonged dependence on the battery system. Also, it will assure you of a quick getaway if there is a need to evacuate the area. Your portable home (RV) enables you to escape from many adverse weather situations. However, when you do have to cope with inclement weather, knowing what to expect, how to react and that you are prepared is half the battle.

Be Certain that Your RV Is Ready

- Full water tank. Water is one of the first things a community loses when a natural catastrophe occurs.

- Fully charged coach batteries with solar panels or a generator to keep them charged. These will supply you with lights and radio communications as well as the power for a furnace in winter or a fan in summer.

- A full fuel and propane tank.

- A catalytic heater if you do much winter traveling.

- A 12-volt radio for getting storm weather warnings.

- CB, ham radio or cellular telephone (preferably all three) for getting help.

- Flares, reflectors and flashlight (s) and extra batteries.

- Fire extinguisher(s) placed where they are accessible.

- Smoke detector with extra batteries.

- Carbon monoxide detector with extra batteries.

- Shovel for throwing sand on fires (such as burning tires).

- An extra water hose with "Y" connection set up and ready to use when you are in a park with water hookups.

- Box of baking soda by the stove to smother fires that are caused by spilled grease.

- Tire chains when you travel in snow areas, which are also helpful when stuck in sand.

- Heat tapes for your water and sewer lines if you stay where temperatures routinely dip below freezing.

- First aid kit with normal emergency supplies.

- A supply of any special medicine required by any member of the family.

Earthquakes
If you are inside your RV when an earthquake occurs, sit quietly until the disturbance subsides. An RV is one of the safest places to be during an earthquake because it was designed to absorb road-shock that may be similar to that of an earthquake. If the RV rocks violently, it may cause a leak in the propane gas system. For that reason, when the quake ends, check gas connections, fittings, and valves for tightness. See Book 4.

If you are outdoors and away from your RV, sit down in an area where there are no overhead wires, poles or anything that might fall on you. This will not be a pleasant experience for you, but you are in a fairly safe place.

If you are driving when a quake occurs, pull over to the side of the road and remain inside the vehicle until it ends. When you continue your trip be on the watch for fallen objects, broken sewer lines, earth slides, damaged bridges or overpasses and undermined roadways.

Tornadoes
Tornadoes are formed from winds rotating at very high speeds around a hollow cavity in which centrifugal forces produce a partial vacuum. As the storm moves, the outer rim of rotating winds becomes thick and black with dust and debris. When condensation occurs around the vortex, a cloud appears, which is the familiar tornado funnel. The funnels usually look like the extension of a black storm cloud stretching downward toward the ground. Some funnels never do touch ground, some touch and then rise again and some travel along the ground giving life to a storm. Accompanying the funnel is a deep roar that has been described as the rumble of many freight trains. It can be heard as far away as 25 miles.

Tornadoes have the concentrated power to cut through a brick house like a buzz saw, uproot a giant tree or lift the roof off a huge supermarket. In 1931 a tornado in Minnesota plucked an 83-ton railroad car with 117 passengers off the track, carrying it 80 feet through the air before dropping it in a ditch. No wonder the RVer finds them so terrifying!

There is a large government/industry infrastructure in place to notify and warn the population of tornadoes, particularly in areas where they commonly occur.

A tornado watch is announced when conditions exist that could develop into a tornado. Radio and television are used to advise the public of this potential. Sometimes the watch goes into effect when there is not even a cloud in the sky. A tornado watch is not a reason to panic, but it does mean you should watch the sky and keep your ear tuned to the radio. Trained meteorologists will continue to advise you until the dangerous weather conditions have passed.

A tornado warning means a tornado has actually been sighted or its presence detected by radar. The report will tell you where the tornado was discovered and the area where it is expected to pass through. When the weather bureau issues a tornado warning, the radio and television media will pass it on. In larger communities, warning sirens will also sound. When you hear a tornado warning, get out of your RV immediately and seek secure shelter! If the tornado touches down and you are in its path, the RV can be rolled over and over until all the objects inside, including people, are crushed. So, get into a shelter as fast as you can to protect yourself from getting blown away or struck by flying objects. If you are staying in an RV park where there is a storm cellar, go there the minute the warning is sounded.

When you are driving in open country and see a tornado in the distance, you may be able to drive away from its path by going at a right angle. Keep watching the sky, especially to the south and southwest. If you see any revolving or funnel-shaped clouds, report them by CB or cell phone to the police. Tornadoes move fast. If you see a bridge, get under it because it may help shelter your rig.

If you are boondocking or driving through flat country, look for a low place between hills, a ditch or a ravine. If you are on flat terrain, get out of your vehicle and lie flat on the ground. Be aware that a thunderstorm that can breed a tornado is often accompanied by a flash flood.

Flash Floods
Heavy rains can cause sudden or "flash" floods that strike with a force that can wash an RV or other vehicle away. Small creeks, gullies, ravines and culverts can flood very quickly--sometimes before even a drop of rain has fallen in the immediate area. Watch the sky for thunderheads, and keep your ear tuned to the weather reports. This is especially true if you are boondocking in canyons or any low-lying ground near dry streambeds. If the weather looks threatening or if heavy rains are predicted, move your rig to higher ground. If it starts raining and you cannot move your rig, it is better to abandon it. Go where it is safe until the sky clears.

AM/FM radios will often give the first warning of severe weather by "static or crackling" sounds. When the sound gets so bad that you can barely stand to listen, you know that severe weather is very close. The radio will also carry the official warnings issued by the National Weather Service.

Hurricanes
Hurricanes and major floods are generally preceded by extended periods of warnings. The RVer in a completely portable home should have plenty of time to get to a safe location. When you are in a hurricane-prone area, listen to the local weather reports, and follow the recommended route if you have to evacuate. If you must travel through a hurricane area right after the storm has passed, watch out for loose or downed electric wires and other fallen objects.

Remember, when the center or eye of a hurricane passes, there will be a temporary lull in the wind. It will then return from the opposite direction, sometimes even more fiercely. The message to learn about hurricanes is not to let your guard down until advised that it is safe to do so by local authorities.

Winter Storms
Usually full-time RVers have already headed south before the first snowflake falls, but sometimes circumstances dictate traveling north while fellow snowbirds are comfortably settled in a southern park.

The challenges winter travelers face are blizzards, ice storms and freezing rains. Listen to weather reports. If you hear a severe blizzard warning, the most dangerous of all winter storms, it means a heavy snowfall is expected with winds of at least 45 miles an hour and temperatures of ten degrees or lower. Such an event can be truly devastating for the unwary RVer. It is advised that RVers seek shelter should they encounter a severe winter storm unexpectedly. Under these conditions, it is just as dangerous to be on the road as it is to be holed-up in the RV; different hazards accompany each of these conditions. On the road, ice is your biggest enemy, and there is little that can be done to offset its effects except to get off the road. When parked, the biggest problem becomes staying warm and well fed along with preventing freeze-up of the water systems on your RV.

If freezing rain or drizzle is predicted, it means that anticipated rain is likely to freeze the instant it hits the ground, putting a thin layer of ice on the roads. When you hear a weather report indicating either of those warnings, you should immediately begin looking for a place to get safely off the road. Gas stations, highway rest areas and shopping centers are safe havens if you cannot find a campground that is open and accessible. Many campgrounds in the northern regions are closed during the winter months. When traveling where temperatures hover near freezing, heed the warning that bridge surfaces can freeze before the road surface does. Drive carefully and very smoothly across bridges to prevent losing control of your RV.

Sometimes an unsuspecting traveler passes from good driving conditions into a storm area without realizing it until it is too late to find a safe haven. If you are forced to park on the side of the road, look for a prepared pull-off area so you can get completely off the highway. Stopping on the shoulder can be very dangerous when visibility is poor. Be aware that the shoulder of the highway may look firm and may even be frozen on the surface, but if it is boggy underneath, when the temperature rises you may find your wheels trapped in deep mud. If you notice deep-rutted tracks left by other vehicles, it indicates a soft base. Hard, shiny tracks probably mean the snow crust is firm. Try to locate a spot where you can point your vehicle toward the road that you want to travel.

Winter storms often last all day or longer, so be conservative on battery use. Furnace blowers drain batteries very quickly, so if you do not have a catalytic heater as a backup, do not waste energy by watching TV or using unnecessary lights. Set your furnace to 60 degrees and put on heavy clothing and a wrap up in a blanket instead of trying to maintain a comfortable coach temperature.

Your propane tank and batteries are your lifeline, so treat them with care. In extremely cold weather, a run-down battery can freeze, further complicating your problems. It may help to insulate it with newspapers or towels. You may also need to protect your water lines. Leaving cabinet doors open will help while you are living with low temperatures in your RV. If you have antifreeze, pour some down the sink and the tub drains and into the holding tank beneath the toilet. Keep the drapes tightly closed to add insulation, because bare glass allows heat to escape easily. If you have newspapers, you may want to cover the windows as well. If cold air is seeping in around door or window cracks, stuff the cracks with paper towels to minimize cold air infiltration. Remember, though, if you are using a catalytic heater, you need to leave one of the windows cracked to allow oxygen to enter. To prevent too much moisture buildup inside the RV, also crack open a vent. You will not lose any appreciable heat by doing this.

A WINTER TRAVEL EMERGENCY KIT FOR RVERS

- Carry extra antifreeze for your radiator and RV holding tanks. Be certain that your cooling system is adequately protected from freezing before leaving home.

- Carry a broom for removing snow from the roof of the RV after a storm ends. Snow is too heavy to leave on your RV roof.

- Carry a canvas tarp to place on the ground so you can lie on it while attaching tire chains. It can also be used to help insulate the wraparound window on a motor home or tow vehicle and for a multitude of other applications.

- Catalytic heaters are ideal because they do not drain the battery the way the RV furnace blower fan does. The catalytic heater is almost 100% efficient; therefore, it uses less propane as well. Suitable catalytic heaters can be mounted permanently or they can remain portable. Be certain to keep free-standing catalytic heaters well away from any combustible material.

- A container of de-icer fluid for cleaning the RV windshield or windshield wiper blades will come in very handy.

- Carry a bright-colored flag (plastic works best) to attach to your antenna when you have to park alongside the highway to alert road crews of your presence. The last thing that you want is to be hit by the snowplow clearing the road.

- Carry road flares. Yellow smoke flares work best in daylight. They can be purchased at any boat supply store. Red safety flares are best for night use and can be purchased at an auto supply store. Red flares are also commonly used during daylight as well.

- A flashlight and extra batteries are essential and should be in every winter survival kit. You will need these if you have to do emergency repair work on your rig or if the battery runs down, cutting off your 12-volt lights. Flashlights and road flares are almost perfect signaling devices during a storm as they can be easily directed where needed.

- Lock graphite (powdered) is used in locks to keep them from freezing or to help in thawing frozen locks.

- An ice scraper is the best way to remove ice and snow from the windshield of your RV.

- A folding ladder adequate to reach the top of an RV roof should be carried.

- Battery or propane-powered lanterns can be very helpful during a storm.

- Carry a bucket of sand for weight and tire traction. This may be the only way to get necessary traction to get your rig back on the road. Remember that during a storm, traditional road assistance may be unavailable.

- Carry a shovel since you may have to dig yourself out. A word of caution: Cold weather puts an extra strain on your heart, so do not overtax yourself.

- Tire chains are often required for travel in severe-weather areas. To be effective, they must be tight, so tension springs are recommended. Remove the chains when you reach dry pavement.

- If you expect to be staying in an area where temperatures often go below freezing, use heat tape to wrap around water and sewer lines. The type with a thermostat works best.

- Carry insulation to wrap around heat tape, sewer outlets, propane regulators and battery box.

- An electric heater to supplement your furnace works well when 110 VAC is available. Never operate a portable electric heater on an RV inverter as it will deplete even a very large battery pack quickly. Every RV has a "cold spot" where the portable electric heater can be directed. At night, direct the heater at the water lines under the sink, particularly when operating at very low temperatures.

- Carry a hair dryer that can be used to thaw out frozen pipes and locks.

DESERT TRAVEL ISSUES

Many RVers find the lure of the deserts of the Southwest to be irresistible. Because many RVers are only snowbirds temporarily enjoying the warm desert climate, they may not fully appreciate the potential danger and unforgiving nature of the desert. With time available to sightsee, they often head into the desert inadequately prepared. The following checklist provides much of what is required; however, the most important point to make is: NEVER TRAVEL ALONE. There is security in company, and there is always someone else anxious to enjoy the wonders the desert offers.

Desert Travel Emergency Procedures

- Always inform someone where you are going, your planned route and when you expect to return. If possible, provide a phone contact number. Once issued, stay with your plan so rescuers can find you if necessary.

- Carefully check your vehicle before departing. Are your hoses and battery good? Is the spare tire properly inflated? Take along a spare fan belt, a can of gasoline and a gallon of radiator water, as well as tools you might need for minor repairs. See Book 3.

- Take at least one gallon of drinking water and some quick-energy foods and candy bars or snacks that do not contain salt, in case you are stranded.

- Take along a blanket, a tarp, a sharp knife, a compass, matches and anything else that may be useful or necessary (such as required medication), if you are stranded.

- If your vehicle breaks down, remain with it. A vehicle can be seen for miles whereas a person on foot is difficult for a rescuer to spot. In addition, your emergency supplies are there, and the vehicle will provide you protection from a sand storm and other elements. Raise the hood and trunk lids to denote that help is needed.

- Use the vehicle and a tarp to produce shade. Sit on a blanket to protect your body, as the ground may be up to 30° hotter than the air. If you have water, drink sparingly. Do not drink alcohol.

- If for some reason you must walk, leave a note in the abandoned vehicle telling rescuers the time you left and the direction you are taking. If you find a road, stay on it.

- When walking, rest frequently, find shade and sit down. When possible, prop your feet up, but do not take off your shoes. You may not be able to get them back on again if your feet swell, making further travel difficult or impossible.

- Clothing helps to reduce your dehydration rate, so leave clothes on even though you are hot. Cover your head!

- If lost, collect brush and set signal fires. Three small fires in a triangle denote help is needed. Set smoke fires in daytime and flaming ones at night.

RVers' Ultimate Survival Guide

SURVIVING "ON THE ROAD" HEALTH PROBLEMS

Being Prepared

As you begin your great adventure as an RVer, you may recall pictures of an RV parked by a bubbling brook, in a lush green forest or in the wide-open spaces where the deer and the buffalo roam. All of that and many more vistas are available to you as an RVer. The trouble is those bubbling brooks, lush green forests and wide-open spaces are a long way from help in case of an emergency. Heart attacks can strike without warning and with terrifying savagery. They can kill you within minutes. Statistics predict that over one-and-a-half million Americans will suffer a heart attack this year, and 400,000 of them will die before they reach a hospital. If getting to a hospital in time is so difficult for the average American living a conventional life, what chance does the RVer have while boondocking where the only neighbors are wandering coyotes? Unless you want the great RVing adventure to be restricted to staying in parks in metropolitan areas, or in the shadow of a hospital where medical help is readily at hand, you must be prepared to deal with emergencies.

Heart Attacks

Imagine for a moment that your mate suddenly complains of a heavy pressure in the middle of the chest. A common reaction is to waste precious minutes asking each other, "Is it a heart attack or just a bad case of indigestion?" To avoid this the first step is quickly and efficiently to recognize the symptoms of a heart attack and react appropriately:

- A feeling that something is seriously wrong.

- A heavy pressure or a choking sensation in the center of chest.

- Pain radiating down either arm or over the back. It may not be a specific pain that you can pinpoint. It may be just underneath the breastbone. If it is in the back only, it is probably between the shoulder blades.

- Perspiration may break out.

- Dizziness sometimes occurs.

Recognize that with a heart attack you may deny the problem (such as, it can't happen to me), so valuable time is often lost while trying to evaluate the situation. When in doubt, proceed as if it is a heart attack. It probably is, even if the only symptom is pain. With the decision that it is a heart attack, you recognize that you need medical help quickly. How will you get that help if you are miles from the nearest town? Your first instinct is to call 911. Your brain screams this at you because of our conditioning to use this lifesaving service. So you try the call only to find you are in one of those "dead" areas where your cell phone does not work. Even if you are able to get through to 911 on your cell phone, sometimes it takes a few minutes to complete the call. Remember that 911 calls on a cellular phone are not automatically located by the emergency operator. You must do that for them. All of this takes time and minutes are precious, so the best procedure is to get someone else to make the call for you. They will have more presence of mind, will do a better job and free you to tend to your loved one.

As an RVer, it is likely that you are miles from town; thus, the chances are that you can get to a hospital quicker than the ambulance can reach you and return to the hospital. Tell the 911 operator that you are heading towards the hospital, what road you are taking and what kind of vehicle you are driving. Ask the ambulance to meet you en route to save as much time as possible. If you have a trailer and it is hitched to the tow vehicle, or if you have a motorhome with a towed car behind, the next serious question becomes, should you unhitch and go in the tow vehicle? The answer is to do whatever is the quickest, but that decision should be made before you call 911 so the ambulance driver will know what vehicle he/she is meeting.

You are now ready to go. Your next consideration is: should you lay the victim down? No, because if it is a heart attack as you expect, laying the victim down will increase the pain and possibly restrict breathing. Also, consider what happens if, while you were placing the call and making the arrangements, the victim loses consciousness and appears to have stopped breathing? Do you know what to do in this case? Or will you have to stand by helplessly and watch your loved one die? Do you know how to administer CPR?

Cardiopulmonary resuscitation (CPR) is an emergency procedure to prevent brain damage incurred when a brain is deprived of oxygen for more than five minutes. CPR is a relatively simple emergency method for getting oxygen to the brain if the heart stops pumping.

There is so much to know about emergency care. We have touched on only a few considerations here. You can begin educating yourself on this critical subject by buying a good first-aid and emergency care book. Your awareness of the situation and the lessons learned will prepare you for that dreaded time when an emergency occurs. You will know what to do. In an emergency, there is not time to stop and look up the directions, so study and practice together and quiz each other before anything happens. You can use the same text for a review of the topic (at least annually) as you travel.

RVers who boondock regularly should also take a Red Cross course in first aid and a course in CPR. These can be truly lifesaving for you and those around you. Check with the Red Cross and the American Heart Association where you will be staying for a few weeks. The courses are very inexpensive and may be free when offered as a community service.

One aspect of CPR and emergency care that will become immediately apparent is that proper techniques require a considerable amount of room. In the tight confines of your RV, a spot suitable to perform CPR will be difficult to come by. Now is the time to consider this limitation and locate the best spot in anticipation of the time when CPR is required to save a life.

Traveler's Disease
Traveler's disease can be contracted anywhere in the world, including the United States. However, if your travels take you into Mexico, the chances are greatly increased that you will contract it.

Traveler's disease has many cute nicknames including "Trotskys," "Turista" and "Montezuma's revenge." You may recall some of the jokes when President Jimmy Carter contracted the disease during a trip to Mexico. If our well-guarded and carefully-fed President could not be protected, you can see just how common this disease really is. RVers can increase their chances of avoiding it if they stay away from certain foods and drinks:

- Fresh dairy products
- Leafy greens
- Cold meats and fish
- Spicy sauces sitting on an open table
- Milk
- Desserts containing dairy products
- Tap water or ice

In addition, do not buy food from a street vendor unless it is something you can boil. Hot tea or coffee are fine and so are bottled or canned soft drinks and beer. However, you should order all drinks without ice. Do not wash fresh fruits and vegetables with local tap water; instead you should peel them with a sterile knife.

Rather than fully live by these rules many RVers eat normally and take their chances. They are commonly rewarded with the disease. There are over-the-counter drugs as well as prescription drugs, that you should carry in your medicine chest on any trip that puts you at risk. Check with your doctor and be prepared.

Normally, the disease runs its course and you will recover in a few days; however, if you run a fever of 102 degrees or higher or if you have severe pain, you should see a doctor NOW.

Consider for a moment that you are ill in a strange town where you do not know anyone--just how do you find a suitable doctor?

LOCATING A DOCTOR WHILE TRAVELING

The local telephone book generally lists name after name under the heading "Physicians." How do you know what distinguishes one from the rest and which one to select? Many experienced RVers have developed their own method of locating a suitable doctor. Some check with a pharmacist in the drugstore because a pharmacist usually knows what doctors are convenient for out-of-towners and which doctors are accepting patients. Some look in the phone book for a medical clinic. This is often the best choice for visitors. Others drive to the nearest hospital and look in that proximity, because they recognize that there is usually a medical clinic in the area surrounding hospitals.

Should the receptionist state that the doctor is not taking any new patients, insist on speaking to one of the nurses. Explain to the nurse that you are travelers just passing through town and are in need of immediate treatment for which you will pay cash. The two key words here are traveler and cash. Even a doctor who is no longer accepting new patients will often see you because it enables him to fulfill ethical obligations without a long-term patient care commitment. This is especially true if that emergency visit involves paying cash. This way they know they will be promptly compensated for their services. An insurance claim that can be turned down long after you are gone offers no such assurance. If you pay cash, they should still help you to file your claim so the insurance company can reimburse you. This is done by completing your claim form and providing detailed receipts for the services performed.

It may cross your mind that it is easier just to go to a hospital emergency room doctor for treatment. The issues with going to an emergency room for non-emergency treatment are threefold:

- If it is not a true emergency per their definition, your insurance company may turn down your claim, resulting in a large out-of-pocket expense.

- An emergency room physician can only treat you for the one-time visit. If follow-up care is required, you will still have to find a physician.

- The rule in emergency rooms is that the sickest patients are seen first. You may feel as if you are dying, but you may be kept waiting as folks with more severe emergencies are treated.

If there are symptoms of a heart attack, a stroke, or any other type of true emergency, do not waste time looking for a doctor. Go directly to the nearest hospital emergency room.

If you are in an RV park and need help for any type of emergency, sound your vehicle horn or use an emergency whistle. Give three blasts, pause, and then give three more. If you are unable to leave the victim, continue this signal until help arrives. Turn on the headlights while sounding the horn so others can determine who (what RV) requires assistance.

Medical Records

It is essential for full-time RVers and anyone who has a medical problem that requires special medication (allergies to specific mediations or treatments) to carry their personal medical records as they travel. This is true even on short trips. Vital information such as diabetic information or the possibility of seizure may be noted on a medical record card you carry in your wallet or a medical record I.D. bracelet you wear in the event you are unable to communicate it yourself. Whether you go to a doctor's office or to an emergency room, your past medical records will make the doctor's job quicker, easier.

You can get copies of pertinent medical records from your current or former doctors if you explain your travel status. The few dollars you pay for the copies can save you from having to undergo a battery of uncomfortable and expensive tests. It is also important to keep your medical records updated so you have a logical reason for refusing to have them repeated without cause.

Please consider that any patient has the right to refuse an X-ray or laboratory test and the doctor has an equal right to refuse to treat a patient that does so; however, the usual reason for doctors ordering a series of tests is that they do not know your medical history. If your past records can provide the needed information, the tests may not be needed.

Carry your records with you and request that each doctor visited update it. If doctors indicate that they can only mail records to another doctor upon request, you may have to educate them about full-time RVing.

To provide a new doctor all the information needed to understand your problem in relation to your past illnesses, there are several pieces of information that your records should contain:

- Any allergic reactions to food or drugs. The record should also detail the type reaction such as rashes, headaches or dizziness.

- A list of the medications you take, including over-the-counter drugs as well as prescription drugs. The doctor needs to consider this information to assure that a new drug will not interact adversely with any you are already taking.

- Results of all past diagnostic procedures, such as X-rays and laboratory tests.

- A list of your medical problems such as past kidney or liver disease, even if you are not presently being treated for them.

What if You Need Surgery "On the Road"?
If a doctor indicates that you require surgery while traveling, you should do as you would at your home base by fully considering all the options before proceeding. Recognize that there are literally thousands of unnecessary operations performed every year. You have the right (perhaps the obligation) to request a second opinion. A good doctor will not try to discourage you from getting a second opinion. He will actually encourage it and cooperate with your choice for a second doctor's opinion. Unless you have great confidence in the new doctor, it may be best to select your own consultant. Selecting your own consultant also gives you two doctors from whom to select as your surgeon. Note that some insurance companies require a second opinion before surgery, or they will refuse the claim. Some insurance companies have stated on your medical insurance card that any surgery must receive an okay from them before it is performed, or they may not honor the claim.

In case of extreme emergency where no time can be lost, it is still best to have the nurse call your insurer requesting authority to proceed even while you are being prepared for surgery. If after hours, have the doctor place the call as soon as possible the next day. Most doctors understand this requirement and will help you fulfill insurance obligations.

In most cases, the first doctor was correct and surgery is necessary. In larger towns, the doctor may be on the staff of more than one hospital, so you may still have to choose a hospital to perform the surgery. Your doctor will most likely consult with you regarding this choice, and your insurance company may be involved as well.

If you are located in a small town with only one hospital, you may wish to get your second opinion from a doctor in a different town to broaden your choice of hospitals.

You can tell a lot about the hospital by just walking through its halls. Are the corridors and patients' rooms clean? Is the hospital well-staffed? Do the nurses look overworked and haggard? Walk through the surgical ward. Are call lights illuminated above many of the rooms? Note how long it takes for the nurse to answer the light. When mistakes are made, it is often a result of poor or inadequate staffing.

Stop at the office and ask if the hospital is accredited. If it is, those in charge will be happy to show you proof. To be accredited, a hospital must meet the minimum standards in its dietary, pharmacy, laboratory and emergency services.

If your visit to the hospital gives you any uneasy feelings, look for a surgeon who has staff privileges at another hospital. There are fine hospitals all over the country, and doctors have a moral obligation to treat a complete stranger with the same concern and respect they show their regular patients.

HAVE PILLS—CAN TRAVEL

If you are getting medicine from a doctor and then leaving town, you need to understand exactly what to expect from the medicine and what it should do.

- Is the medicine necessary? Many patients feel they must have a prescription when they leave a doctor's office or somehow the doctor is not doing his job.

- What is the medicine supposed to do? Learn the name of the drug and specifically what results you should expect and when.

- Determine what are the possible side effects. Many drugs have side effects such as nausea or drowsiness or have precautions necessary to minimize side effects.

- Can you still drive after taking this medicine?

- Ask your doctor about interactions with other medications you are taking.

- How should it be taken? How many times a day? With meals? Does it make any difference? During the night?

- You should read and keep any directions for use or data sheets that came from the pharmacy with the medicine.

- Should you take the medicine until it is all gone or just until you feel better?

- Ask the doctor if there is a "generic equivalent" to the prescription. If one is available will he/she write the prescription for it. Many states permit a pharmacist to substitute a generic drug. It is best to get the doctor's okay before substituting generics.

Literature published by the U.S. Department of Health states that all drugs, whether sold under their brand or their generic names, must meet the same FDA standards for purity, effectiveness, strength and safety. Yet there may be a considerable difference in price! There is also a price difference between pharmacies. Many patients who buy medicine need it in a hurry, so they go to the nearest, most convenient place. If you have time and inclination, it does pay to comparison shop as there is often a significant variation in price between various retailers.

If you get your prescriptions filled at pharmacies of a national chain connected by a computer system (Walmart, Eckerd, Walgreens, etc.), the prescription can be easily refilled (if authorized by the original prescription) at other stores even in other states. Many medicines require an ongoing medical follow-up or blood test before they can be continued beyond the original prescription, so your doctor must approve any refills. Sometimes this can be accomplished by phone when you are traveling and find that you require a refill or a new prescription. Most pharmacies are happy to make the required calls for you.

Mail-order pharmacies are allowed to fill and refill drugs (except narcotics) and mail them to all 50 states regardless of the state in which the prescribing physician was licensed. It generally takes seven to ten days for medicine to reach you by mail unless you want to pay for an overnight delivery service. This is possibly the most convenient way to obtain any required drugs for RVers who are on the road all or most of the time.

Emergency Air Transport Service
Emergency medical evacuation is a service RVers should seriously consider. In the event of an accident or severe illness, the emergency air transport service will arrange for and transport the patient and a companion to a hospital near your home base after initial emergency treatment is completed at the nearest hospital. The company may even fly you home for prolonged physical therapy or to recuperate. The eligibility requirements and different company offerings vary, so be sure you read the contract.

Some also provide a driver to return your RV to your listed home base. In event of a death, the service transports the body to your home base. There are differences in price and in services provided so be sure to compare everything before selecting a medical evacuation company.

SUMMARY

Having completed Book 9, you no doubt have a much better perspective as to what safety and personal well-being issues we face as RVers. You also know what can be done to minimize our exposure to the hazards that threaten our lifestyles and our lives. When viewed in the concentrated format of this book, it may seem intimidating or overwhelming. In reality, RVers have one of the safest most pleasurable lifestyles around. Yet, we do not want to be lulled into a false sense of security. We must understand the hazards and be determined to avoid any unnecessary exposure by controlling our environment.

Much of this book on personal safety was developed and offered by members of the Escapees RV Club. This organization is recognized as a significant contributor to the welfare and security of serious RVers everywhere. Our thanks to Joe and Kay Peterson, Dave Balaria and others within the Escapees RV Club organization for their contributions.

(proposed in [**54**]) was analyzed by A. Blass and Yu. Gurevich in [**2**]. They showed that, in contrast to simple backtracking (see above), Matiyasevich's method requires (on average) exponential time on random formulas. In other words, without a modification, this method is not very efficient.

Intuitively, this negative result is consistent with the fact that Matiyasevich used the chemical kinetic equations that describe *slow* reactions. O. Fuentes has experimentally shown that if we use *fast-reaction* equations instead, the method becomes very efficient [**17**], [**18**], [**37**], [**16**].

Meanwhile, the very idea of chemical computing was independently rediscovered in [**23**] and [**24**].

Finally, in 1994, the real boom started when L. Adleman *actually performed chemical computations* "in vitro" [**1**]: namely, he used actual chemical reactions between DNA fragments to solve a particular case of the traveling salesman problem (another problem known to be intractable). After Adleman's sensational experiment, chemical computing has joined the mainstream of theoretical computer science. Dozens of papers are being published every year. At present, this area is developing so rapidly that any attempt to summarize its state will be outdated by the time the book is out. (Interested readers are advised to browse through the Net for the most recent papers.)

3.3.2. *New developments in discrete optimization techniques.* The new approach to discrete optimization developed by the Davydovs in [**5**] has been continued in their papers [**6**]–[**12**]:

- [**9**] presents the main results and concepts from [**5**] in a brief form; the main emphasis is on the main notions of *duality*, *closeness*, and *non-tree-like* search schemes.
- [**7**] describes the relation between dual structures (as defined in [**5**]), flow problems from linear programming, and known NP-problems such as satisfiability and graph coloring.
- Papers [**8**], [**10**], and [**11**] show how the dual structures (or, what is equivalent, nonsatisfiable formulas) can be used for the analysis of the matrices A for which the system $Ax = 0$ has a nontrivial nonnegative solution. Namely, nonsatisfiability turns out to be related to the existence of solutions that are *stable* (in some reasonable sense).
- Papers [**6**] and [**12**] use methods developed in [**5**] to design new modifications of the branch-and-bound method of discrete optimization. These new modifications are called the *Kowalski tree* method and the *plait-and-bound* method.

3.4. New heuristics for satisfiability related to Maslov's method.

In 1991, O. Dubois *et al.* developed a new heuristic for satisfiability [**13**], [**14**]; this heuristic is based on ideas that are quite in line with the "increasing freedom of choice" described above.

Yu. Matiyasevich and O. Dubois have experimentally compared Dubois' and Maslov's methods (the author is thankful to Yu. Matiyasevich, who kindly described to him the results of these unpublished experiments). Based on the results of their experiments, Dubois' method is definitely as good as Maslov's original one, and probably even somewhat better.

3.5. Applications of similar ideas to new problems (knapsack, artificial intelligence, logic programming, interval computations).

3.5.1. *Knapsack.* In [47] and [62], S. Shukeilo et al. used the freedom of choice strategy to develop a new algorithm for yet another intractable problem: the *knapsack* problem (for a detailed description of different known intractable problems, see, e.g., [19]). This algorithm is based on probabilistic estimates of the number $N(x_i, \varepsilon_i)$ of solutions that are similar (in idea) to Dubois' estimates for satisfiability [13], [14]. Computer experiments have shown that this algorithm works well on random knapsack problems.

3.5.2. *Artificial intelligence (AI).* Traditionally, the problems of applied mathematics consist of finding a solution that satisfies one or several precisely defined conditions. If it is impossible to satisfy all these conditions, then the only answer we want is that this problem is not solvable.

In many AI problems, however, these conditions are often formulated non-precisely: for example, a person who plans to fly from the US to Paris may want to fly by Air France, to take a window seat, and to leave and arrive at convenient times. However, if it is impossible to satisfy all these conditions, the traveler would like to satisfy at least some of them.

If we do not take this flexibility into consideration, then we can reformulate the original problem as a propositional satisfiability problem, and apply Maslov's method. However, due to this flexibility, it is not necessary to make all parts of the resulting formula true. In [35], [36], and [41], the resulting problem is formulated in precise terms, and a modification of Maslov's method is developed for solving this problem.

In particular, in [35] and [36], this idea is applied to formalizing informal reasoning in physics.

3.5.3. *Logic programming.* Traditional programming languages describe, step by step, what the computer should do. Ideally, we should be able to formulate what we *want*, and let the computer decide how to compute it. A natural universal language for describing what we want is the language of mathematical logic. So, the natural idea is to formulate our requirements in logical terms, and let the computer find a solution. In this case, the logical statement serves as a program for the computer; hence, this approach is called *logic programming*.

One of the problems with this approach is that, as Church has shown, mathematical logic is undecidable. So, no algorithm can serve as an absolutely correct "compiler" for this language: no algorithm can take an arbitrary logical statement and decide whether it is true. As a result, we have to use "approximate" compilers that sometimes return results *different* from what we would expect from mathematical logic.

This approximate character of logic programming was initially viewed as a drawback, until researchers realized that in many cases when there is a difference between the results of a logic program and the result of mathematical logic, the logic program is *closer* to commonsense reasoning. Thus, logic programming is a nice method of formalizing commonsense reasoning. Hence, the nontraditional "logic" behind logic programming is of great importance.

In particular, for this new logic, we can formulate the analogues of the propositional satisfiability problem. The natural analogue of a satisfying vector is a so-called *stable model* [20], [21], [22].

O. Fuentes *et al.* modified Maslov's iterative method so that instead of satisfying vectors, it now looks for stable models [**17**], [**18**], [**37**], [**16**]. The main idea behind this modification came from a rather unusual source: an attempt to formalize the ... Mexican national character [**18**].

The resulting method of computing stable models was successfully tested both on random logic programs and on the benchmark logic programs coming from practical problems (such as technical diagnostics).

Similarly to Maslov's original method, this modification can be naturally reformulated in terms of *chemical computing*.

3.5.4. *Interval computations.* Not only *discrete* problems are intractable (NP-hard); many *continuous* problems (in which we process real numbers) are intractable as well. Moreover, in continuous problems, there is an additional complexity:

- If input data consist of elements of discrete sets, then we can usually safely assume that we know the data precisely.
- In *continuous* problems, when we apply an algorithm $f(x_1, \ldots, x_n)$ to real numbers $x_1, \ldots, x_n$, the situation is more complicated. Real numbers x_i usually come from measurements, and measurements are never 100% precise; hence, the result $\tilde{x}_i$ of measuring a physical quantity may differ from the actual value x_i of this quantity.

In some cases, we know the *probabilities* of different possible values of measurement error $\Delta x_i = \tilde{x}_i - x_i$, but in many real-life situations, all we know about this error is that it is bounded by some bound Δ_i (this bound is usually provided by the manufacturer of the measuring instrument). Hence, when the measurement result is $\tilde{x}_i$, the only thing we know about the actual value x_i is that it belongs to the interval $[\tilde{x}_i - \Delta_i, \tilde{x}_i + \Delta_i]$.

Traditionally, the data processing algorithm is applied to the measurement results $\tilde{x}_1, \ldots, \tilde{x}_n$. Ideally, we would like to know not only the result $\tilde{y} = f(\tilde{x}_1, \ldots, \tilde{x}_n)$ of applying this algorithm, but also how accurate this result is. In other words, we would like to know the set of all possible values of $y = f(x_1, \ldots, x_n)$:

$$\{f(x_1, \ldots, x_n) \mid x_1 \in [\tilde{x}_1 - \Delta_1, \tilde{x}_1 + \Delta_1], \ldots, x_n \in [\tilde{x}_n - \Delta_n, \tilde{x}_n + \Delta_n]\}.$$

For algorithms f that compute continuous functions, this set is an interval, so, all we need to know is its endpoints. Computation of this interval's endpoints is a particular case of the so-called *interval computations*.

It is known (see [**65**] for references) that even for polynomial algorithms f, the problem of computing the endpoints is NP-hard (it is actually NP-hard even for quadratic f).

This problem is of great practical importance, so no wonder many heuristic algorithms have been developed for it. Since this interval computation problem is NP-hard, we can reformulate other intractable problems in these terms, and hence we can apply known interval heuristics to other intractable problems.

In particular, in [**65**], B. Traylor *et al.* have applied this idea to *propositional satisfiability*. For some of the interval heuristics, the resulting method turned out to be ... very similar to Maslov's original method. Thus, we get a new *justification* of Maslov's method. But not only that: this reduction to interval computations provides us with *a* reasonable *way* of *choosing* some *parameters* of Maslov's method, parameters which the previous justifications did not help to choose.

Acknowledgments. First of all, I want to thank Grigory Mints, whose energy, persistence, and thoroughness made both this book and its current translation possible. I am also very thankful to all the authors of this book, especially to Evgeny Dantsin, Gennady Davydov, Inna Davydova, and Michael Zakharevich, for their help, and to Michael Gelfond, Yuri Gurevich, and Vladimir Lifschitz for valuable discussions. We are also very thankful to Nina B. Maslova and Elena Maslova, who helped us to read through Maslov's unpublished manuscripts.

The author of was partially supported by NASA Grant No. NAG 9-757. This work was partially carried out while he was a Visiting Professor at LAFORIA, University of Paris VI, Summer 1996.

References

1. L. Adleman, *Molecular computation of solutions to combinatorial problems*, Science **266** (11 Nov., 1994), 1021-1024.
2. A. Blass and Yu. Gurevich, *On Matiyasevich's nontraditional approach to search problems*, Information Processing Letters **32** (1989), 41-45.
3. B. Bouchon-Meunier, V. Kreinovich, A. Lokshin, and H. T. Nguyen, *On the formulation of optimization under elastic constraints (with control in mind)*, Fuzzy Sets and Systems (to appear).
4. S. A. Cook, *The complexity of theorem-proving procedures*, Proc. Third Annual Sympos. Theory of Computing, ACM, New York, 1971, pp. 151-158.
5. G. V. Davydov and I. M. Davydova, this book.
6. _____, *Non-tree-like coverings in discrete optimization*, Sov. Math. (Izv.Vuzov) **32** (1988), no. 3, 93-97.
7. _____, *A flow interpretation of NP-complete problems*, Sov. Math. (Izv. Vuzov) **32** (1988), no. 11, 96-101.
8. _____, *Solvability of the system $Ax = 0, x \geq 0$, with indeterminate coefficients*, Sov. Math. (Izv. Vuzov) **34** (1988), no. 9, 108-112.
9. _____, *Duality and non-tree-like search in discrete optimization*, Izv. Akad. Nauk SSSR Tekhn. Kibernet. **1988**, no. 1, 86-93. (Russian)
10. _____, *Tautologies and positive solvability of linear homogeneous systems*, Ann. Pure Appl. Logic **57** (1992), 27-43.
11. _____, *Solvable matrices*, Vestnik St. Petersburg Univ. Math. **26** (1993), no. 1, 1-6.
12. _____, *The plaits and bounds method*, Operations Research and Statistical Modeling, vol. 6, Saint Petersburg, 1994, pp. 14-30. (Russian)
13. O. Dubois, *Counting the number of solutions for instances of satisfiability*, Theoret. Computer Sci. **81** (1991), 49-64.
14. O. Dubois and J. Carlier, *Probabilistic approach to the satisfiability problem*, Theoret. Computer Sci. **81** (1991), 65-75.
15. R. I. Freidzon, M. I. Zakharevich, E. Ya. Dantsin, and V. Ya. Kreinovich, *Hard problems: formalizing creative intelligent activity (new directions)*, Proc. Conf. Semiotic Aspects of Formalizing Intelligent Activity Borzhomi–88, Moscow, 1988, pp. 407-408. (Russian)
16. L. O. Fuentes, *Applying uncertainty formalisms to well-defined problems*, Master thesis, Department of Computer Science, University of Texas at El Paso, 1991.
17. L. O. Fuentes and V. Ya. Kreinovich, *Simulation of chemical kinetics as a promising approach to expert systems*, Abstracts of the Southwestern Conference on Theoretical Chemistry (Univ. of Texas at El Paso, November 1990), p. 33.
18. _____, *A touch of Mexican soul makes computers smarter*, University of Texas at El Paso, Department of Computer Science, Technical Report UTEP-CS-91-6 (can be accessed by anonymous ftp to cs.utep.edu, directory pub/reports, file utep-cs-91-6.tex in plain TeX), 1991.
19. M. Garey and D. Johnson, *Computers and intractability: a guide to the theory of NP-completeness*, Freeman, San Francisco, CA, 1979.

20. M. Gelfond and V. Lifschitz, *The stable model semantics for logic programming*, Logic Programming: Proc. Fifth Internat. Conf. and Sympos. (R. Kowalski and K. Bowen, eds.), MIT Press, Cambridge, MA, 1988, pp. 1070-1080.
21. _____, *Logic programs with classical negation*, Logic Programming: Proc. Seventh Internat. Conf. (D. Warren and P. Szeredi, eds.), MIT Press, Cambridge, MA, 1990, pp. 579-597.
22. _____, *Classical negation in logic programs and disjunctive databases*, New Generation Computing **9** (1991), 365-385.
23. A. Hjelmfelt, E. D. Weinberger, and J. Ross, *Chemical implementation of neural networks and Turing machines*, Proc. Natl. Acad. Sci. USA **88** (1991), 10983-10987.
24. _____, *Chemical implementation of finite-state machines*, Proc. Natl. Acad. Sci. USA **89** (1992), 383-387.
25. S. Kamat, *Efficient space allocation for restructurable VLSI RAM chips*, Master thesis, Department of Electrical and Computer Engineering, University of Texas at El Paso, 1993.
26. V. Kozlenko and V. Kreinovich, *Using computers for solving optimal control problems in case of uncertain criteria*, International Radioelectronics Surveys, No. 8 (1989), 60-66. (Russian)
27. V. Kozlenko, V. Kreinovich and M. G. Mirimanishvili, *An optimal method of describing expert information*, Applied Problems of Systems Analysis, Georgian Polytechnical Institute, Tbilisi, 1988, no. 8 (337), pp. 64-67. (Russian)
28. V. Ya. Kreinovich, *Foundations of S. Maslov's operator*, Proc. Third All-Union Conf. Applications of Methods of Mathematical Logic (Tallinn 1983), pp. 80-81. (Russian)
29. _____, In this volume.
30. _____, *Group-theoretic approach to intractable problems*, Proc. Internat. Conf. Computer Logic COLOG-88 (Tallinn 1988), vol. 1, pp. 31-42 [same as [32]].
31. _____, *How to describe certainty values: an axiomatic approach*, Proceedings of the Conference on Semiotic Aspects of Formalizing Intelligent Activity Borzhomi-88, Moscow, 1988, pp. 141-145. (Russian)
32. _____, *Group-theoretic approach to intractable problems*, Lecture Notes in Computer Science, vol. 417, Springer-Verlag, Berlin, 1990, pp. 112-121.
33. _____, *Knowledge representation for measurable quantities: group-theoretic approach*, Mathematical Methods of Algorithm Design and Analysis, Akad. Nauk SSSR 1990, Leningrad, pp. 64-72. (Russian)
34. V. Kreinovich, Ching-Chuang Chang, L. Reznik, and G. N. Solopchenko, *Inverse problems: fuzzy representation of uncertainty generates a regularization*, Proc. NAFIPS'92: North American Fuzzy Information Processing Society Conference (Puerto Vallarta, Mexico, December 15-17, 1992), vol. II, NASA Johnson Space Center, Houston, TX, 1992, pp. 418-426.
35. V. Kreinovich and A. M. Finkelstein, *Perspectives of using personal computers when solving creative problems in physics*, Proc. Conf. Dialogue on Personal Computers IVERSI-85 (Tbilisi 1985). (Russian)
36. _____, *Formalization of various methods of solving creative problems in physics*, Proc. Conf. Semiotic Aspects of Formalizing Intelligent Activity Kutaisi-85, Moscow, 1985, pp. 146-149. (Russian)
37. V. Kreinovich and L. O. Fuentes, *Simulation of chemical kinetics—a promising approach to inference engines*, Proc. World Congr. Expert Systems (Orlando, Florida, 1991) (J. Liebowitz, ed.), vol. 3, Pergamon Press, N.Y., 1991, pp. 1510-1517.
38. V. Kreinovich and S. Kumar, *Optimal choice of &- and ∨-operations for expert values*, Proc. Third Univ. of New Brunswick Artificial Intelligence Workshop (Fredericton, N.B., Canada, 1990), pp. 169-178.
39. _____, *How to help intelligent systems with different uncertainty representations communicate with each other*, Cybernetics and Systems: Internat. J. **22** (1991), 217-222.
40. V. Kreinovich, R. Lea, O. Fuentes, and A. Lokshin, *Fuzzy control is often better than manual control of the very experts whose knowledge it uses: an explanation*, Proc. 1992 Internat. Conf. Tools with Artificial Intelligence, (Arlington, VA), IEEE Computer Science Press, Los Alamitos, CA, 1992, pp. 180-185.
41. V. Ya. Kreinovich and A. Lokshin, *An iterative method for the propositional satisfiability problem with possibly unreliable knowledge*, Abstracts Amer. Math. Soc. **11** (1990), 475.

42. V. Kreinovich, Ch. Quintana, and R. Lea, *What procedure to choose while designing a fuzzy control? Towards mathematical foundations of fuzzy control*, Working Notes First Internat. Workshop on Industrial Applications of Fuzzy Control and Intelligent Systems (College Station, TX, 1991), pp. 123-130.
43. V. Kreinovich, Ch. Quintana, R. Lea, O. Fuentes, A. Lokshin, S. Kumar, I. Boricheva, and L. Reznik, *What non-linearity to choose? Mathematical foundations of fuzzy control*, Proc. 1992 Internat. Conf. Fuzzy Systems and Intelligent Control (Louisville, KY, 1992), pp. 349-412.
44. V. Kreinovich, Ch. Quintana, and L. Reznik, *Gaussian membership functions are most adequate in representing uncertainty in measurements*, Proc. NAFIPS'92: North American Fuzzy Information Processing Society Conference (Puerto Vallarta, Mexico, December 15-17, 1992), vol. II, NASA Johnson Space Center, Houston, TX, 1992, pp. 618-624.
45. V. Kreinovich and L. K. Reznik, *Methods and models of formalizing a priori information (on the example of processing measurements results)*, Analysis and Formalization of Computer Experiments, Mendeleev Metrology Inst., Leningrad, 1986, pp. 37-41. (Russian)
46. _____, *Prospects of using expert systems in intelligent measuring instruments*, Proc. Workshop on Aspects of Intelligent Measurement (Dagomys, Sochi, USSR, 20-30 October, 1989), Moscow, 1990, Part 2, pp. 97-110. (Russian)
47. V. Kreinovich and S. Yu. Shukeilo, *A new probabilistic approach to the knapsack problem*, Proc. Third National Workshop on Discrete Optimization and Computers, Moscow, 1987, pp. 123–124. (Russian)
48. V. Kreinovich and D. Tolbert, *Minimizing computational complexity as a criterion for choosing fuzzy rules and neural activation functions in intelligent control*, Intelligent Automation and Soft Computing. Trends in Research Development and Applications. Proc. First World Automation Congress (WAC'94) (Maui, Hawaii, August 14-17, 1994) (M. Jamshidi et al., eds.), vol. 1, TSI Press, Albuquerque, NM, 1994, pp. 545-550.
49. S. Yu. Maslov, *Calculi with monotonic deduction*, Zap. Nauchn. Sem. Leningrad. Otdel. Mat. Inst. Steklov. (LOMI) **88** (1979), 90–105; English transl. in J. Soviet Math. **20** (1982), no. 4.
50. _____, *Iterative methods in intractable problems as a model of intuitive methods*, Abstracts Ninth All-Union Sympos. Cybernetics, 1981, pp. 52-56. (Russian)
51. _____, *Asymmetry of cognitive mechanisms and its implications*, Semiotika i Informatika **20** (1983), 3-31. (Russian)
52. _____, *Theory of deductive systems and its applications*, MIT Press, Cambridge, MA, 1987.
53. S. Yu. Maslov and Yu. N. Kurierov, *Strategy of increasing the freedom of choice when recognizing propositional satisfiability*, Abstracts All-Union Conf. "Methods of Mathematical Logic in Artificial Intelligence and System Programming." Part 1, Vilnius, 1980, pp. 130-131. (Russian)
54. Yu. V. Matiyasevich, In this volume.
55. H. T. Nguyen, V. Kreinovich, R. N. Lea, and D. Tolbert, *How to control if even experts are not sure: robust fuzzy control*, Proc. Second Internat. Workshop Industrial Applications of Fuzzy Control and Intelligent Systems (College Station, TX, December 2-4, 1992), pp. 153-162.
56. H. T. Nguyen, V. Kreinovich, and D. Tolbert, *On robustness in fuzzy logics*, Proc. IEEE-FUZZ Internat. Conf. (San Francisco, CA, March 1993), vol. 1, pp. 543-547.
57. _____, *A measure of average sensitivity for fuzzy logics*, Internat. J. on Uncertainty, Fuzziness, and Knowledge-Based Systems **2** (1994), 361-375.
58. P. W. Purdom and C. A. Brown, *Polynomial-average-time satisfiability problems*, Inform. Sci. **41** (1987), 23-42.
59. A. Ramer and V. Kreinovich, *Maximum entropy approach to fuzzy control*, Proc. Second Internat. Workshop Industrial Applications of Fuzzy Control and Intelligent Systems (College Station, TX, December 1992), pp. 113-117.
60. _____, *Maximum entropy approach to fuzzy control*, Inform. Sci. **81** (1994), 235-260.
61. _____, *Information complexity and fuzzy control*, Fuzzy Control Systems (A. Kandel and G. Langholtz, eds.), CRC Press, Boca Raton, FL, 1994, pp. 75-97.
62. S. Shukeilo, *A new probabilistic approach to the knapsack problem*, Master thesis, Leningrad Electrical Engineering Institute, 1988. (Russian)

63. O. Sirisaengtaksin, L. O. Fuentes, and V. Kreinovich, *Non-traditional neural networks that solve one more intractable problem: propositional satisfiability*, Proc. First Internat. Conf. Neural, Parallel, and Scientific Computations (Atlanta, GA, May, 1995), vol. 1, 1995, pp. 427-430.
64. M. H. Smith and V. Kreinovich, *Optimal strategy of switching reasoning methods in fuzzy control*, Theoretical Aspects of Fuzzy Control (H. T. Nguyen et al., eds.), Wiley, New York, 1995, pp. 117-146.
65. B. Traylor and V. Kreinovich, *A bright side of NP-hardness of interval computations: interval heuristics applied to NP-problems*, Reliable Computing **1** (1995), 343-360.
66. M. I. Zakharevich, In this volume.
67. _____, Proc. Conf. Semiotic Aspects of Formalizing Intelligent Activity (Borzhomi, 1988), Moscow, 1988, pp. 141-145. (Russian)
68. _____, Unpublished manuscripts and technical reports, 1991-95.

Selected Titles in This Series

(Continued from the front of this publication)

147 **I. G. Bashmakova et al.,** Nine Papers from the International Congress of Mathematicians, 1986
146 **L. A. Aĭzenberg et al.,** Fifteen Papers in Complex Analysis
145 **S. G. Dalalyan et al.,** Eight Papers Translated from the Russian
144 **S. D. Berman et al.,** Thirteen Papers Translated from the Russian
143 **V. A. Belonogov et al.,** Eight Papers Translated from the Russian
142 **M. B. Abalovich et al.,** Ten Papers Translated from the Russian
141 **H. Draškovičová et al.,** Ordered Sets and Lattices
140 **V. I. Bernik et al.,** Eleven Papers Translated from the Russian
139 **A. Ya. Aĭzenshtat et al.,** Nineteen Papers on Algebraic Semigroups
138 **I. V. Kovalishina and V. P. Potapov,** Seven Papers Translated from the Russian
137 **V. I. Arnol′d et al.,** Fourteen Papers Translated from the Russian
136 **L. A. Aksent′ev et al.,** Fourteen Papers Translated from the Russian
135 **S. N. Artemov et al.,** Six Papers in Logic
134 **A. Ya. Aĭzenshtat et al.,** Fourteen Papers Translated from the Russian
133 **R. R. Suncheleev et al.,** Thirteen Papers in Analysis
132 **I. G. Dmitriev et al.,** Thirteen Papers in Algebra
131 **V. A. Zmorovich et al.,** Ten Papers in Analysis
130 **M. M. Lavrent′ev, K. G. Reznitskaya, and V. G. Yakhno,** One-dimensional Inverse Problems of Mathematical Physics
129 **S. Ya. Khavinson,** Two Papers on Extremal Problems in Complex Analysis
128 **I. K. Zhuk et al.,** Thirteen Papers in Algebra and Number Theory
127 **P. L. Shabalin et al.,** Eleven Papers in Analysis
126 **S. A. Akhmedov et al.,** Eleven Papers on Differential Equations
125 **D. V. Anosov et al.,** Seven Papers in Applied Mathematics
124 **B. P. Allakhverdiev et al.,** Fifteen Papers on Functional Analysis
123 **V. G. Maz′ya et al.,** Elliptic Boundary Value Problems
122 **N. U. Arakelyan et al.,** Ten Papers on Complex Analysis
121 **V. D. Mazurov, Yu. I. Merzlyakov, and V. A. Churkin, Editors,** The Kourovka Notebook: Unsolved Problems in Group Theory
120 **M. G. Kreĭn and V. A. Jakubovič,** Four Papers on Ordinary Differential Equations
119 **V. A. Dem′janenko et al.,** Twelve Papers in Algebra
118 **Ju. V. Egorov et al.,** Sixteen Papers on Differential Equations
117 **S. V. Bočkarev et al.,** Eight Lectures Delivered at the International Congress of Mathematicians in Helsinki, 1978
116 **A. G. Kušnirenko, A. B. Katok, and V. M. Alekseev,** Three Papers on Dynamical Systems
115 **I. S. Belov et al.,** Twelve Papers in Analysis
114 **M. Š. Birman and M. Z. Solomjak,** Quantitative Analysis in Sobolev Imbedding Theorems and Applications to Spectral Theory
113 **A. F. Lavrik et al.,** Twelve Papers in Logic and Algebra
112 **D. A. Gudkov and G. A. Utkin,** Nine Papers on Hilbert's 16th Problem
111 **V. M. Adamjan et al.,** Nine Papers on Analysis
110 **M. S. Budjanu et al.,** Nine Papers on Analysis
109 **D. V. Anosov et al.,** Twenty Lectures Delivered at the International Congress of Mathematicians in Vancouver, 1974

(See the AMS catalog for earlier titles)

DATE DUE